The Dogs Coloring Book

by Jeri Lee C.Ht.

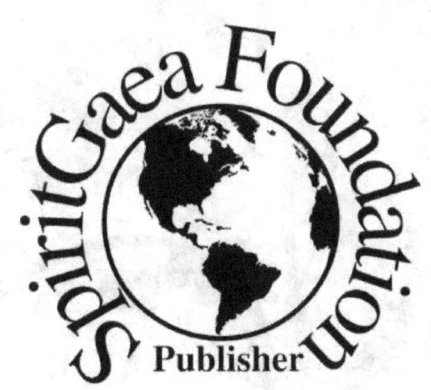

Copyright Jerilee.com
2022
All rights Reserved

ISBN: 9798356673023

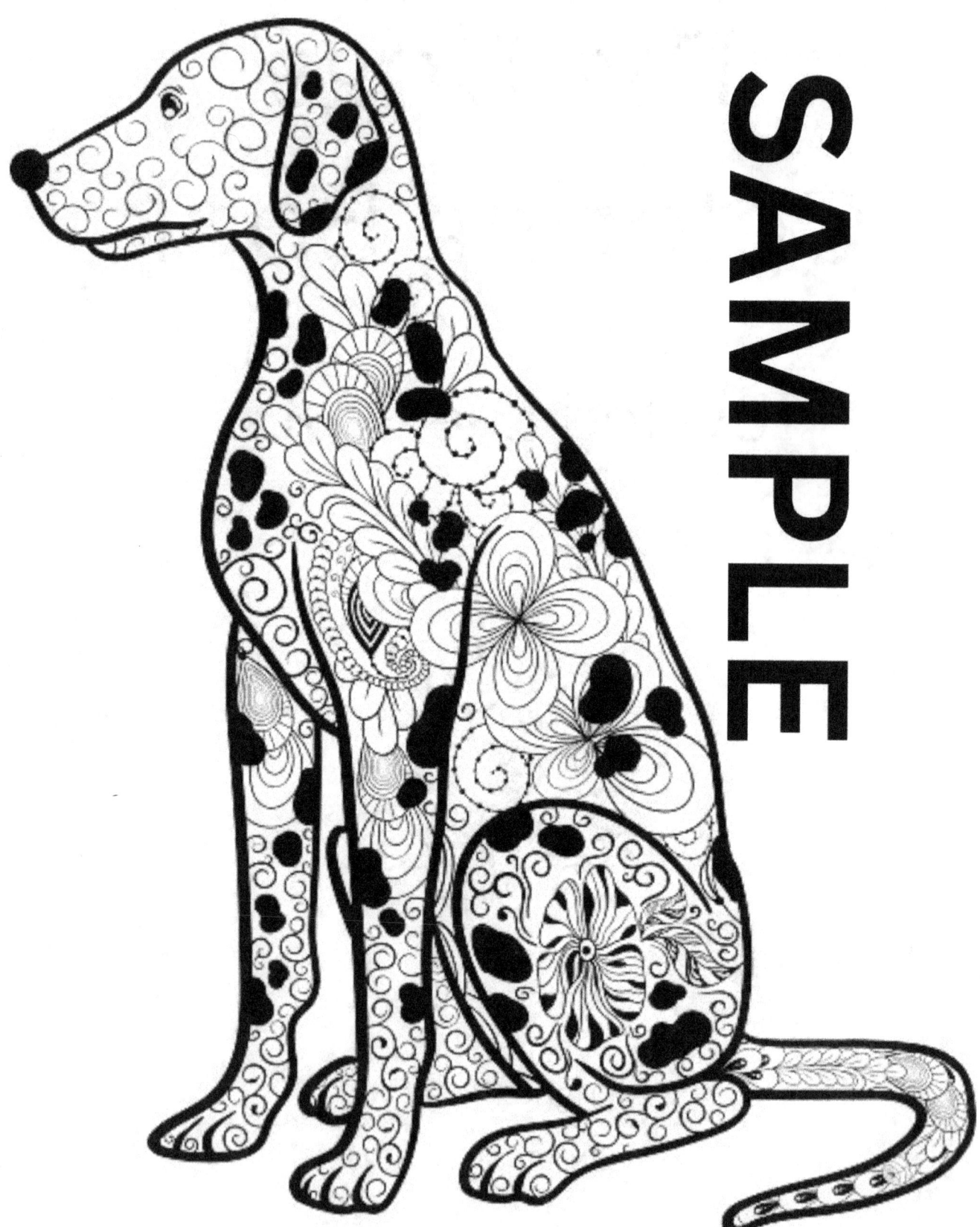

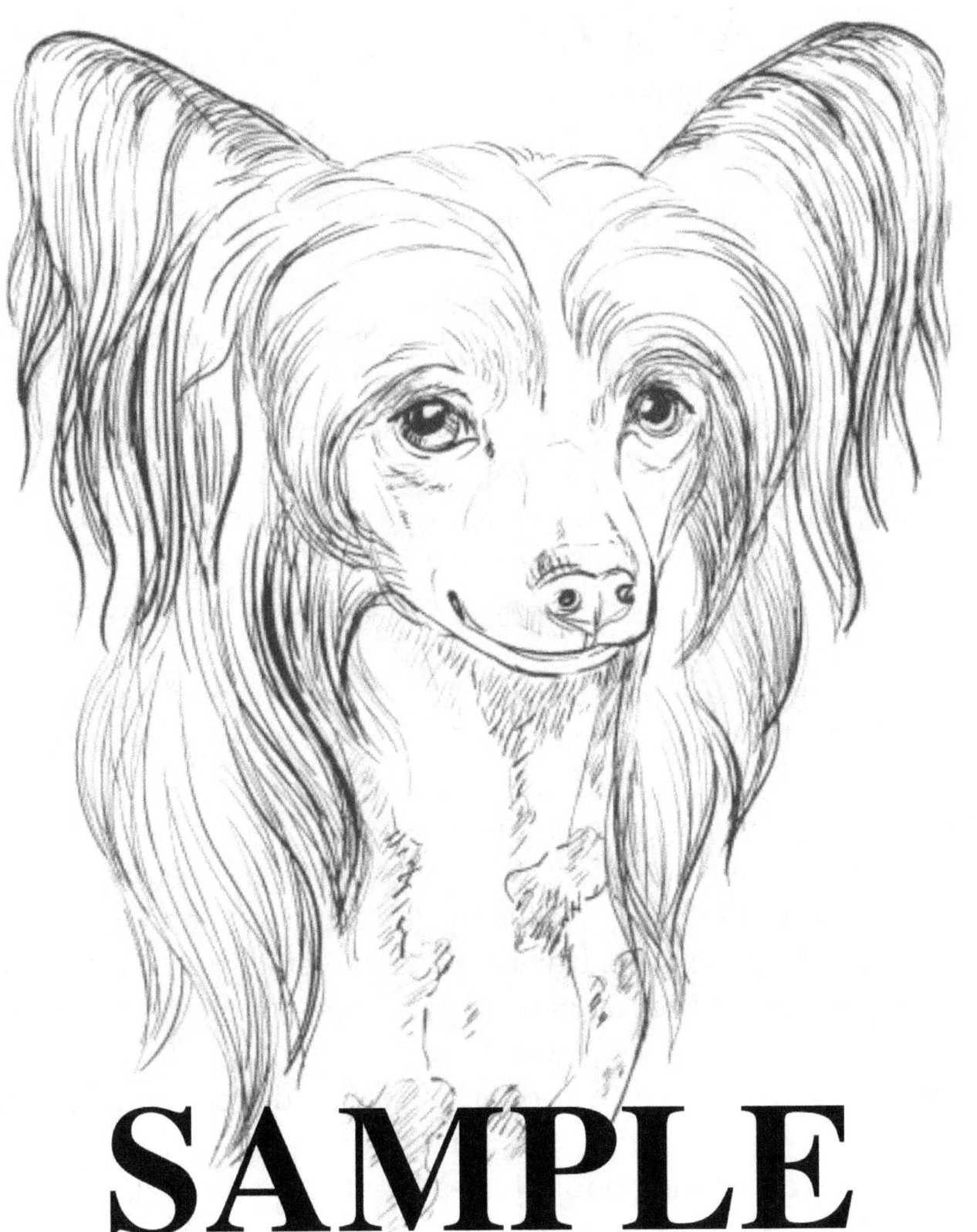

Author
and
Artist
Jeri LeeC.Ht.

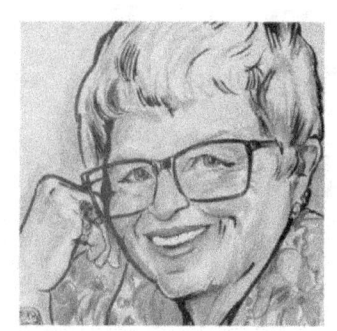

I was born on a farm in 1939, and the world was different. My grandmother said that's a dog, an animal that lives in the barn with the horses, cows, pigs, and chickens. My mother said that dog is an animal and can only come into the house in bad weather but must stay in the laundry room. I told my kids that it's your pet that can live in our home.

My son said, I love my dog, and it can sleep with me. How times have changed.

According to national surveys, 63% of American households have a pet. No one seems to be immune to the love and loyalty of domestic animals.

Pets are not just for children. They are members of your family, and whether it's a dog, cat, bird, fish, or other small creature that needs your care, it willingly gives you love and loyalty.

Pets do affect your health and general disposition. Statistics show your pets have the capability of raising your feelings and well-being.

Pets can give you health and happiness, and most people love animals.

This series of coloring books is designed to be fun, relaxing and enjoyable. Your best friend is often your dog, cat or other pet.

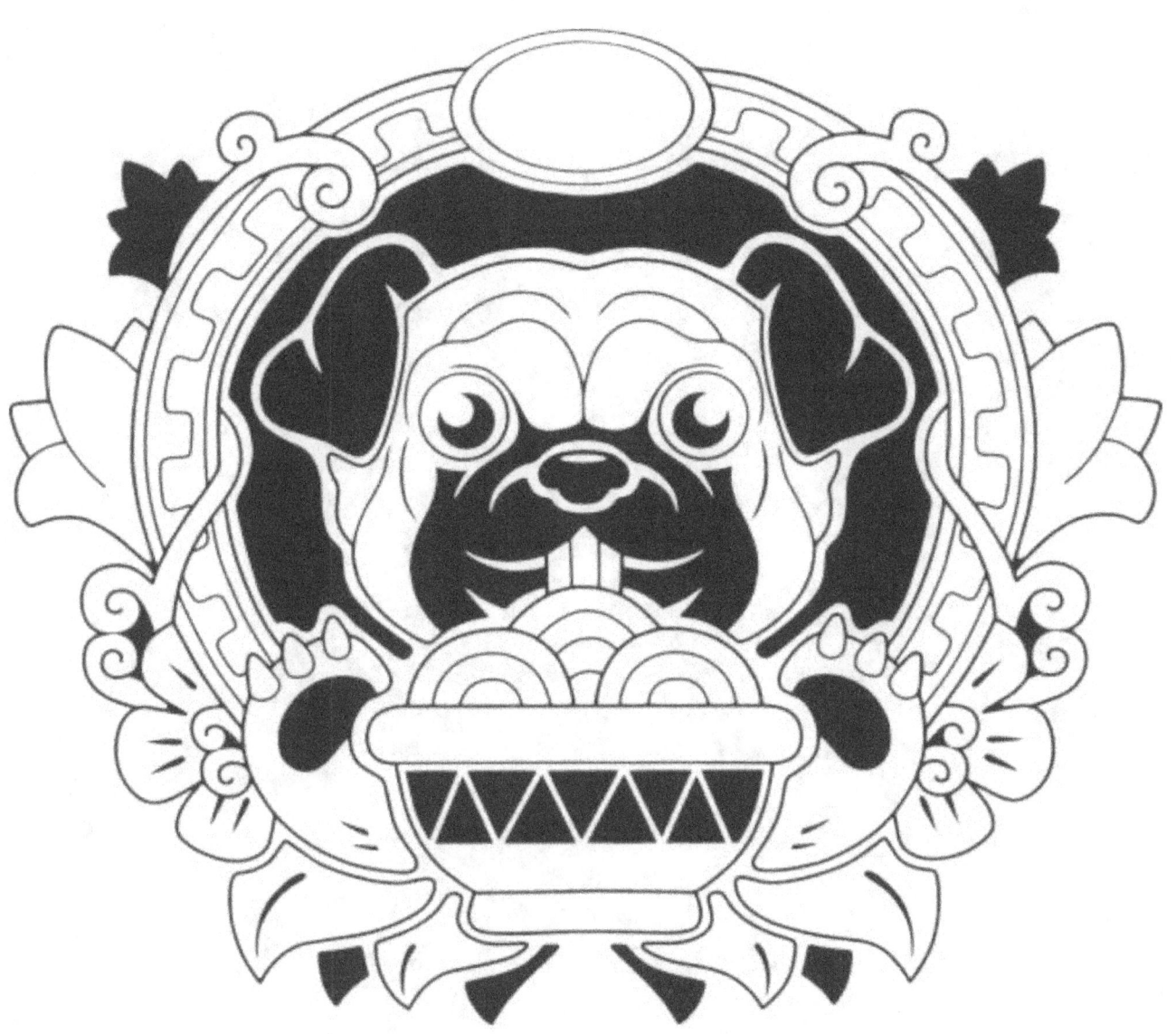

This Book
Belongs To

_____
Your Name

_____
Date

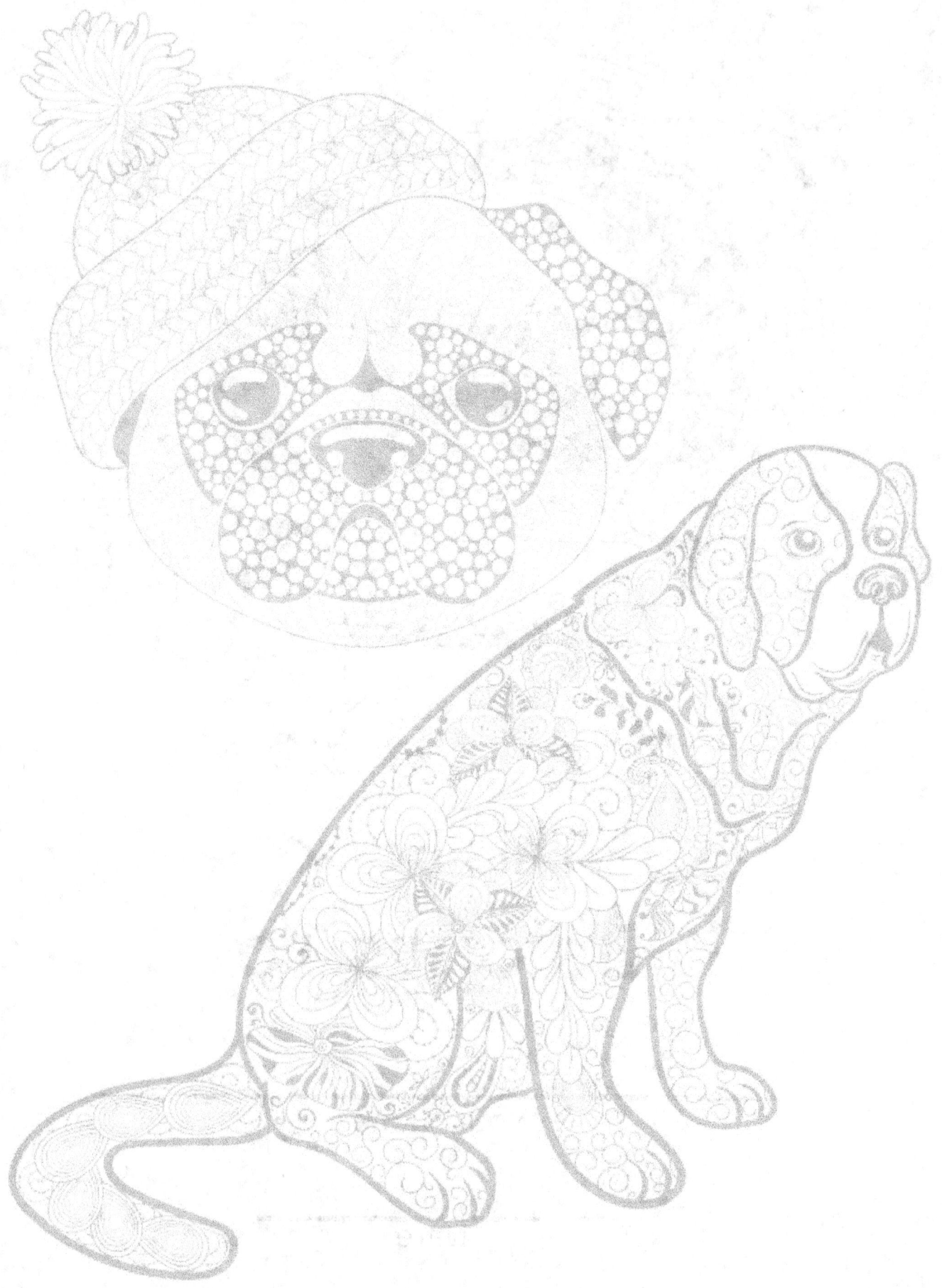

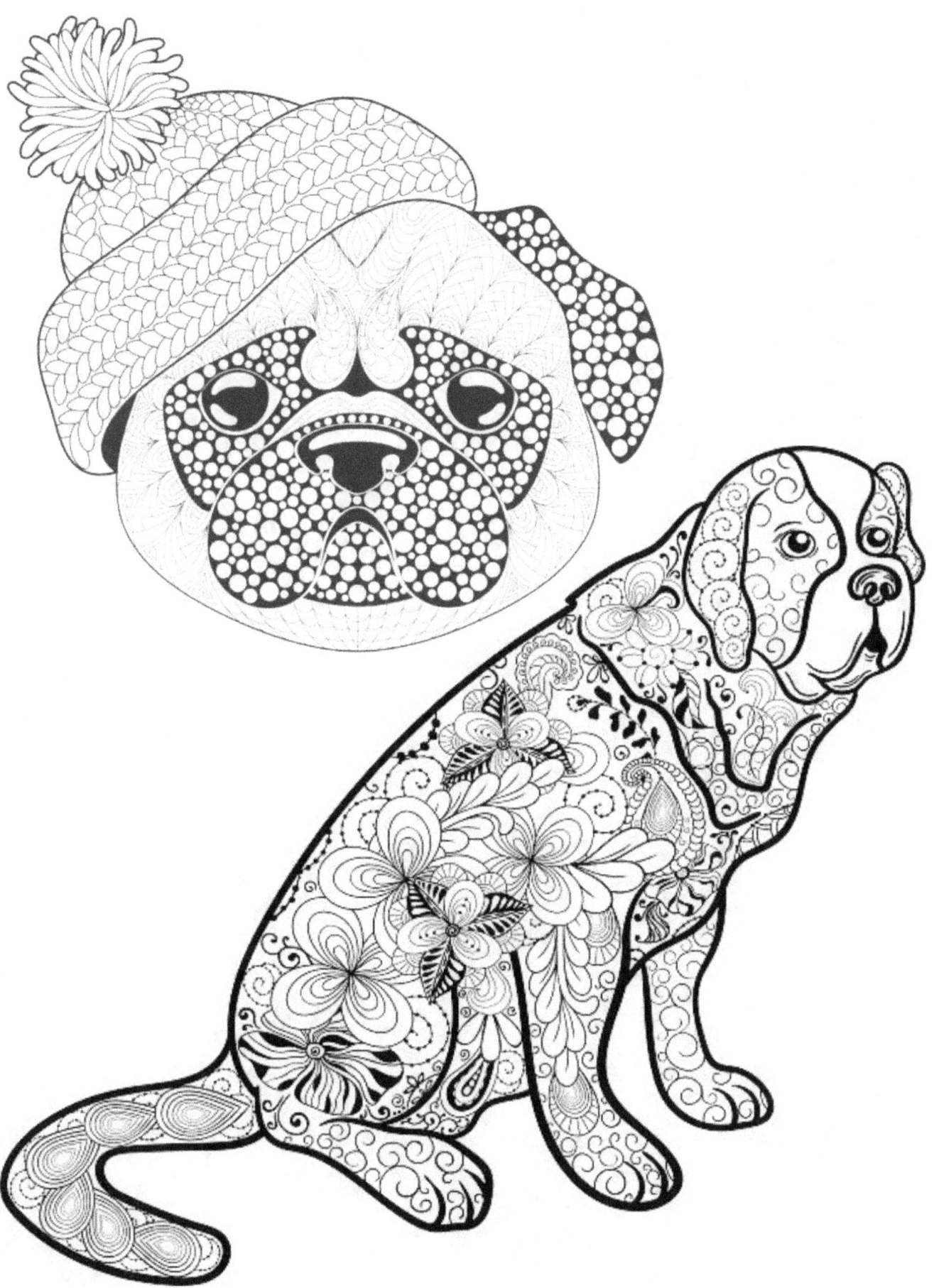

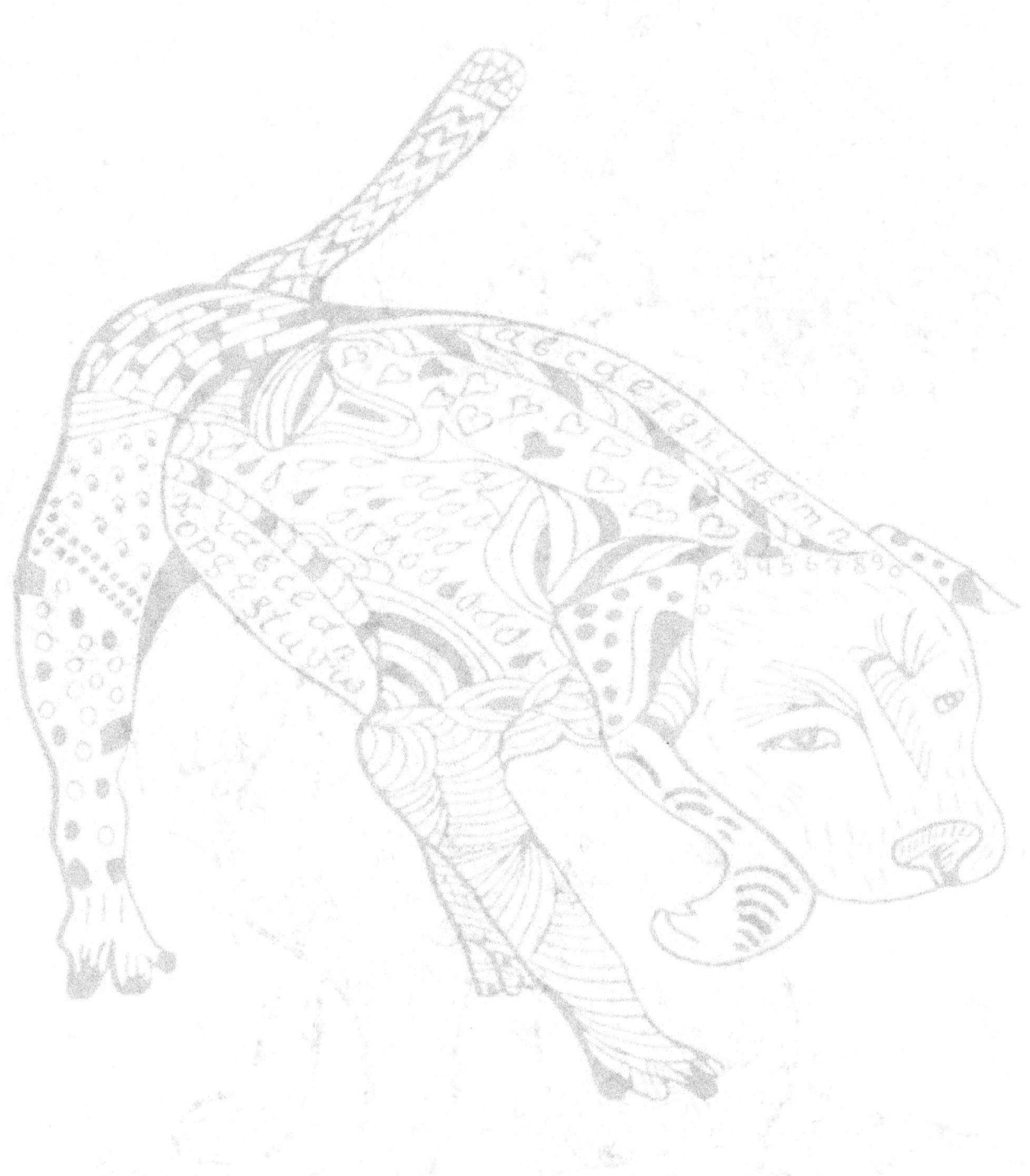

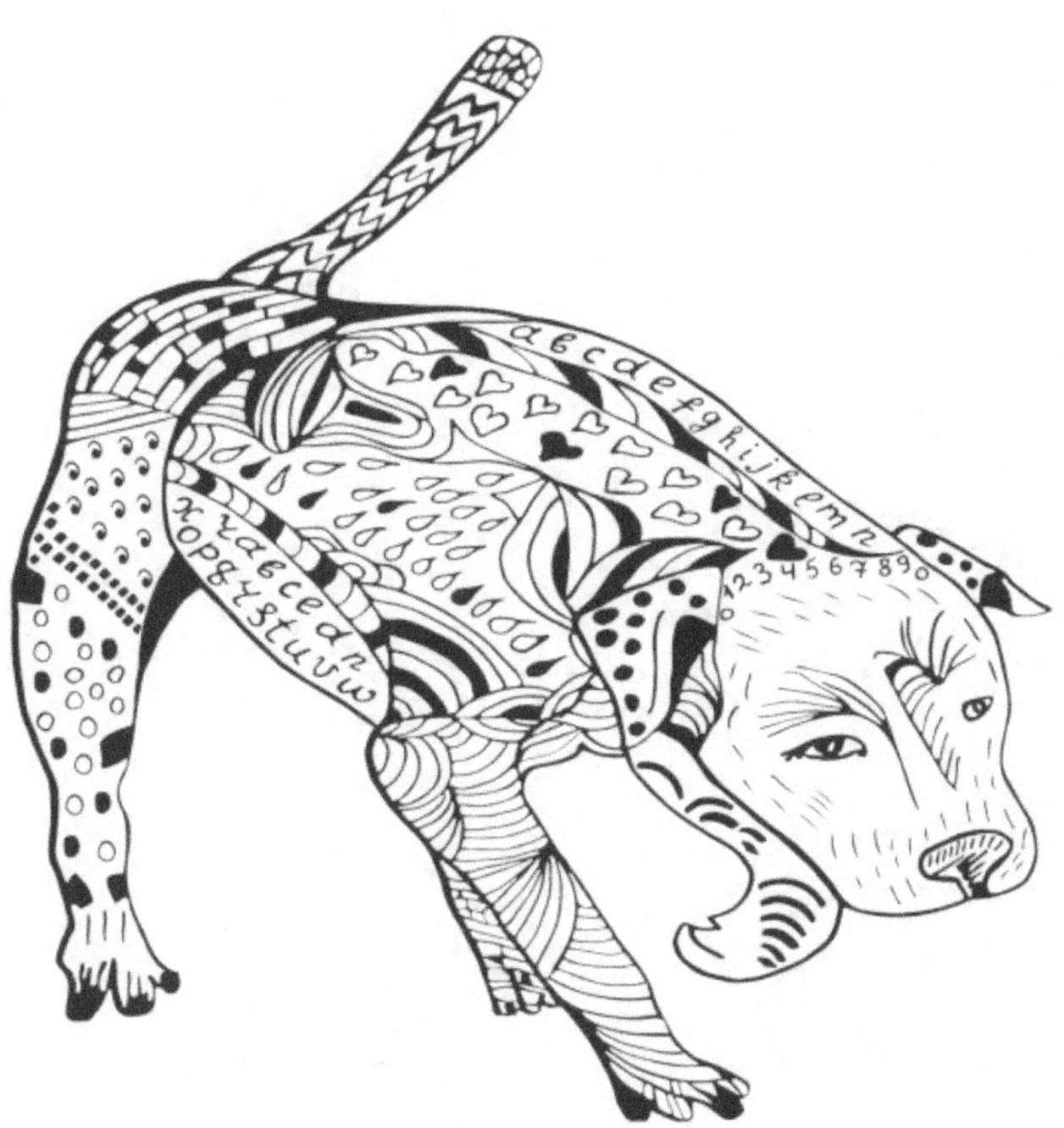

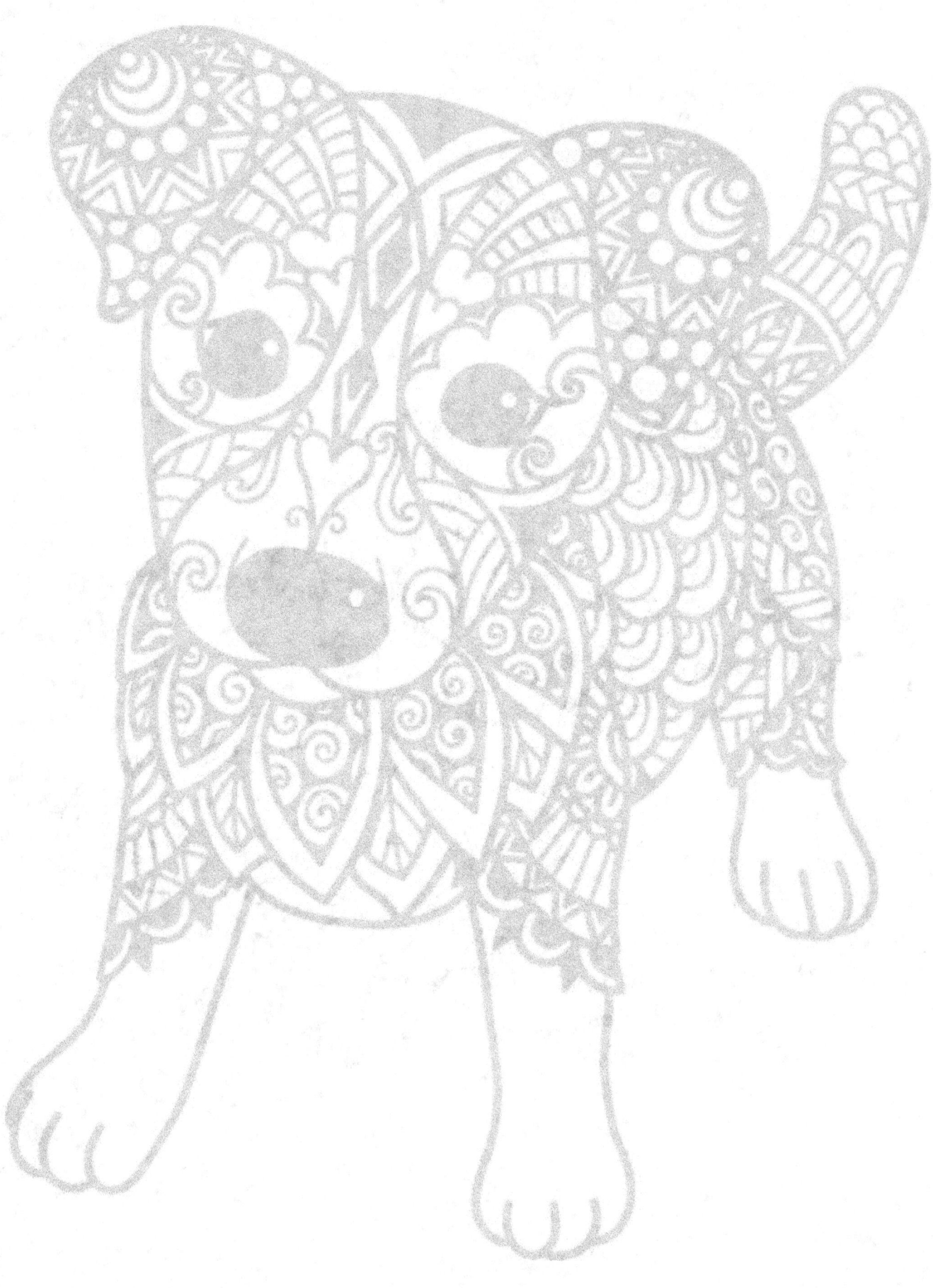

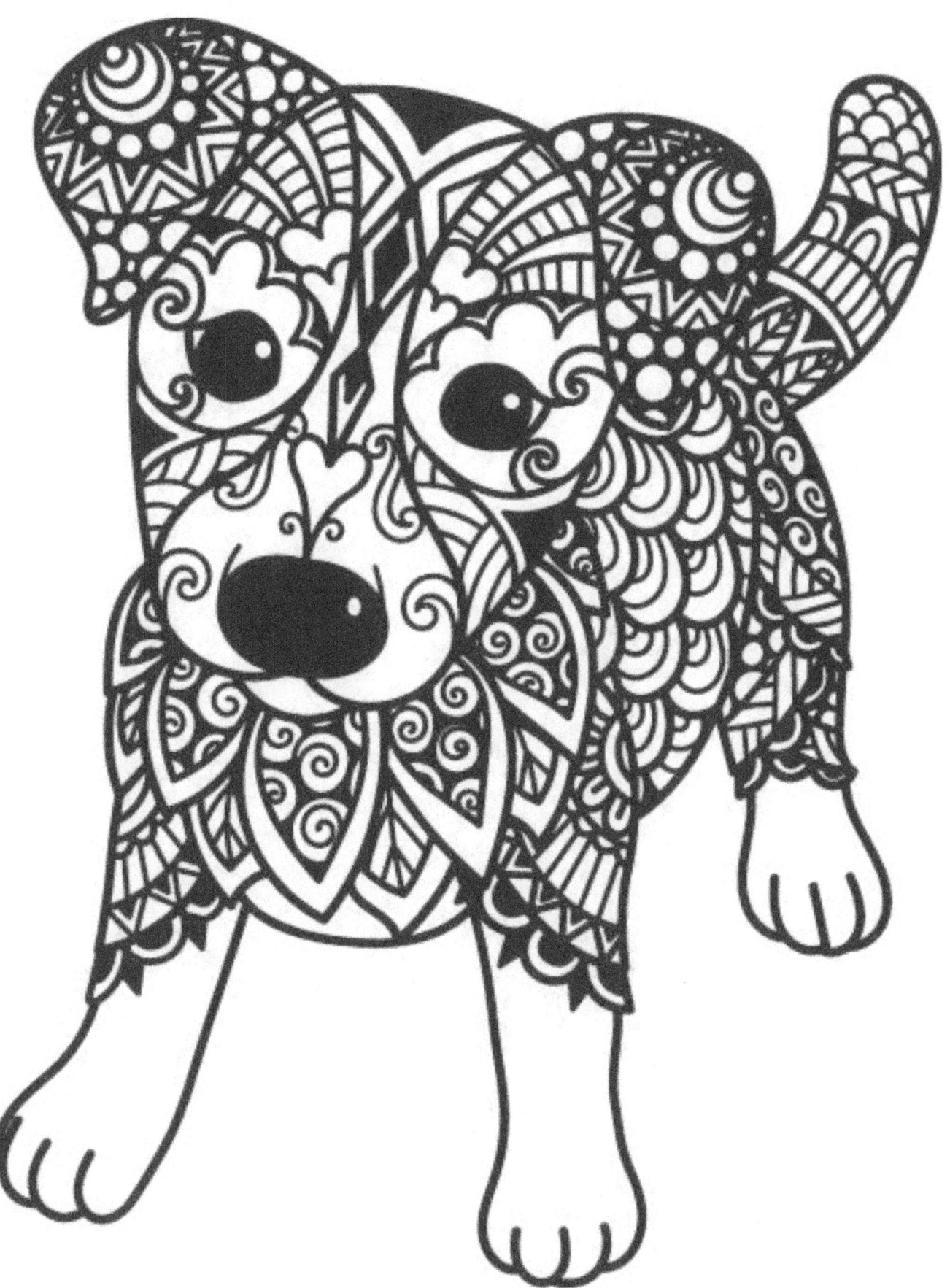

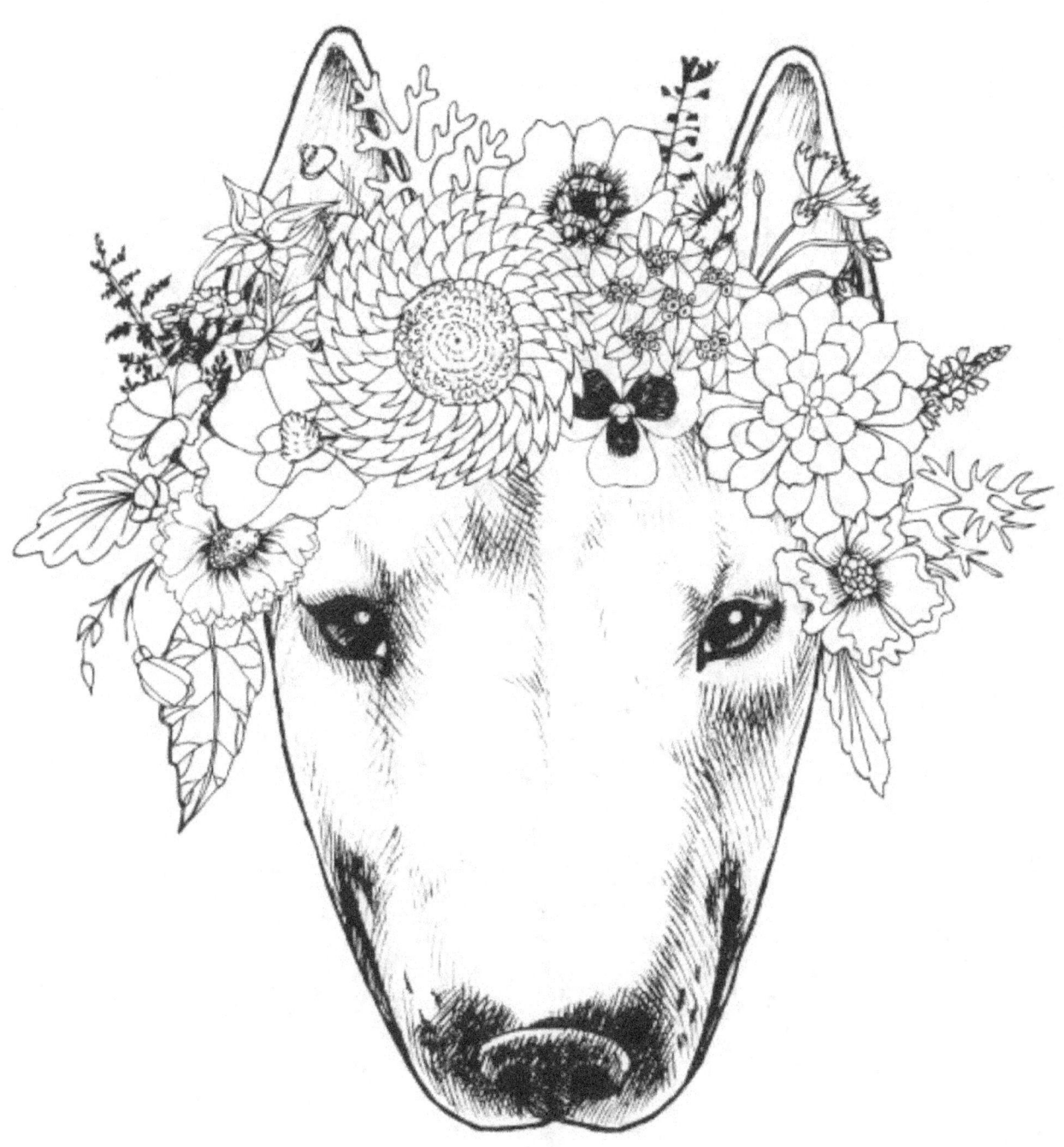

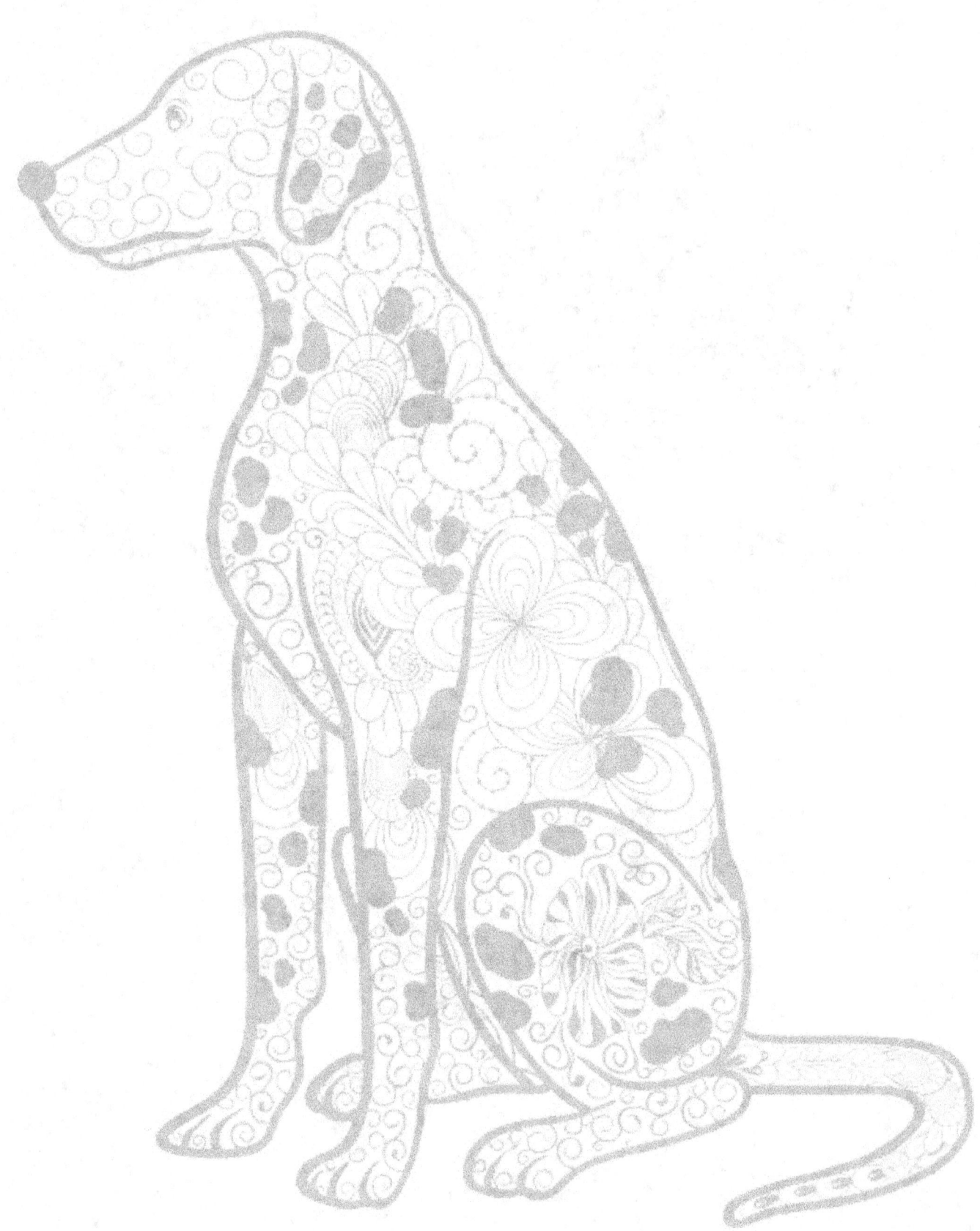

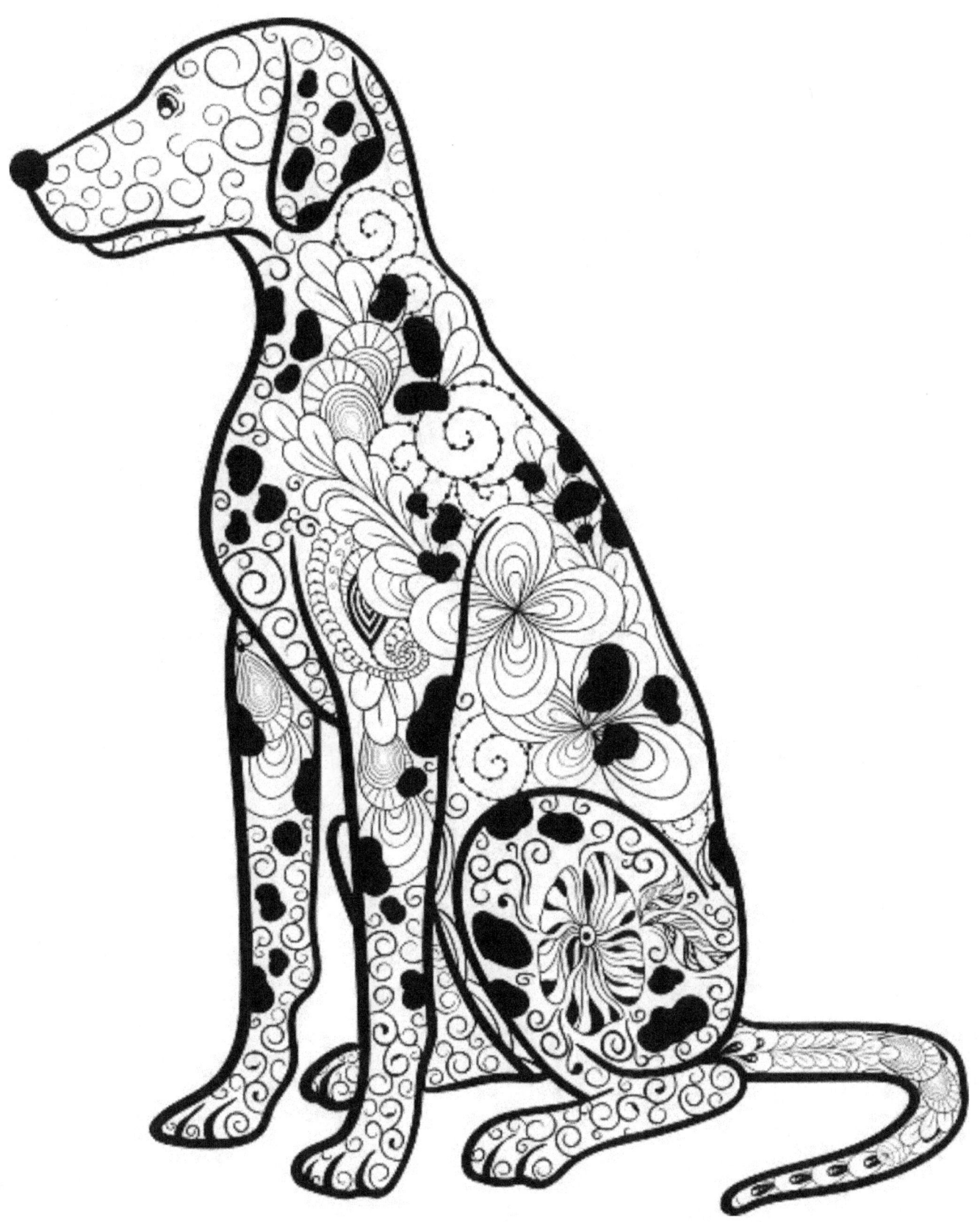

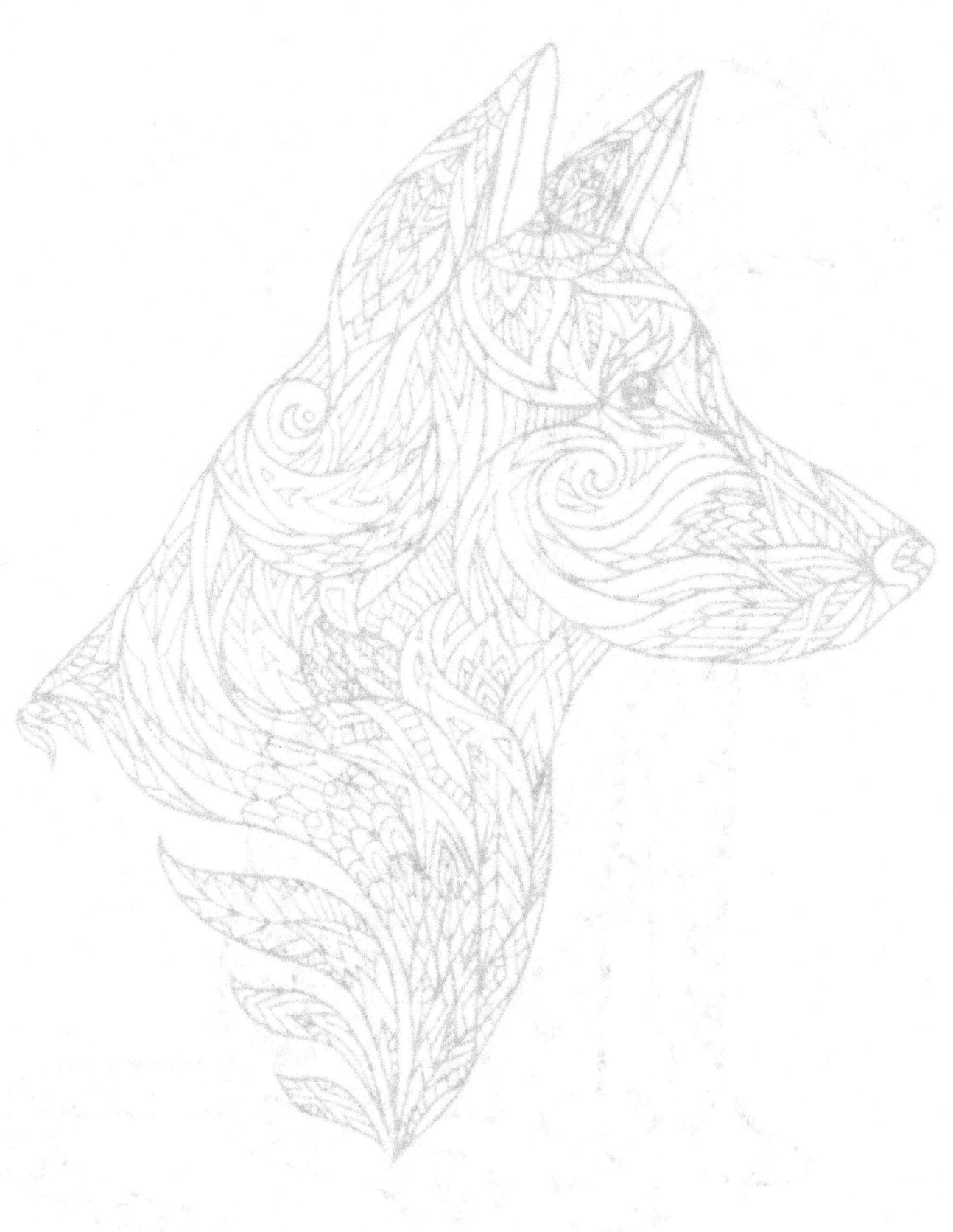

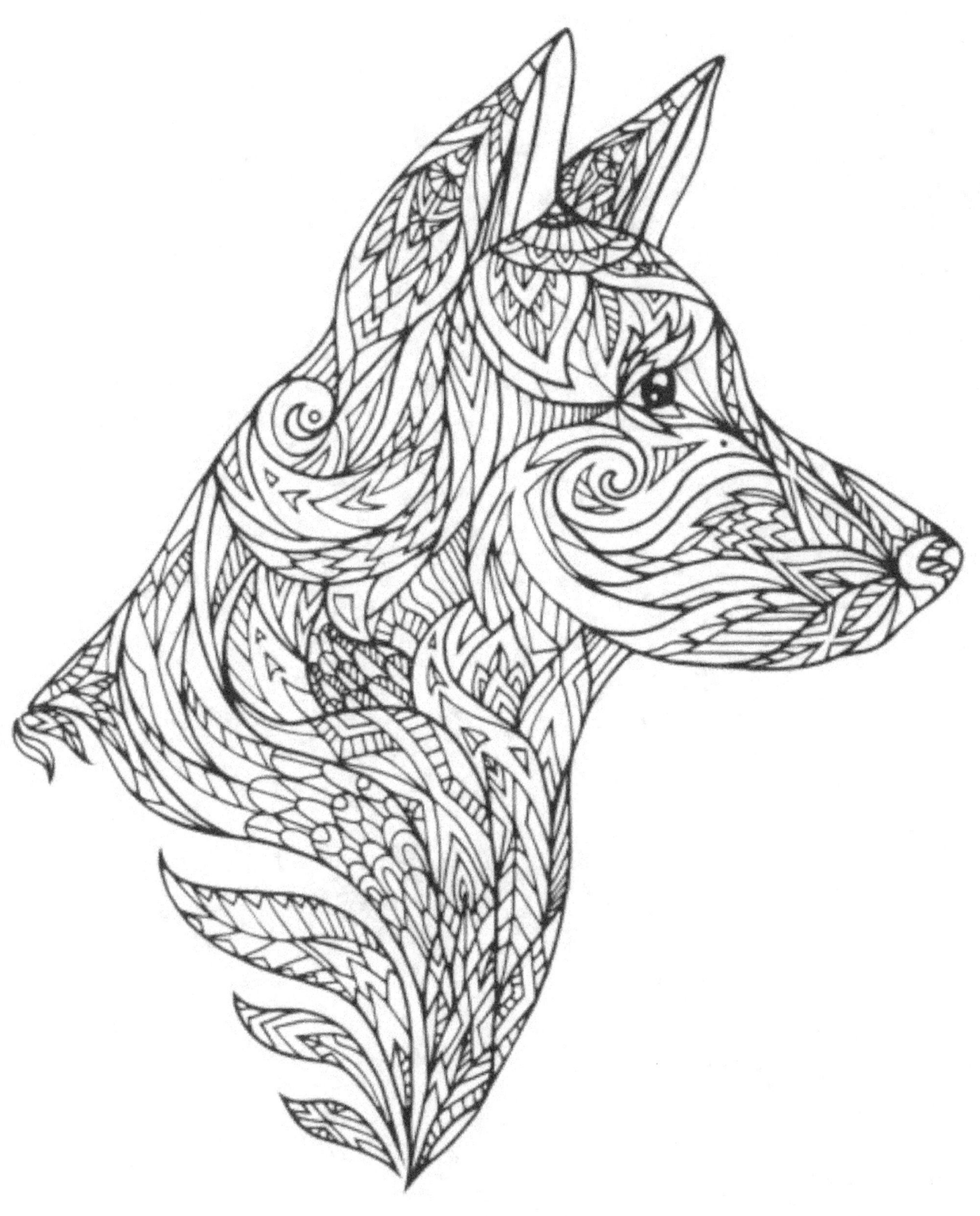

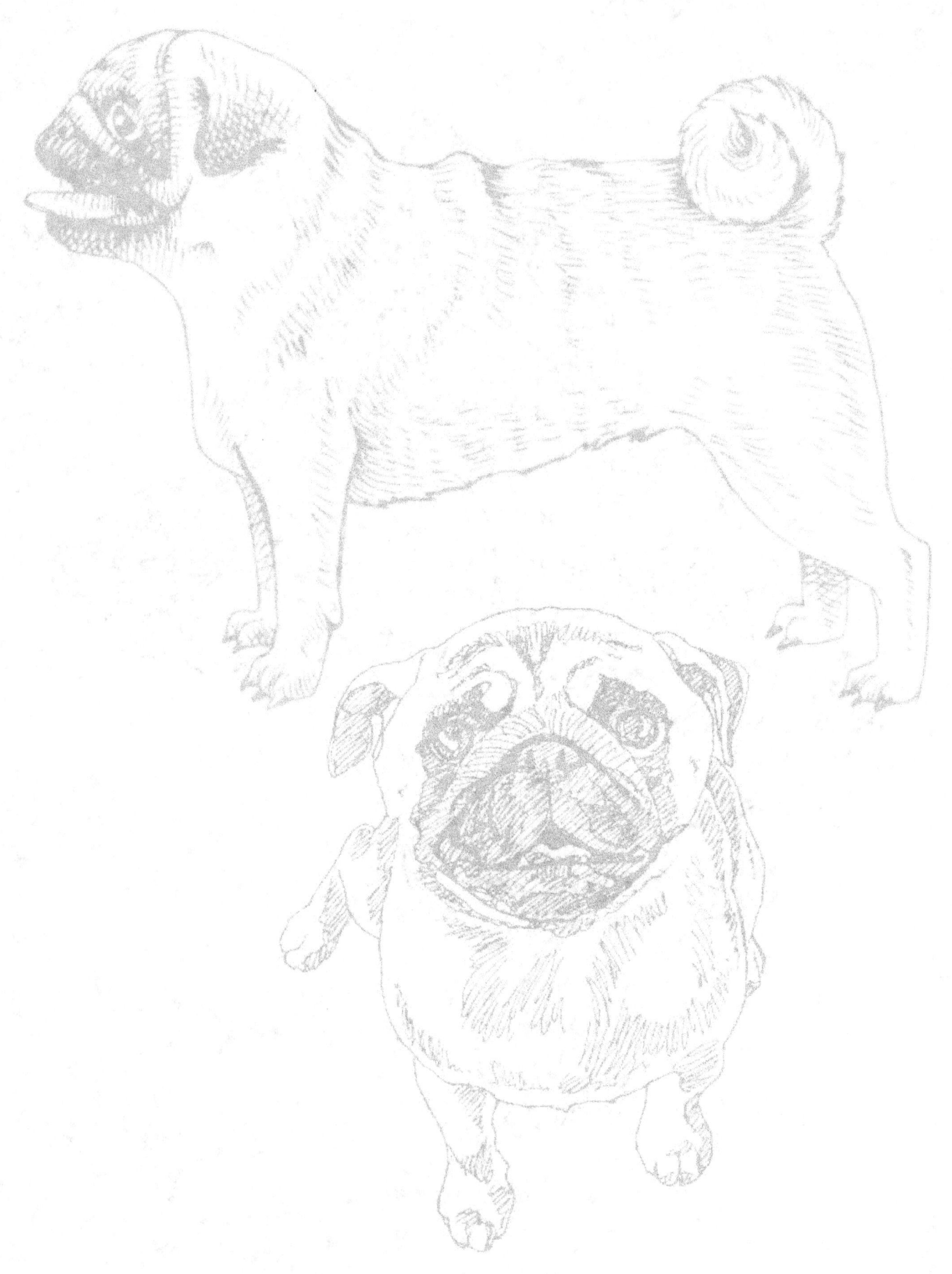

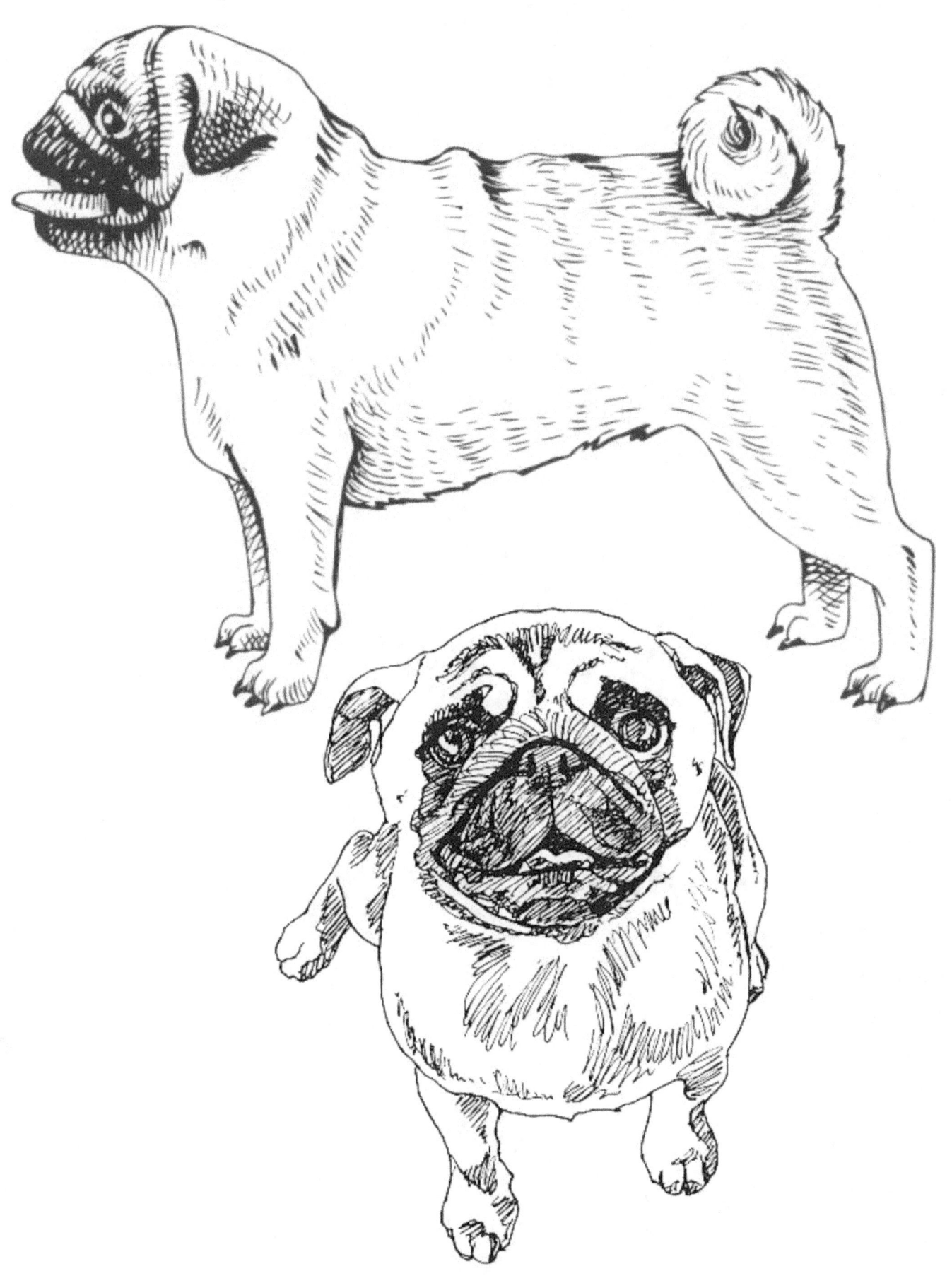

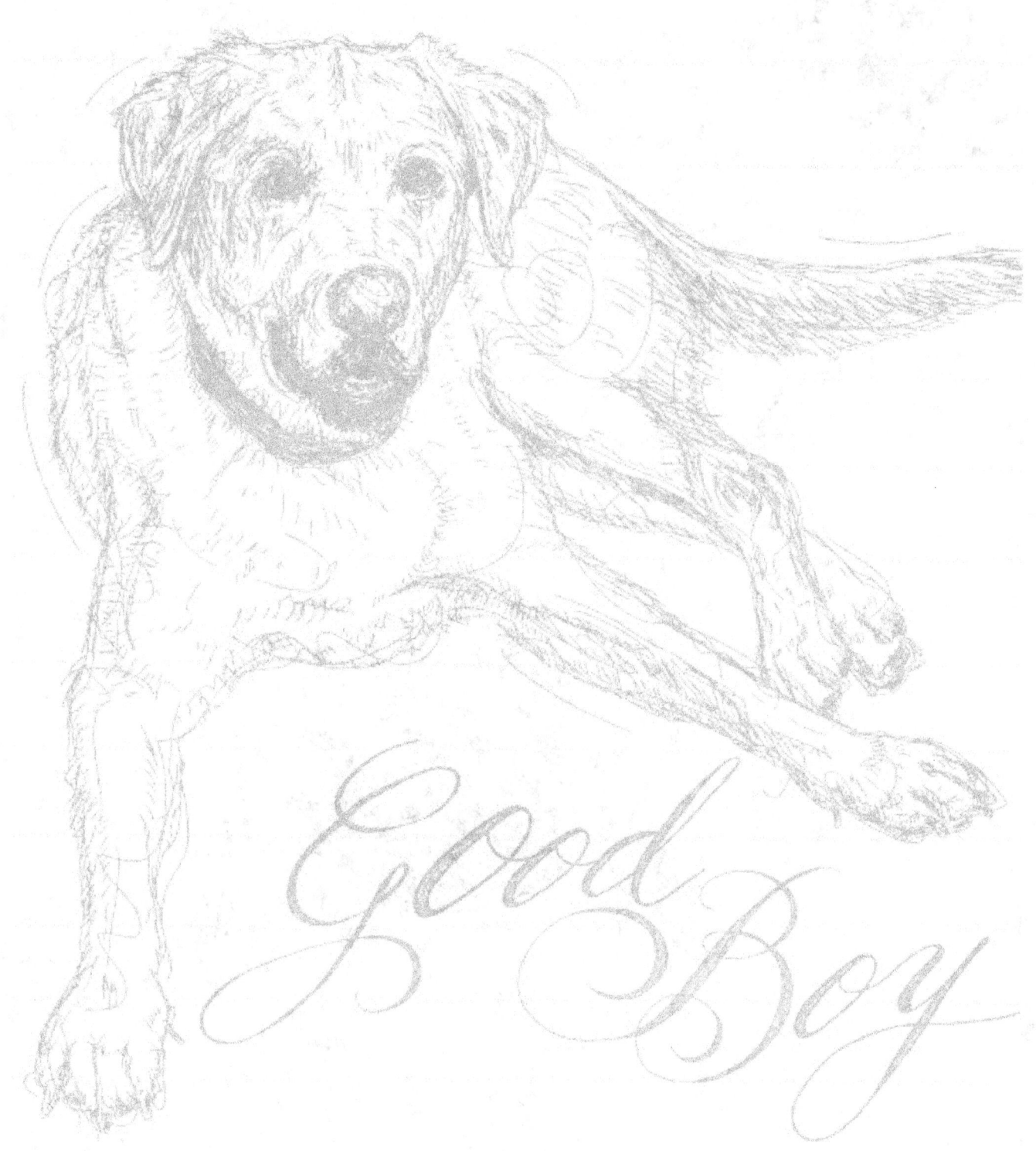

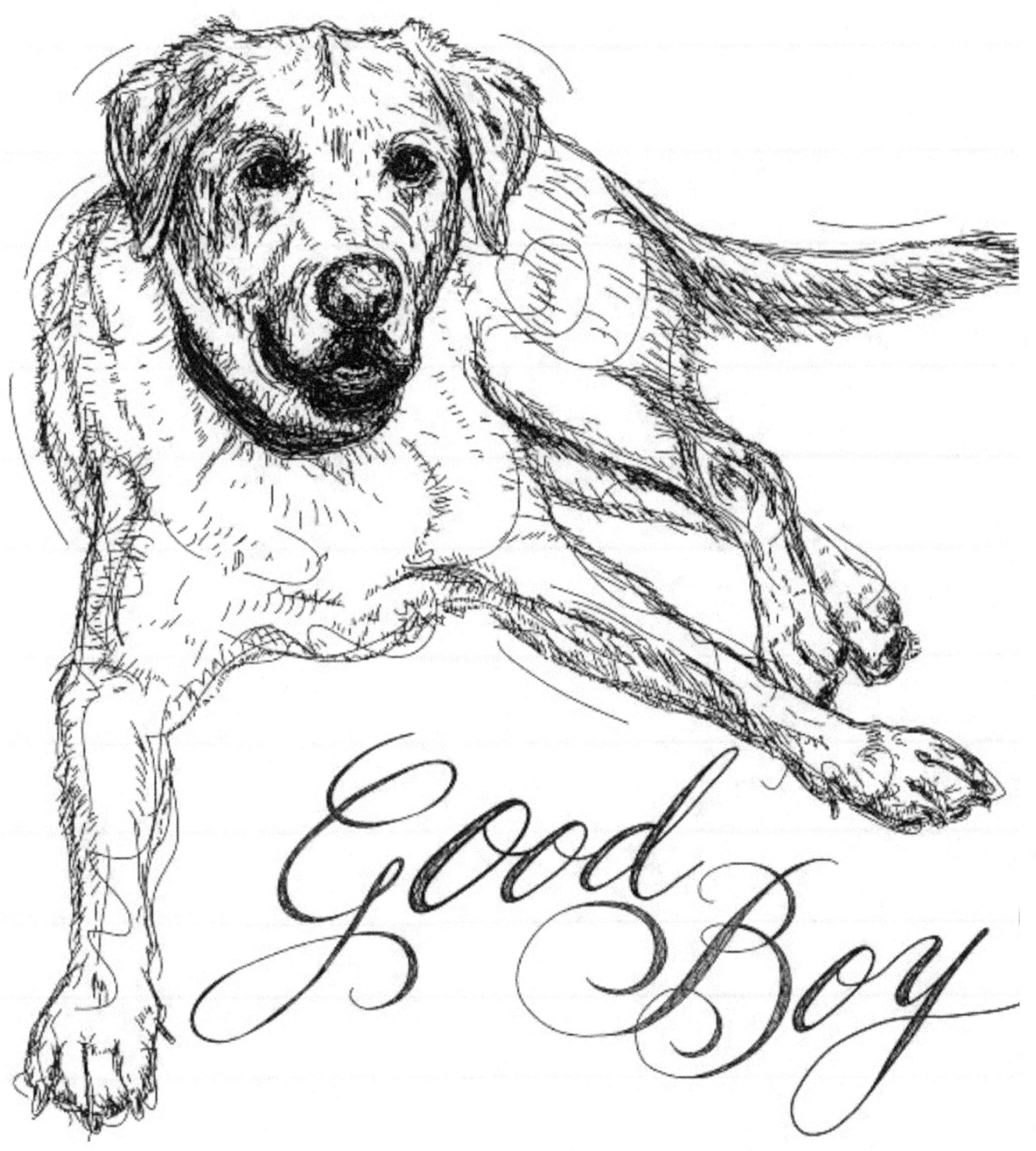

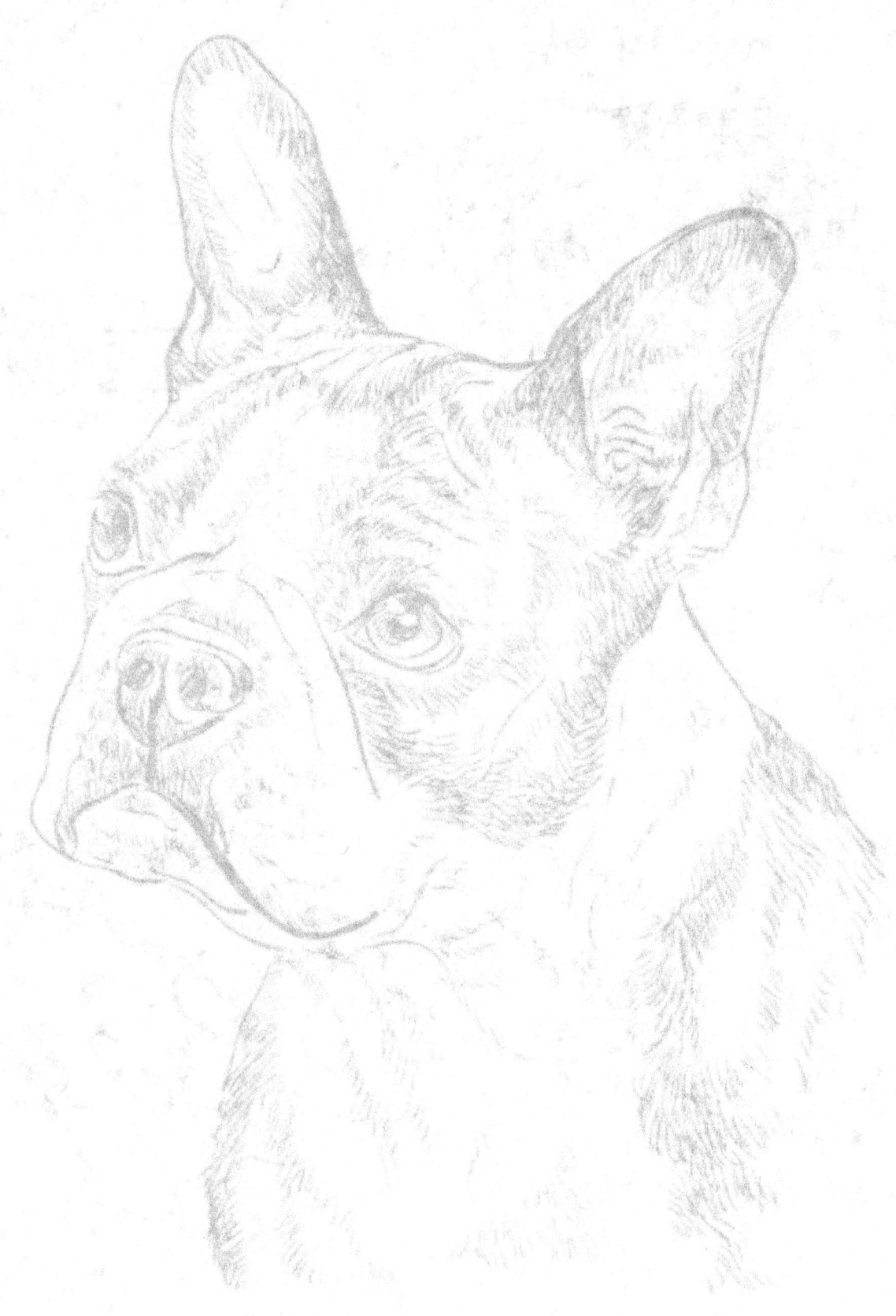

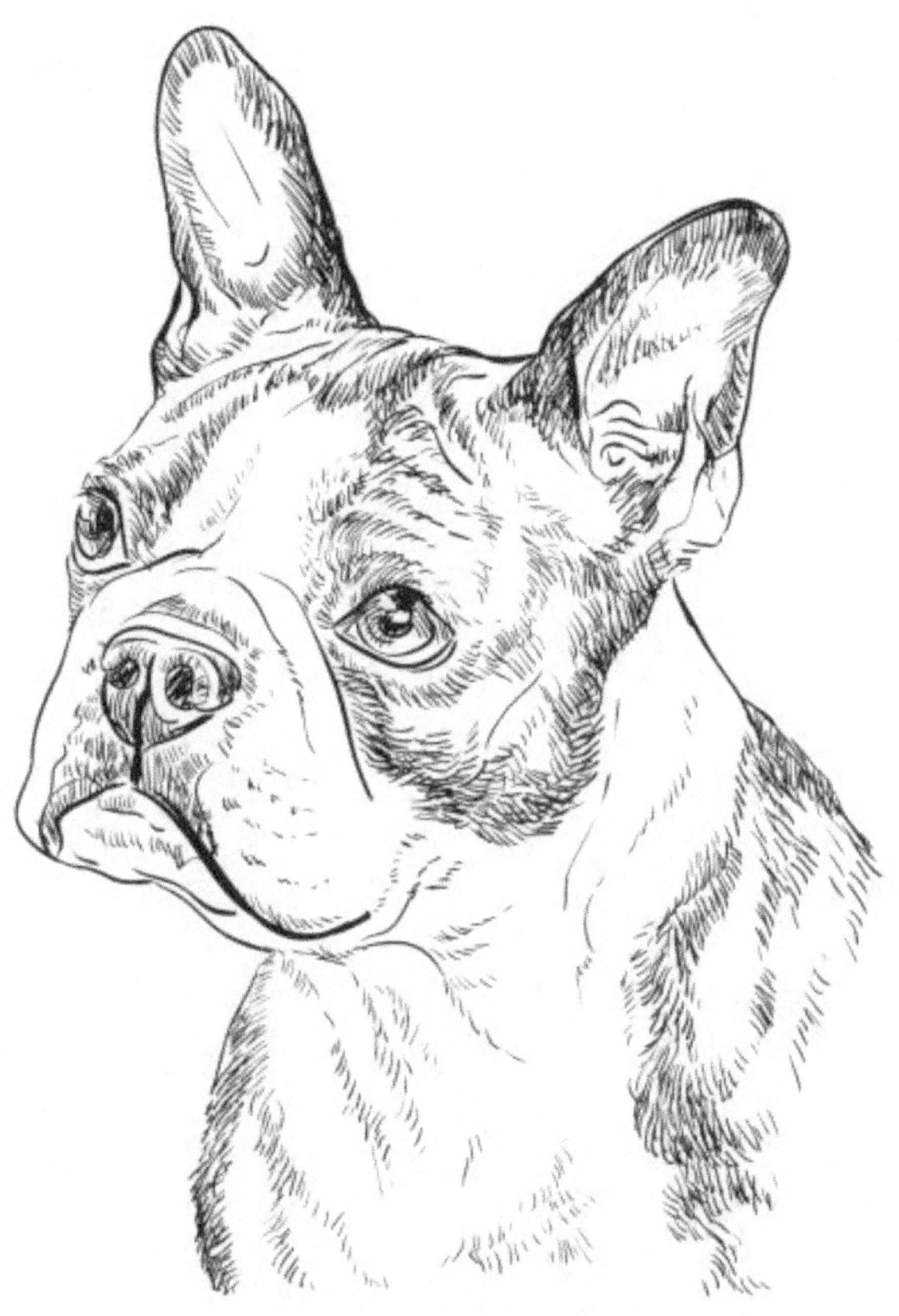

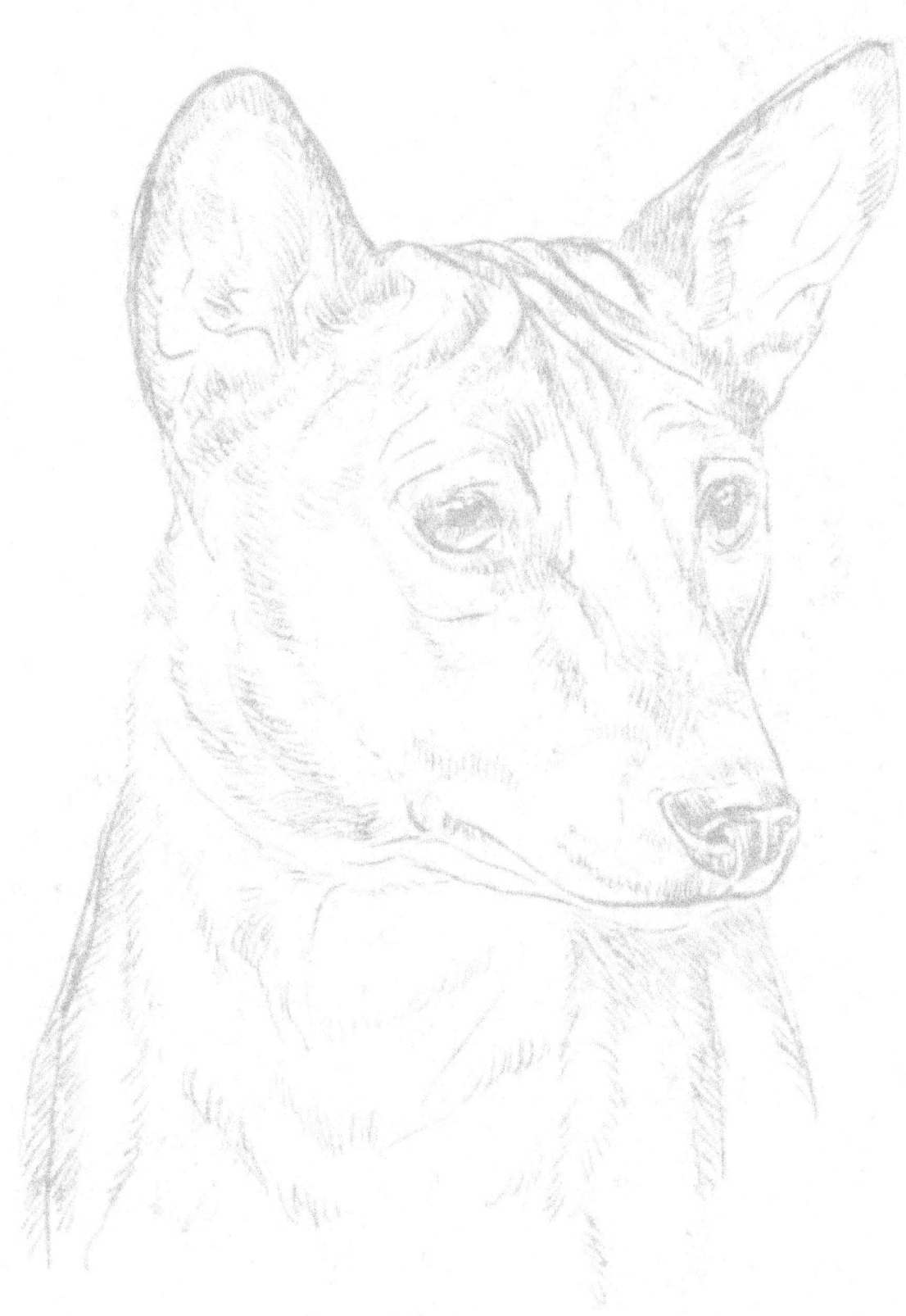

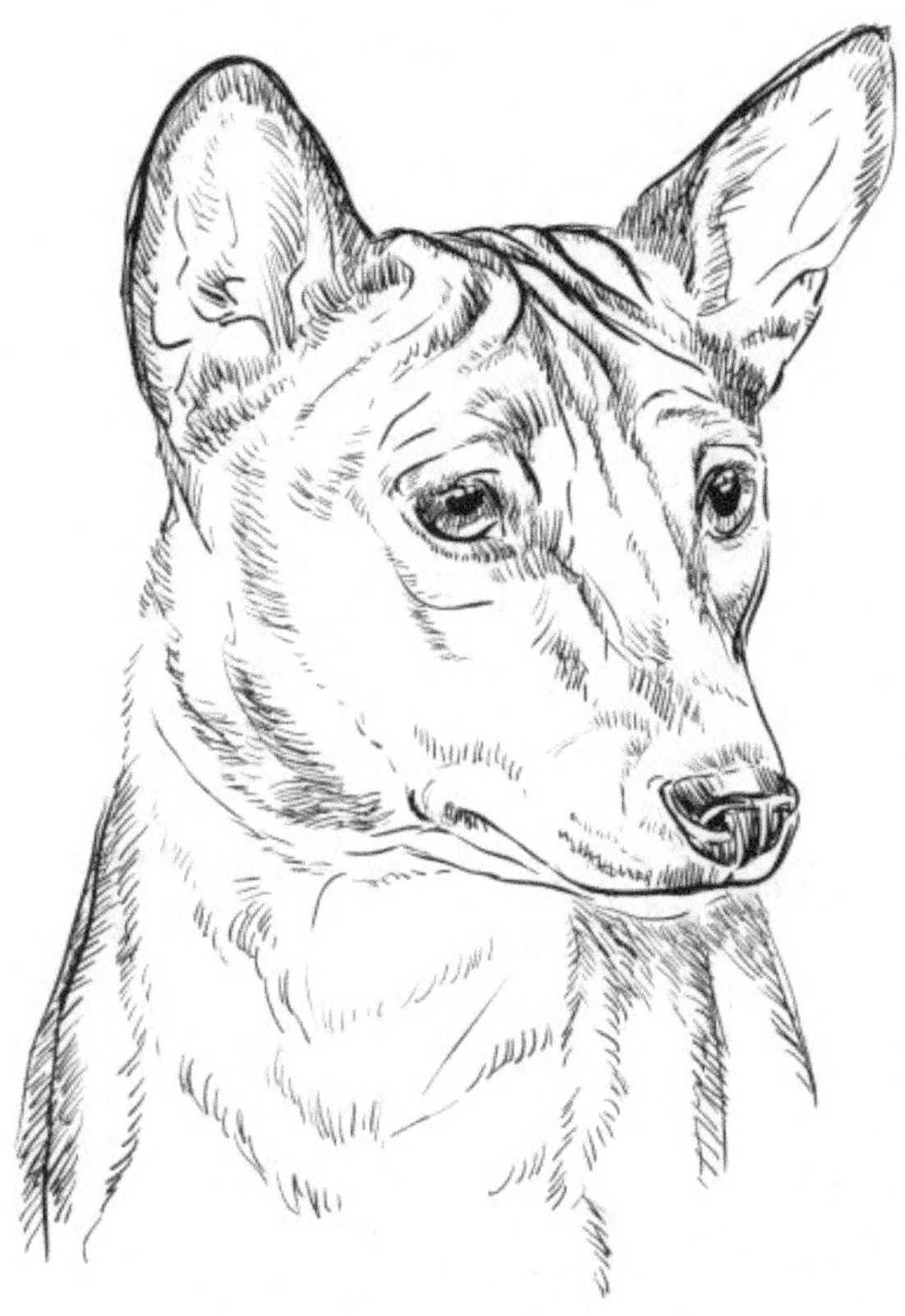

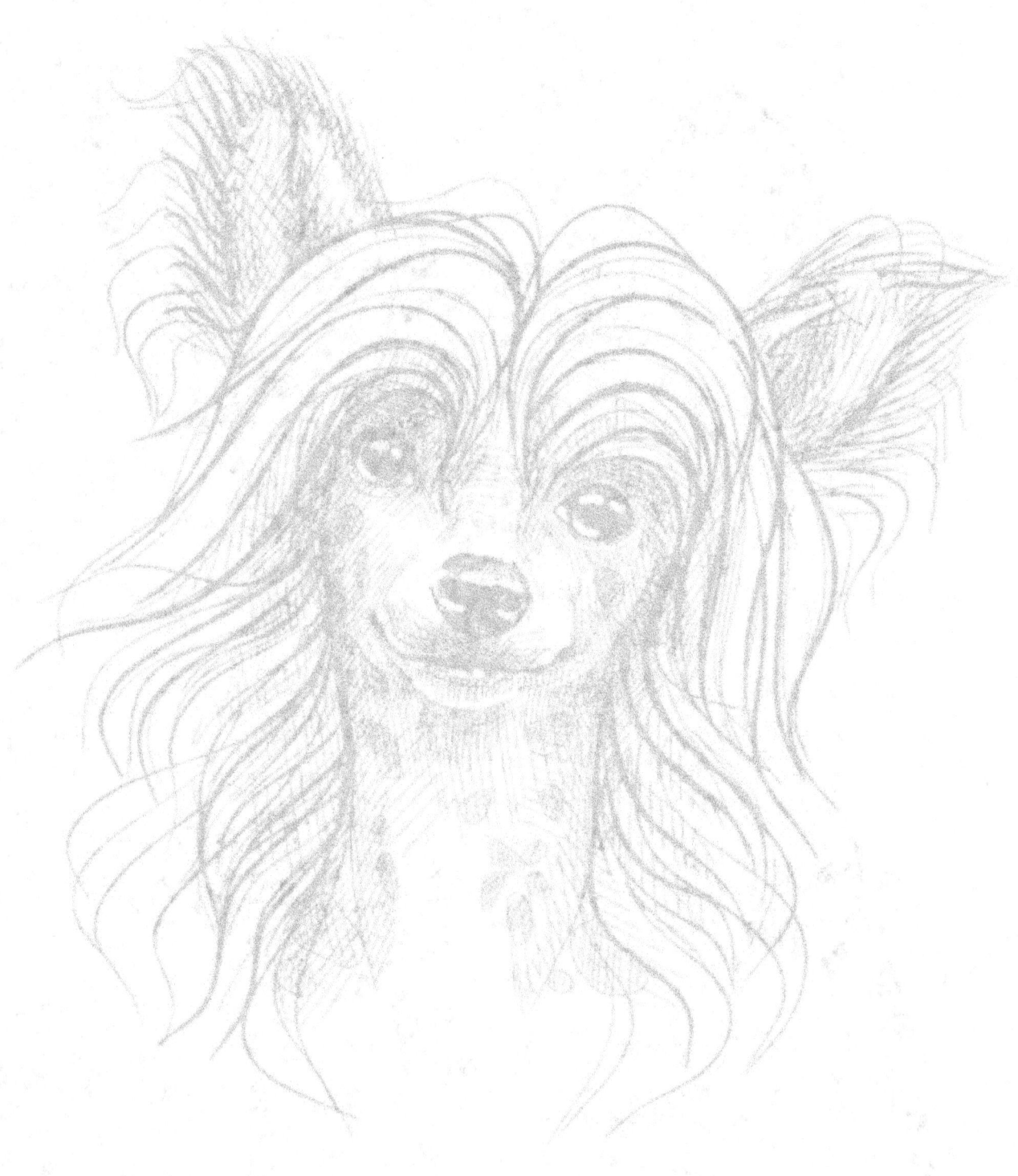

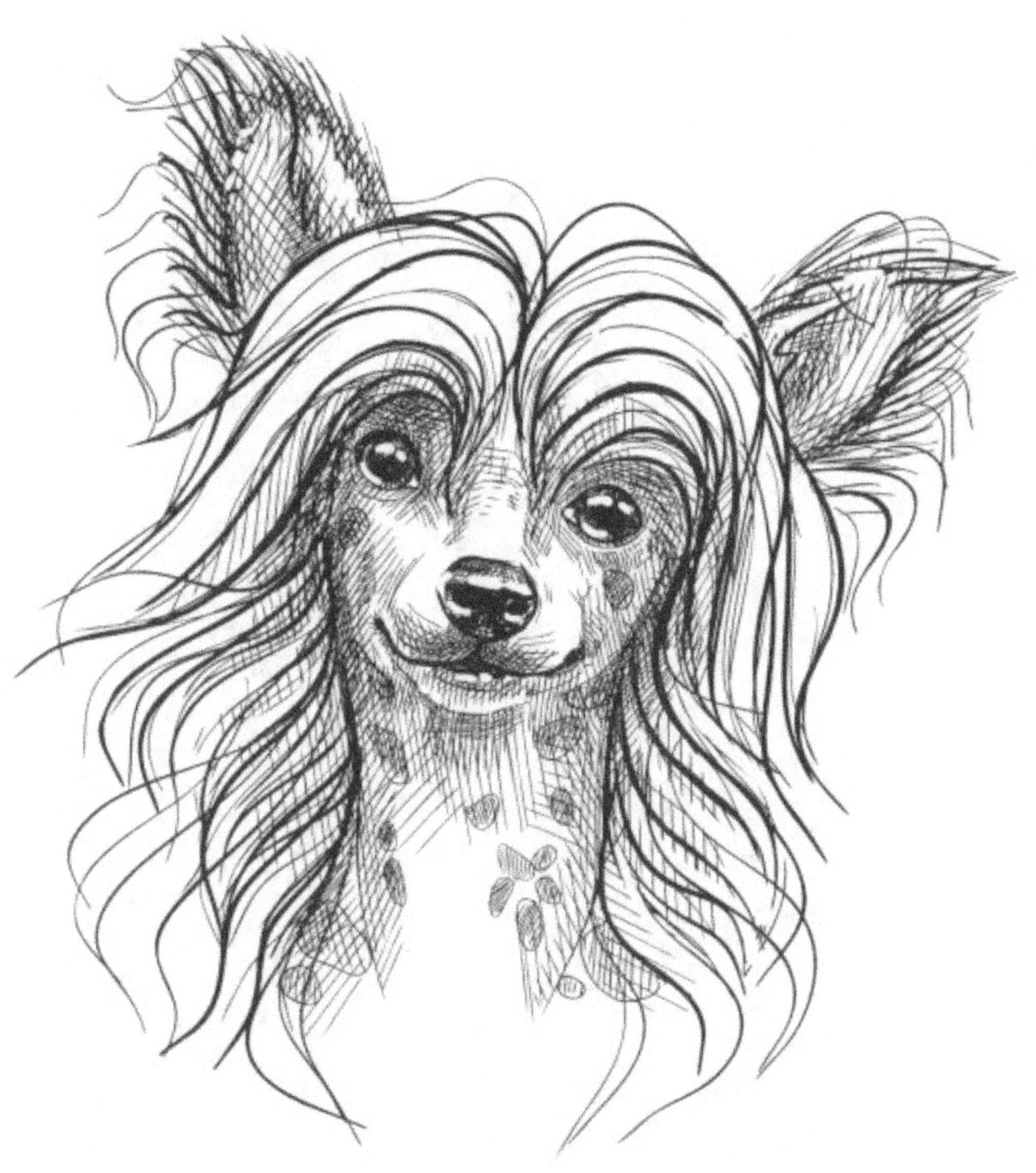

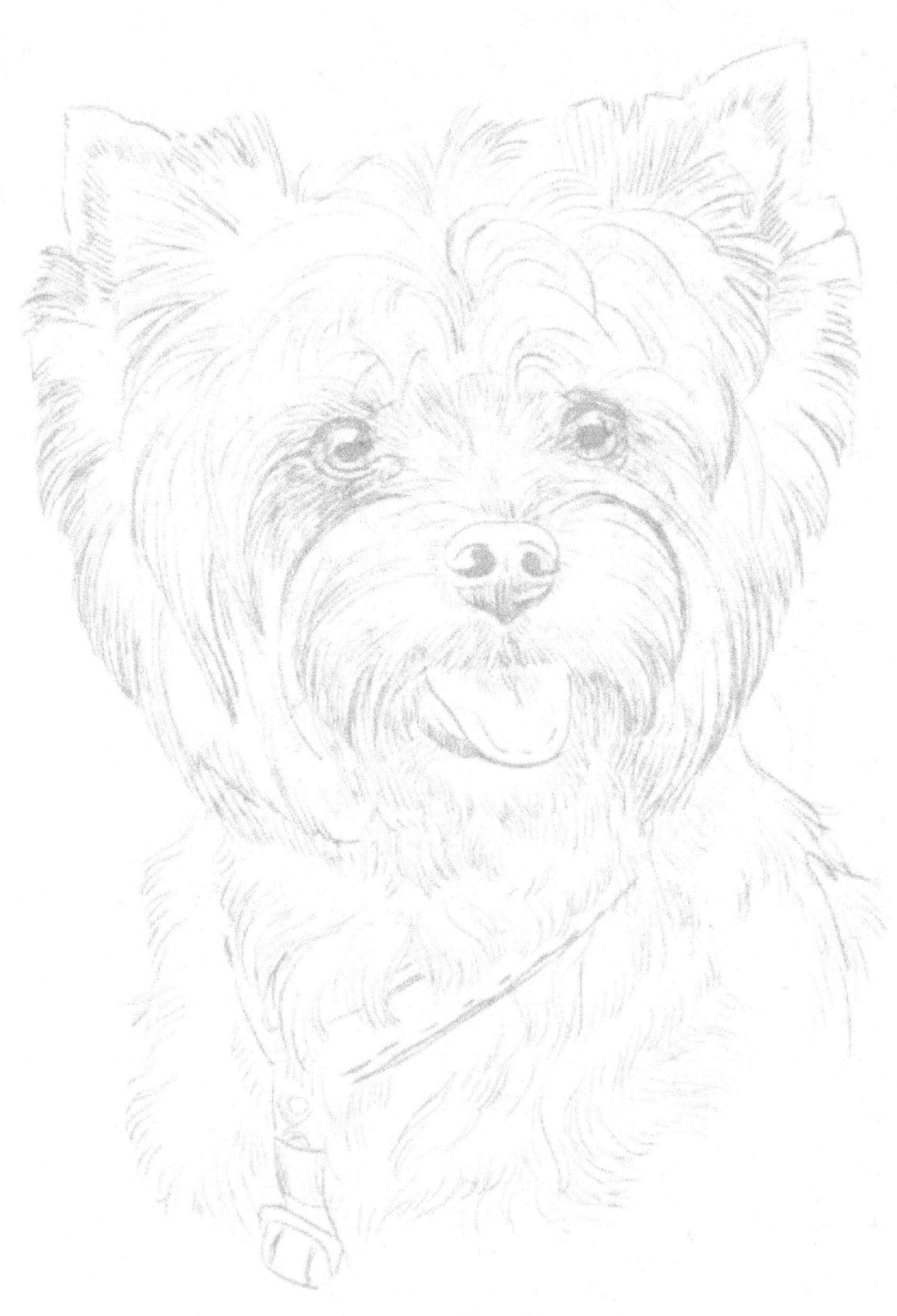

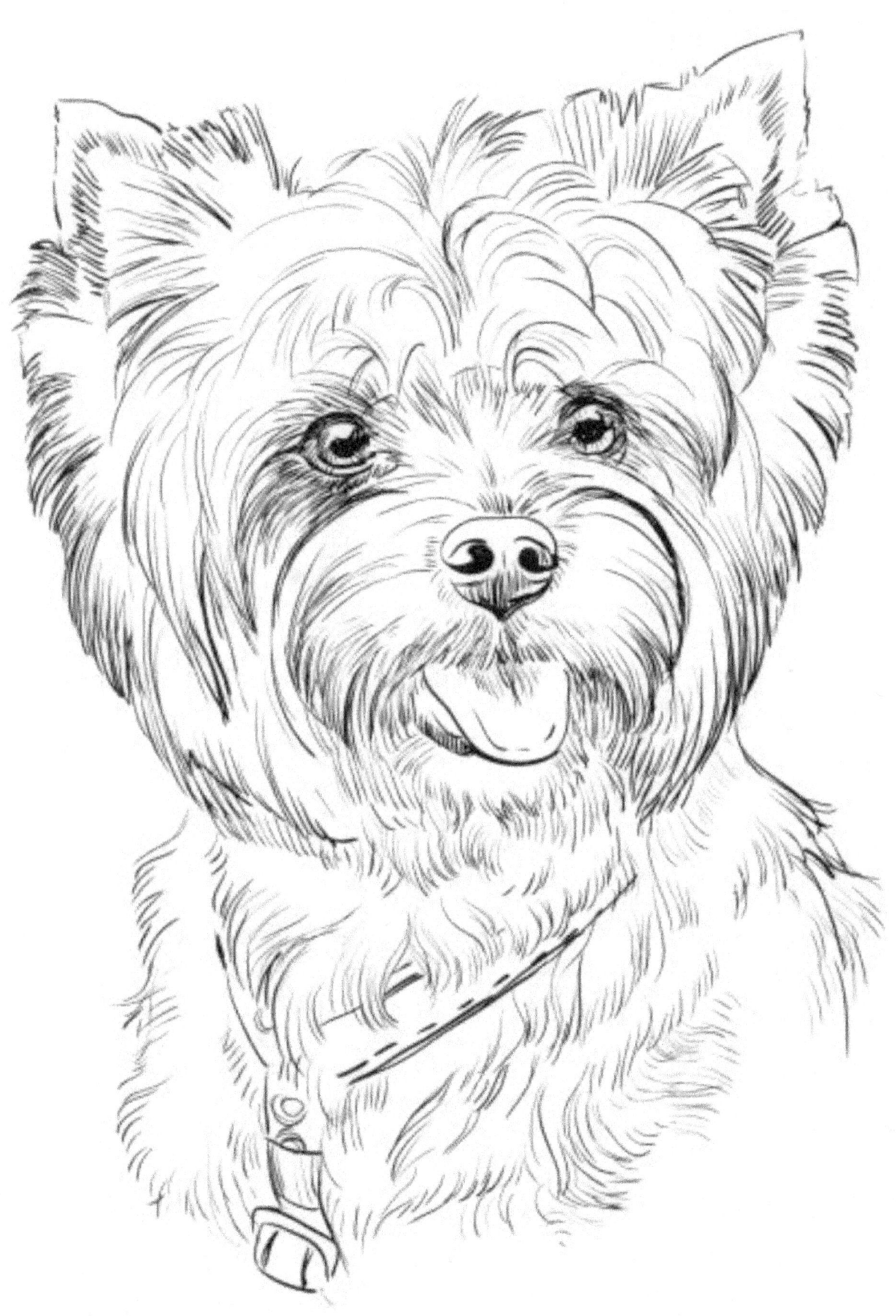

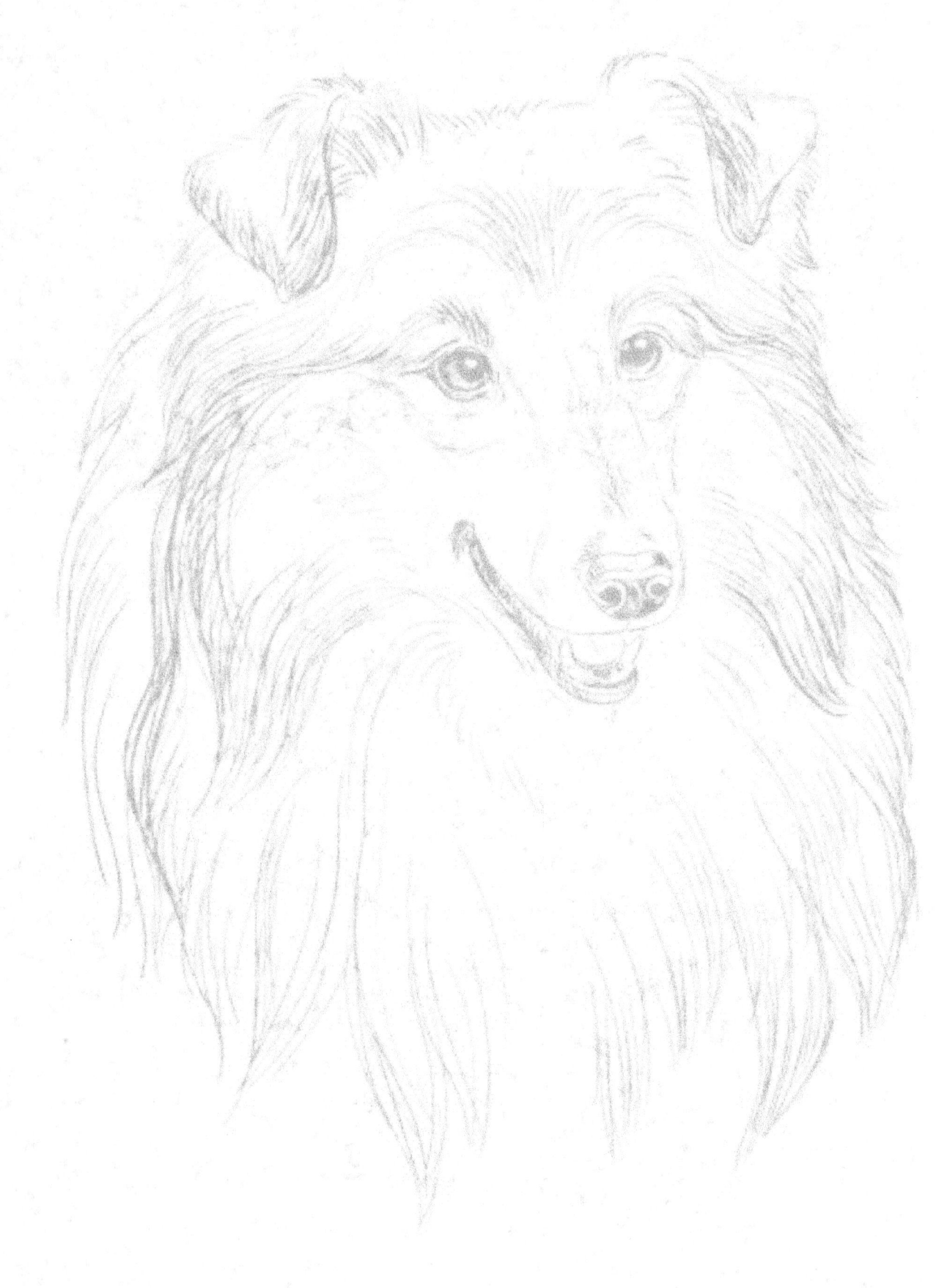

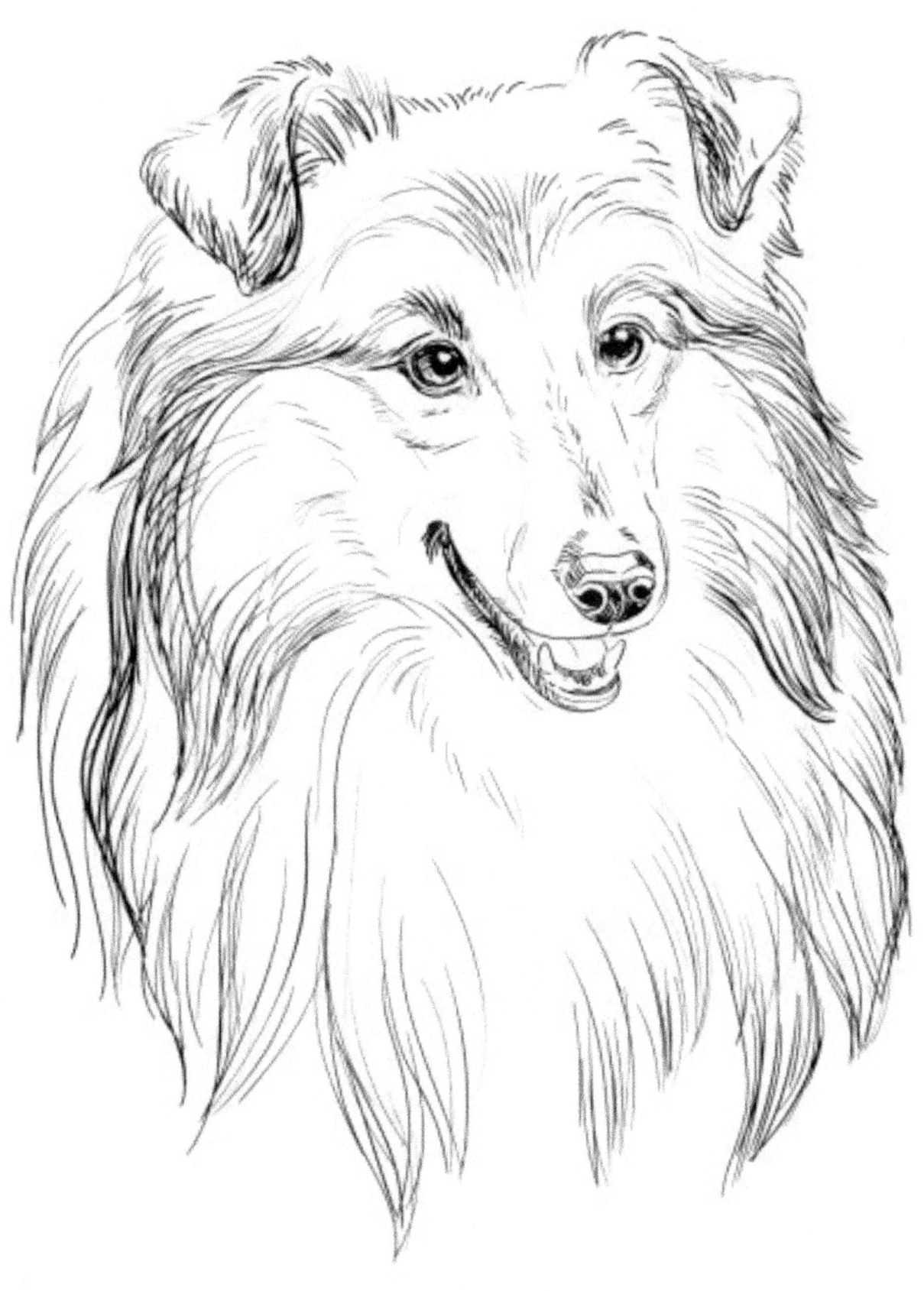

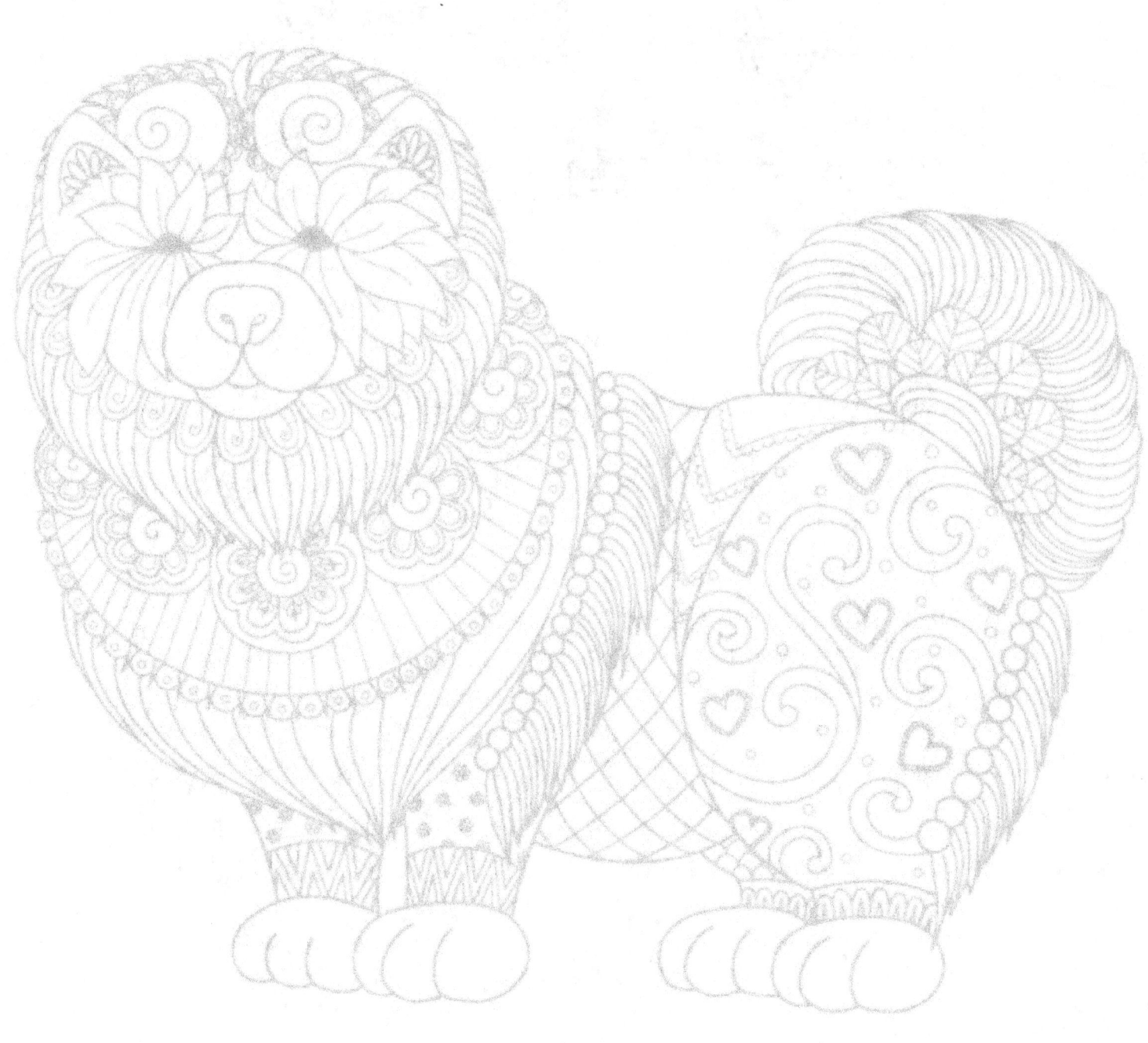

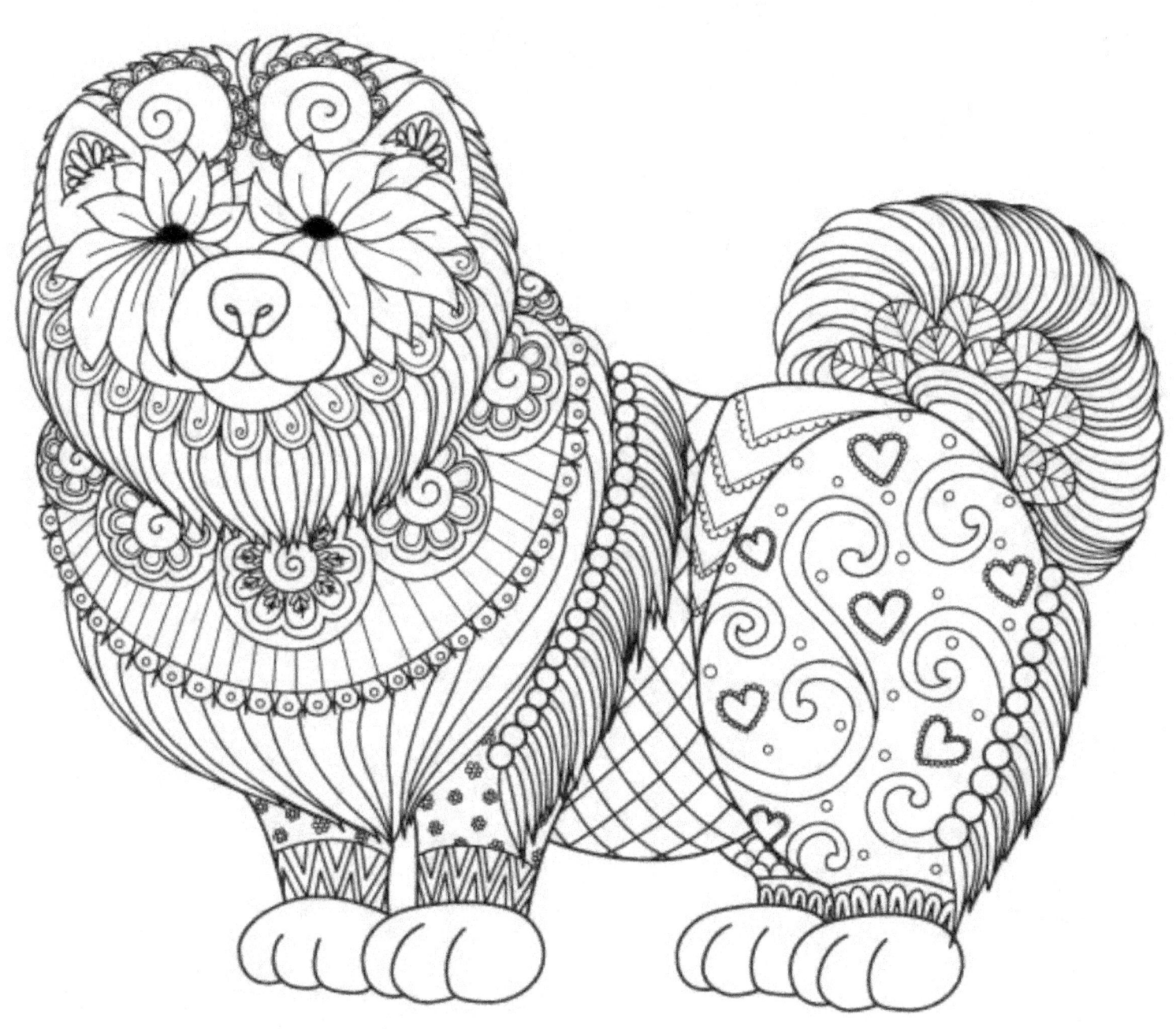

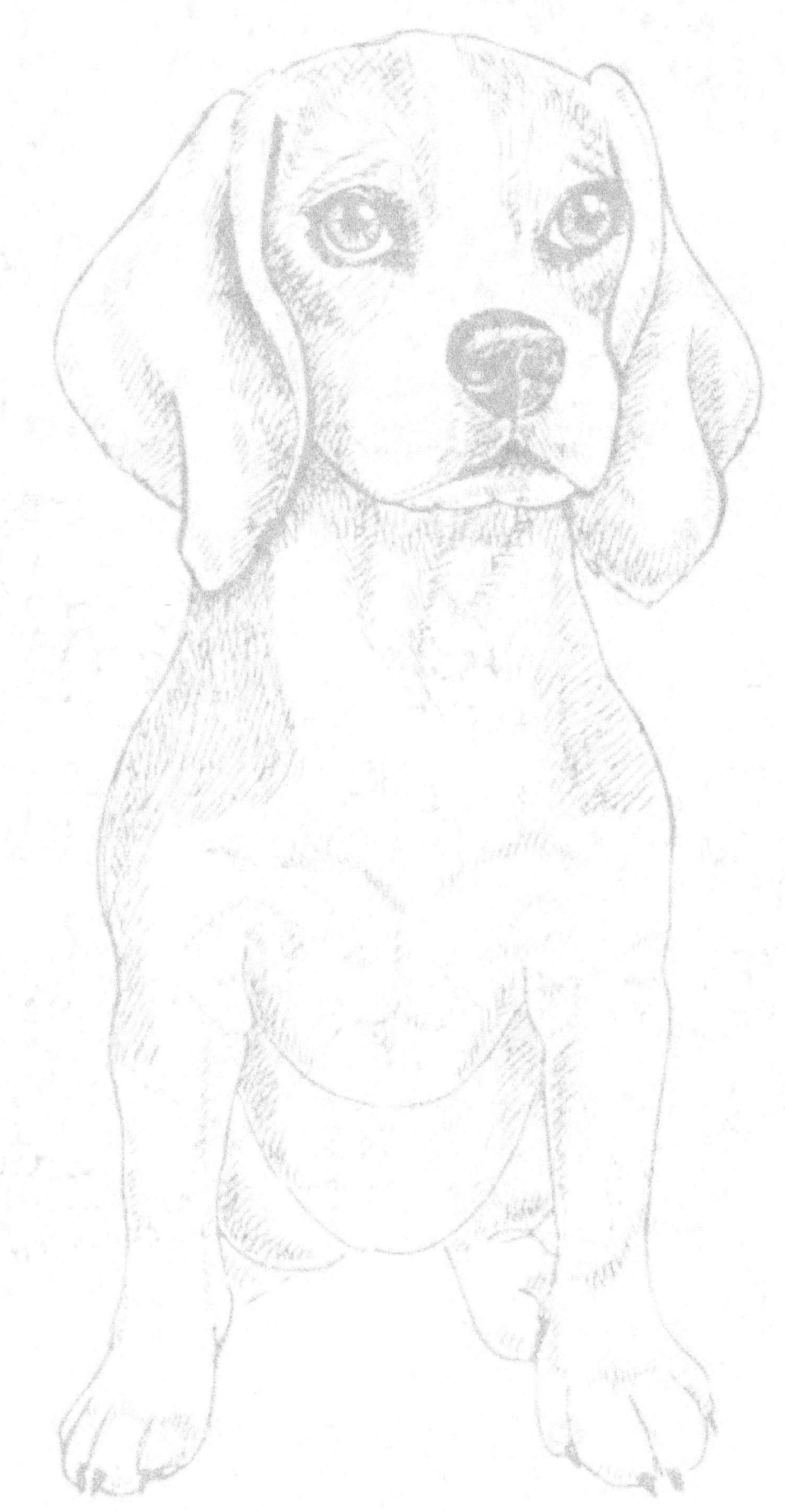

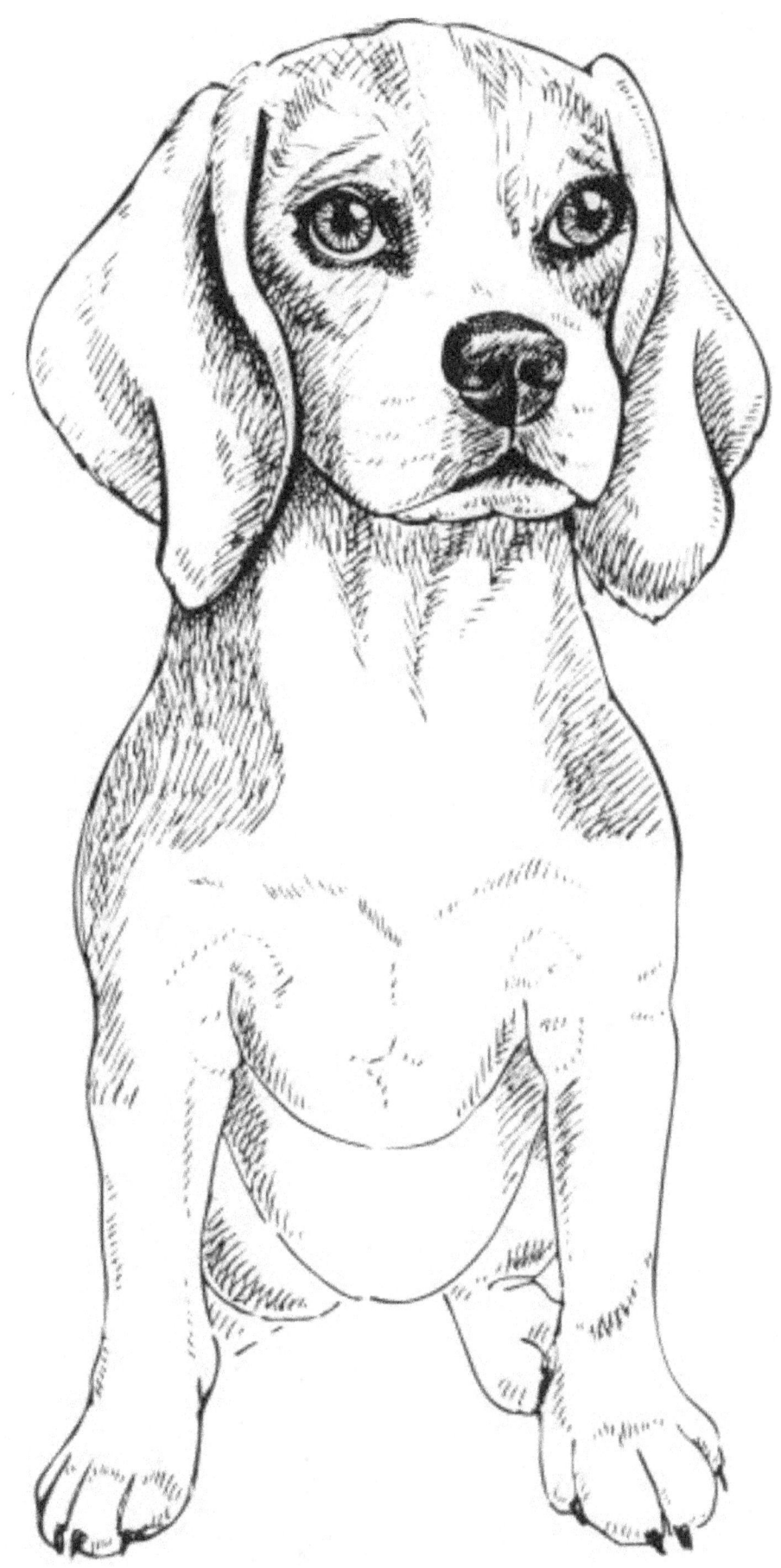

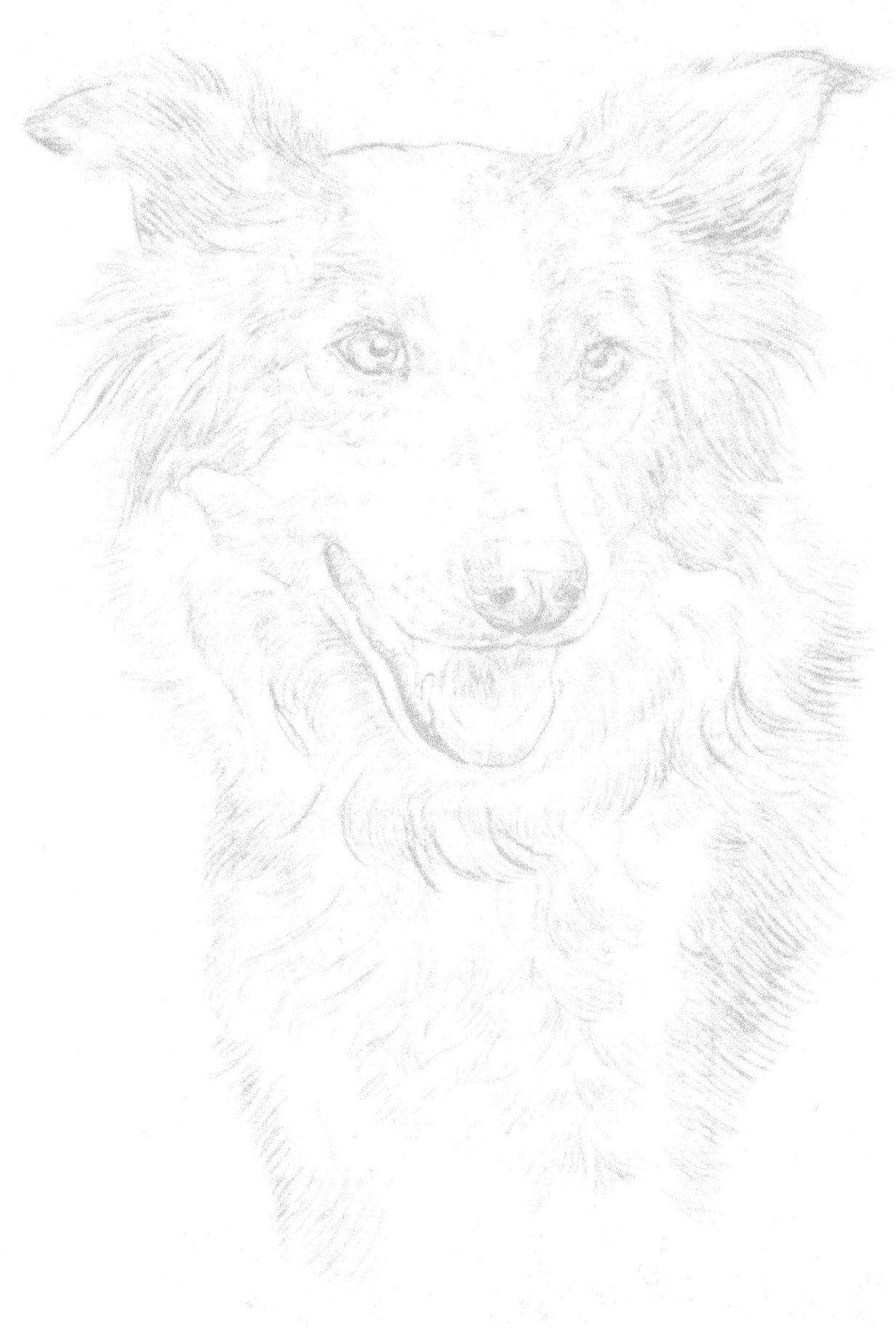

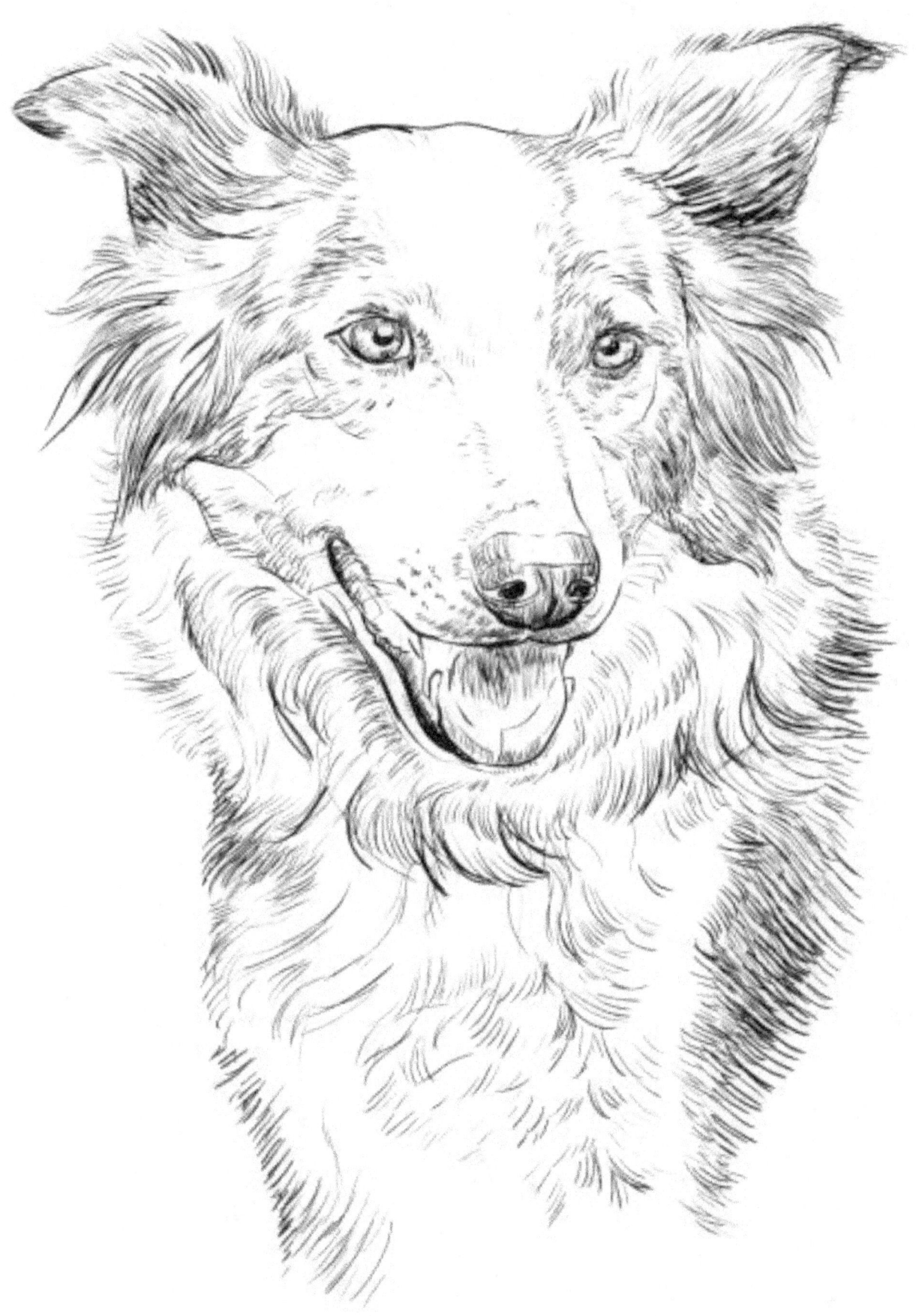

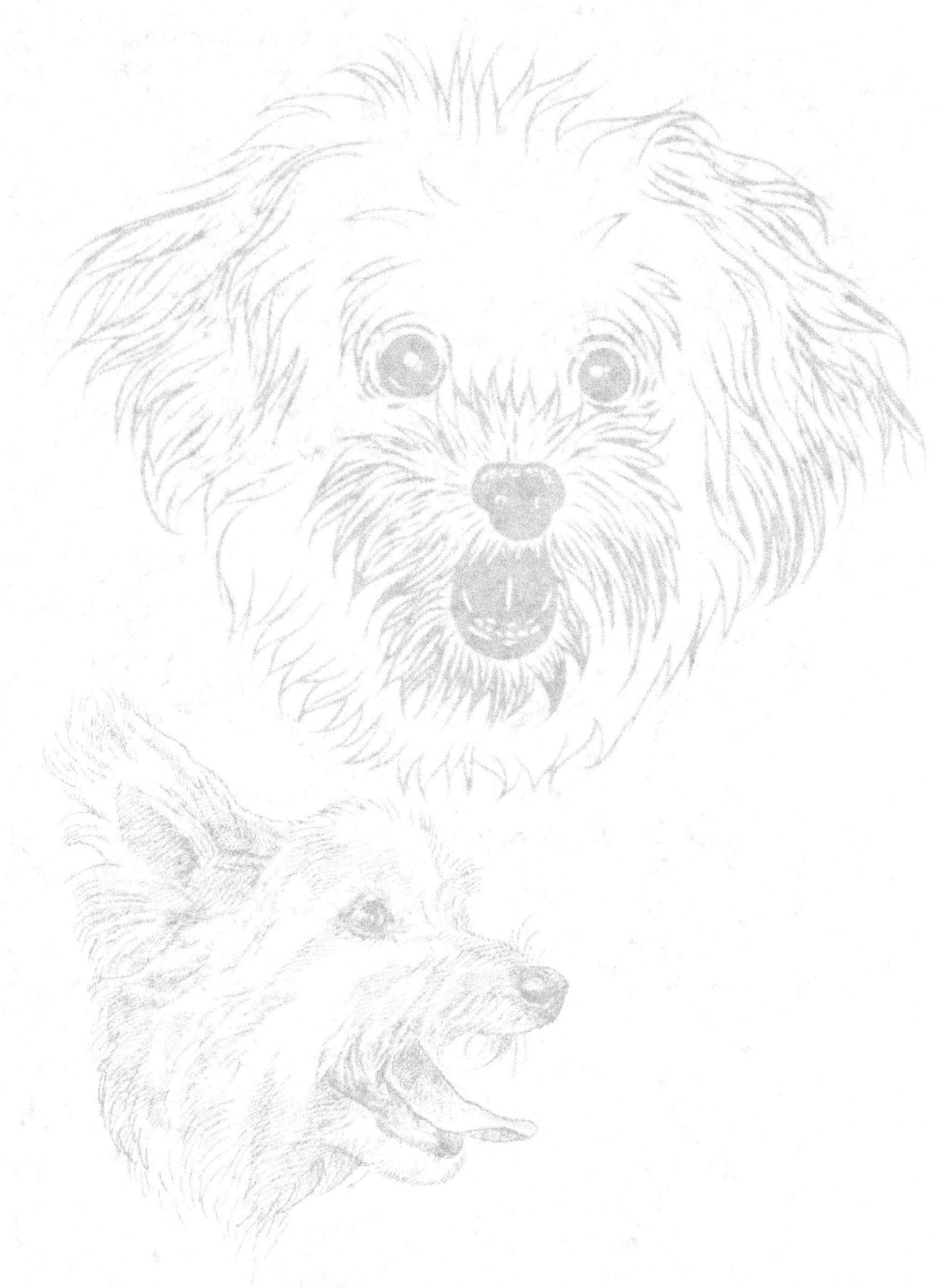

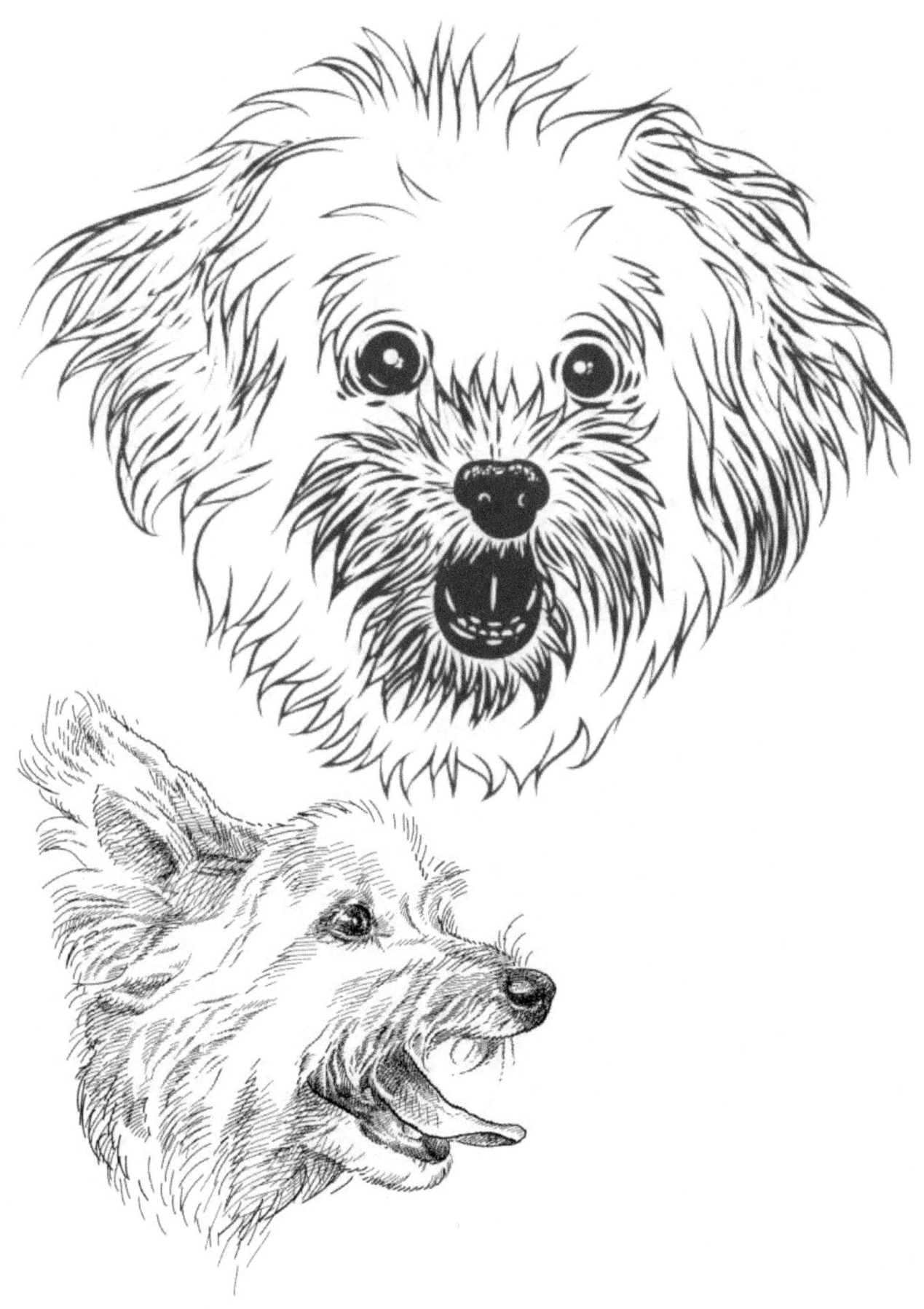

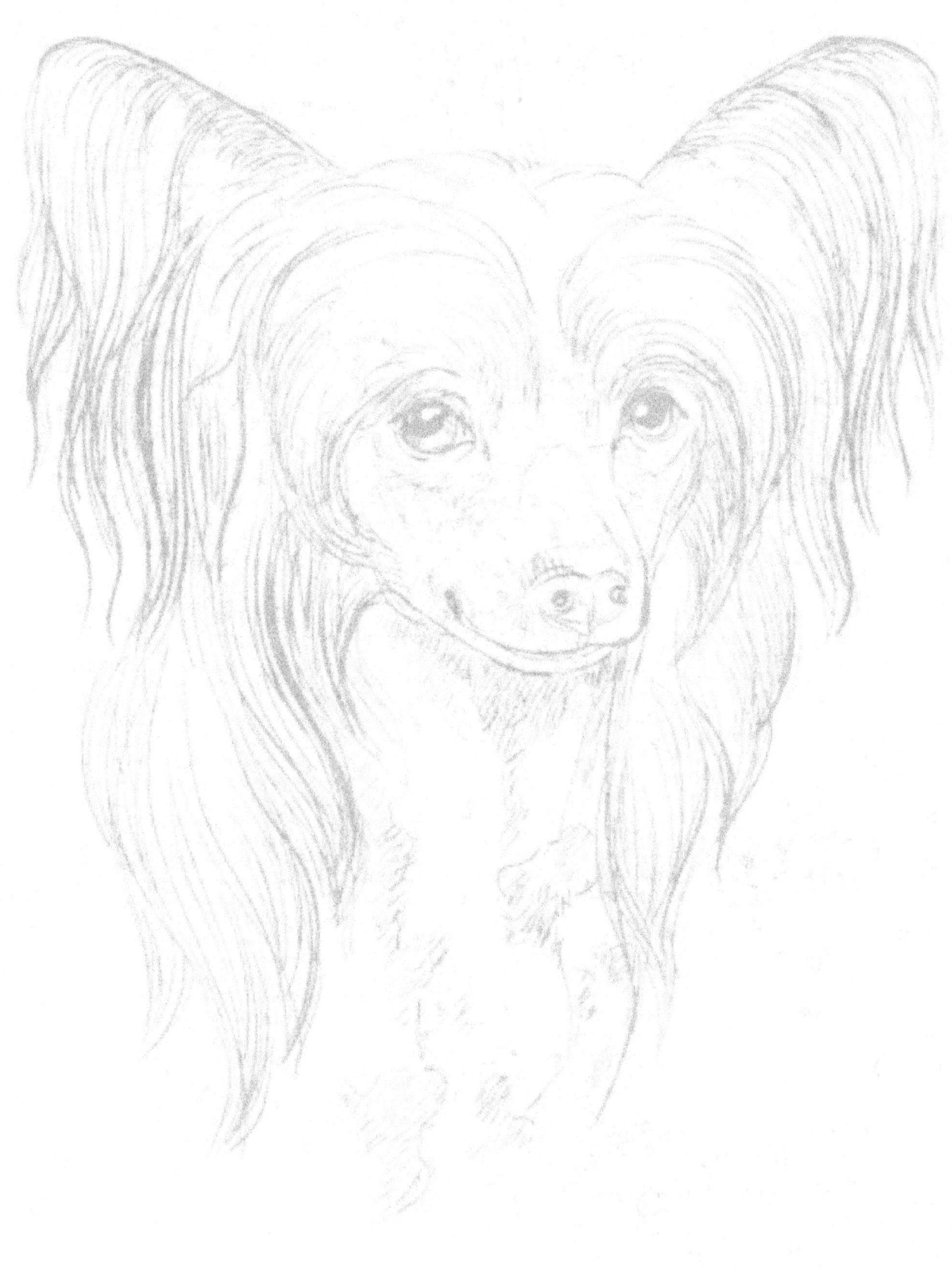

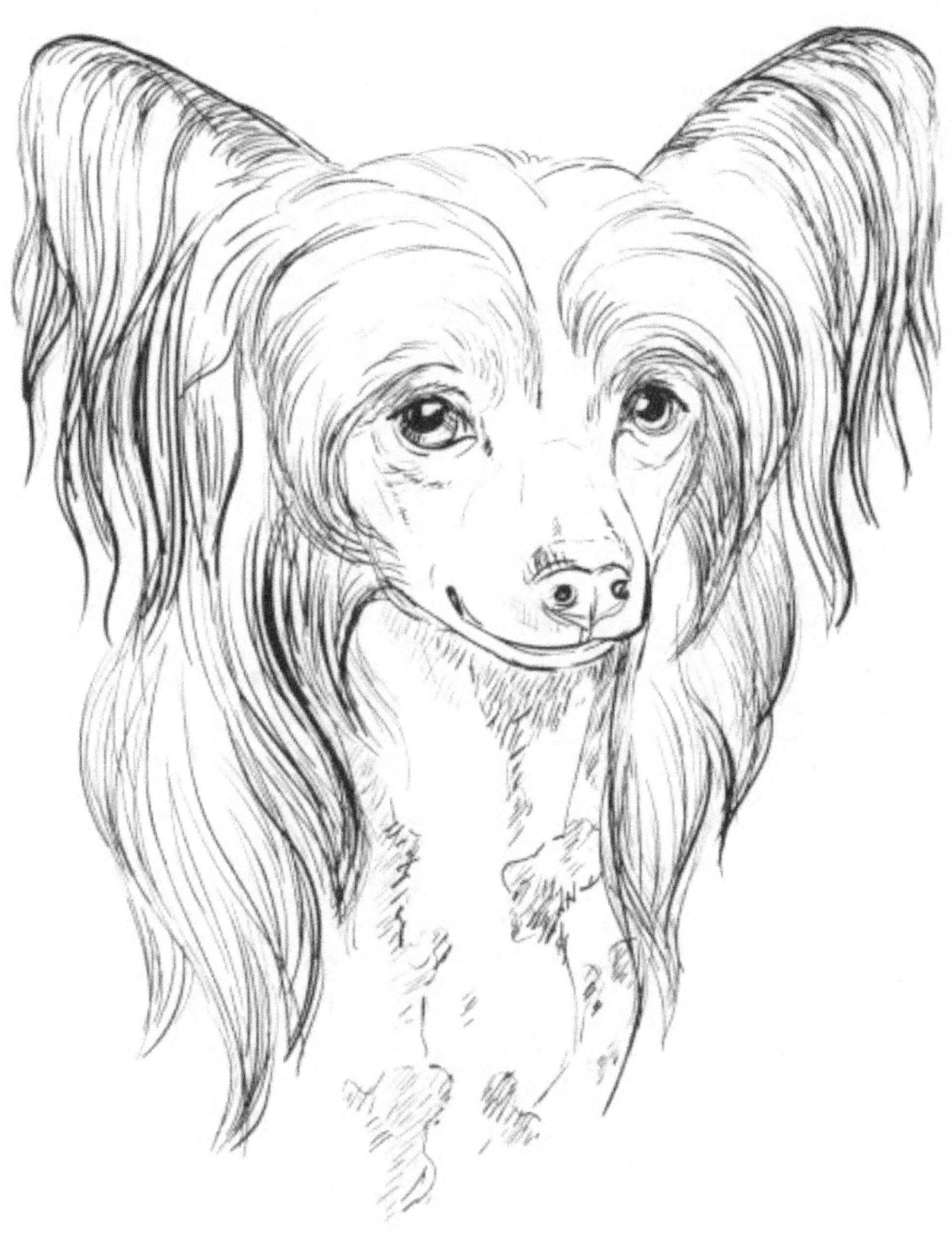

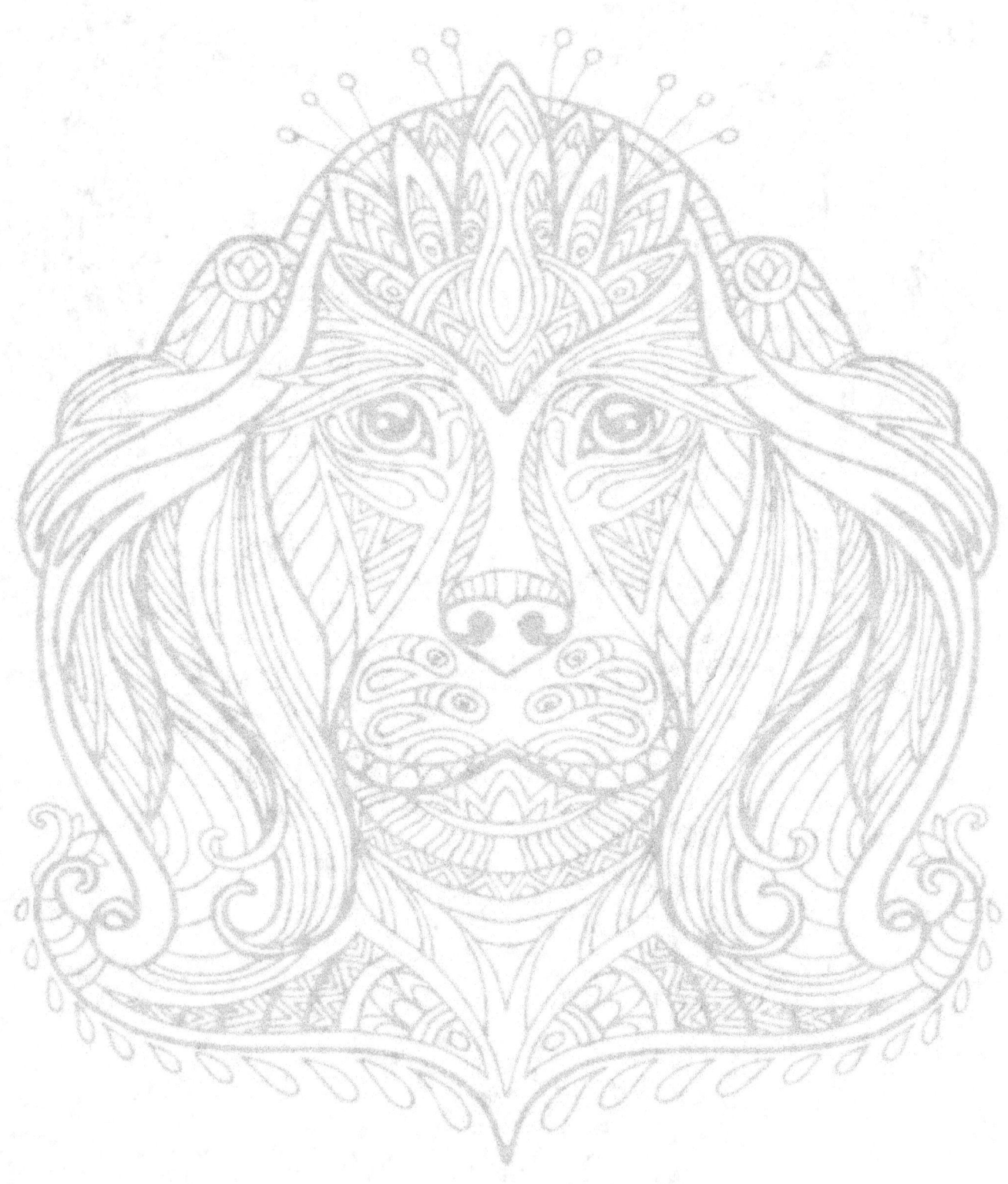

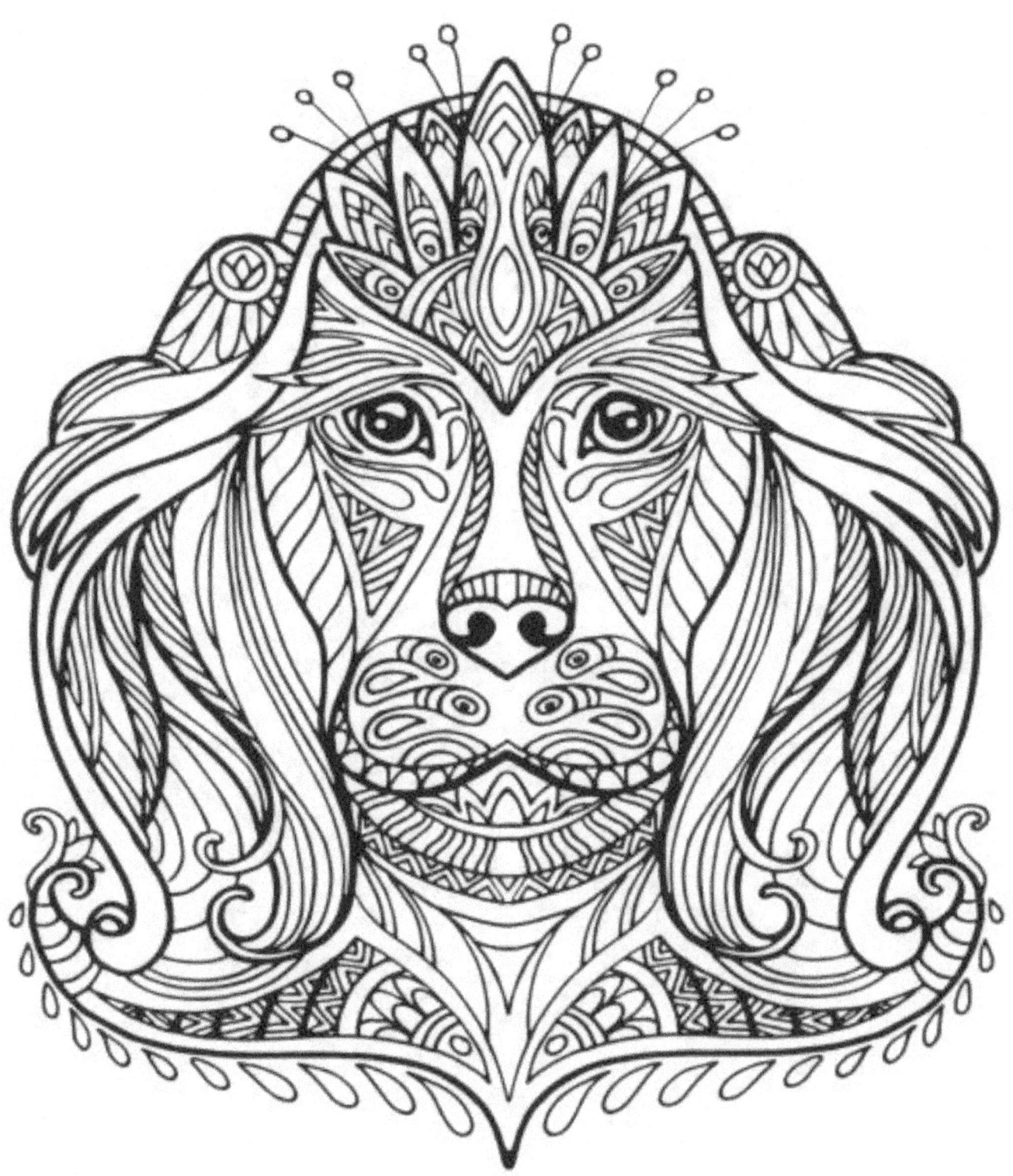

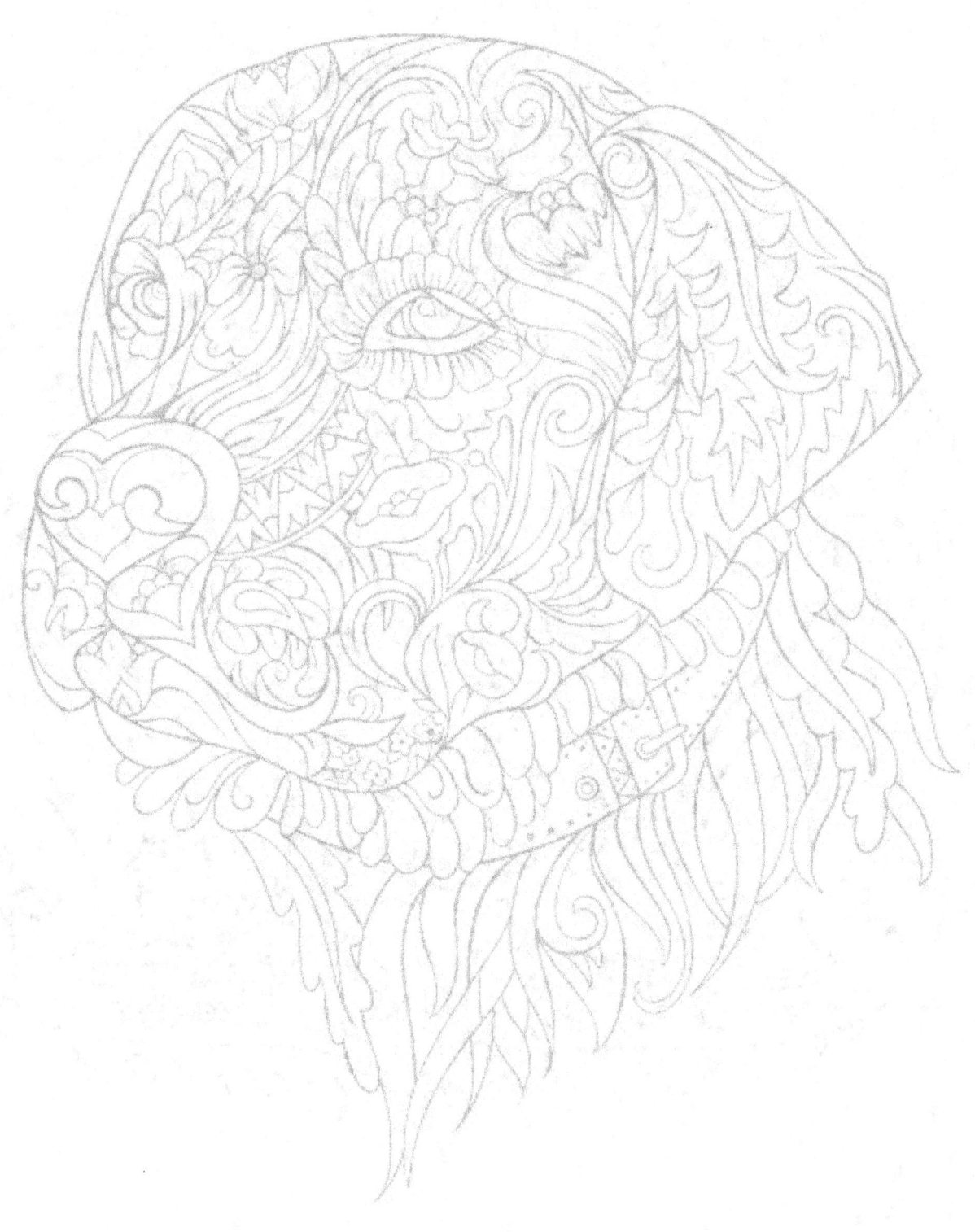

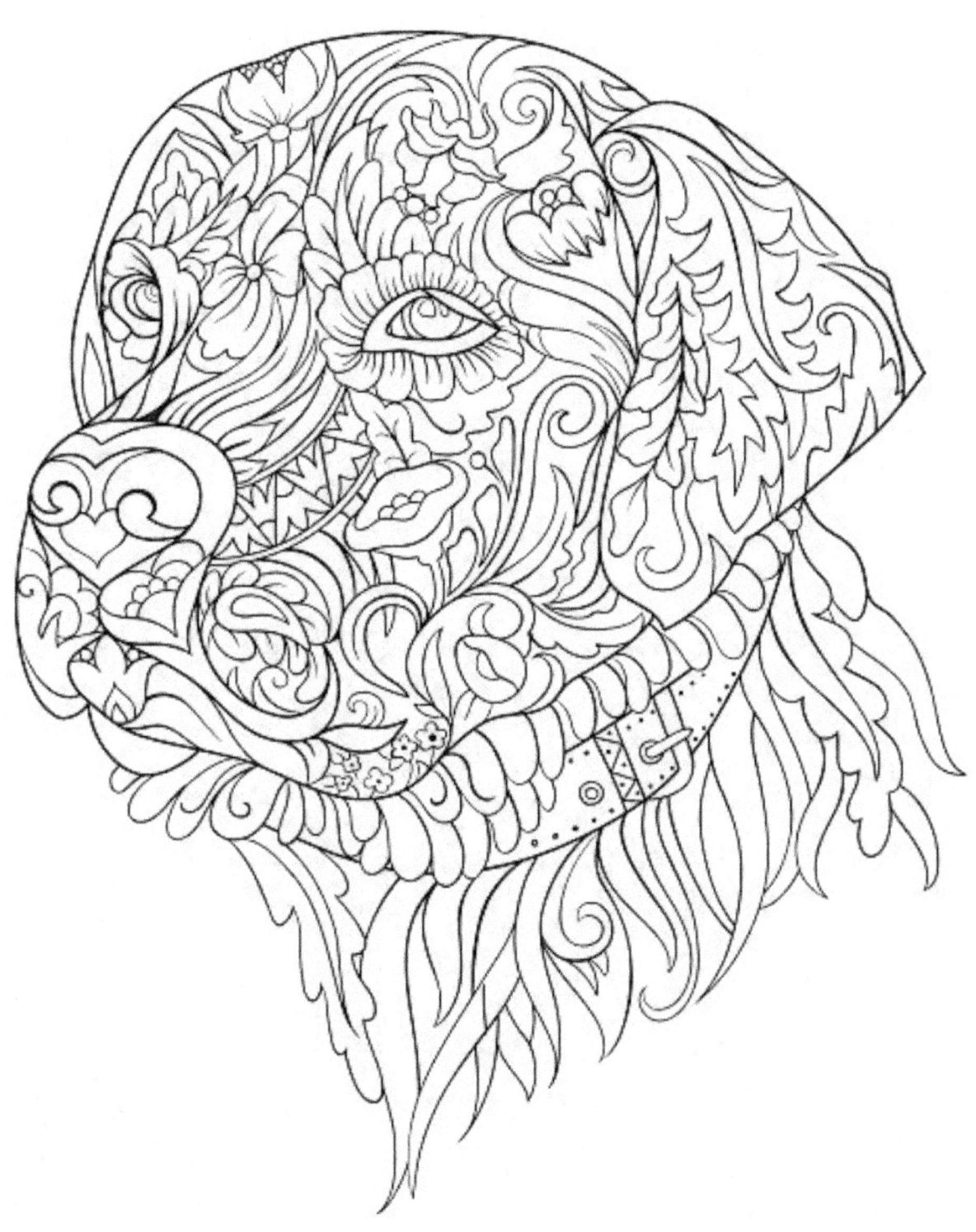

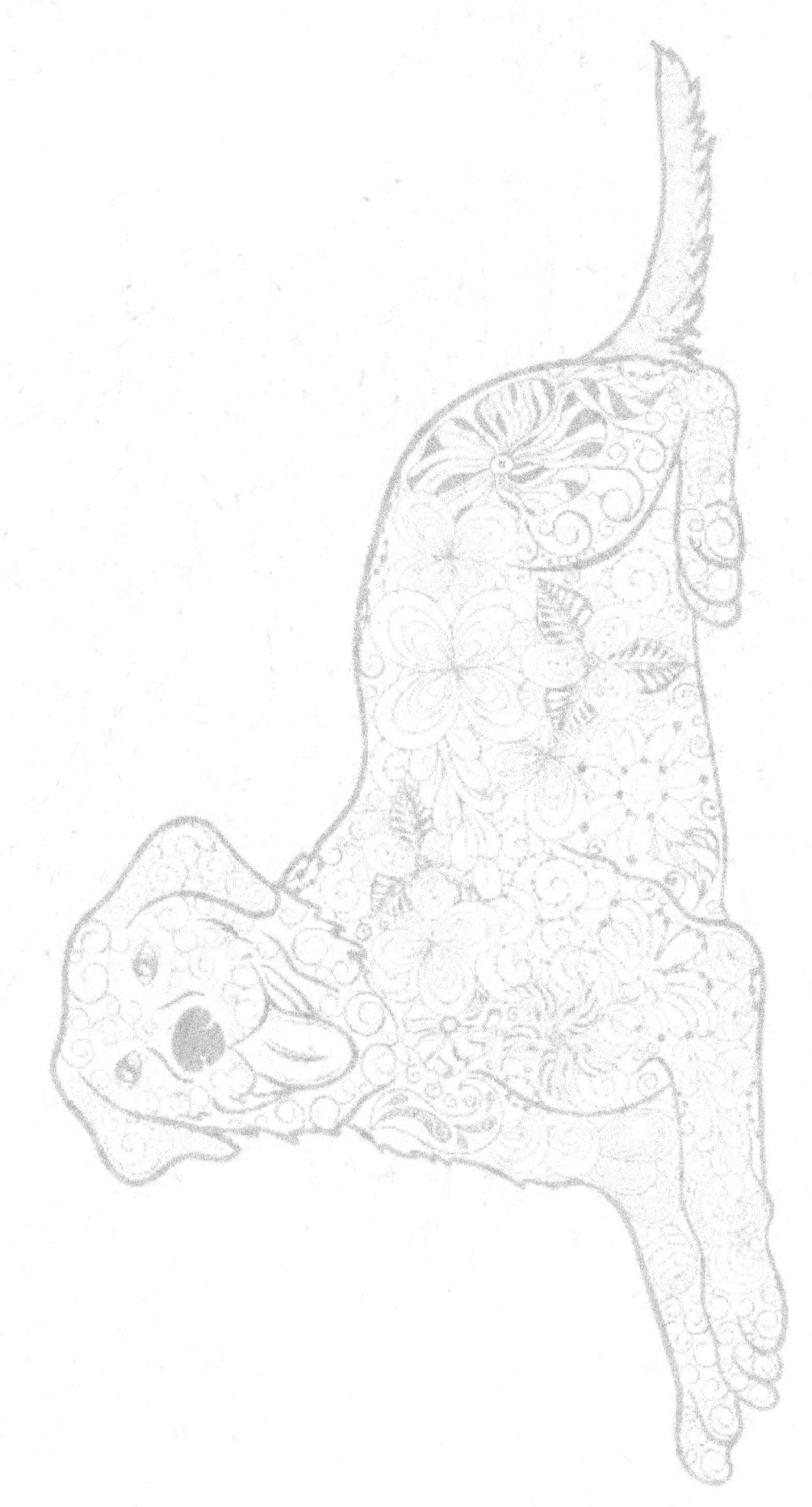

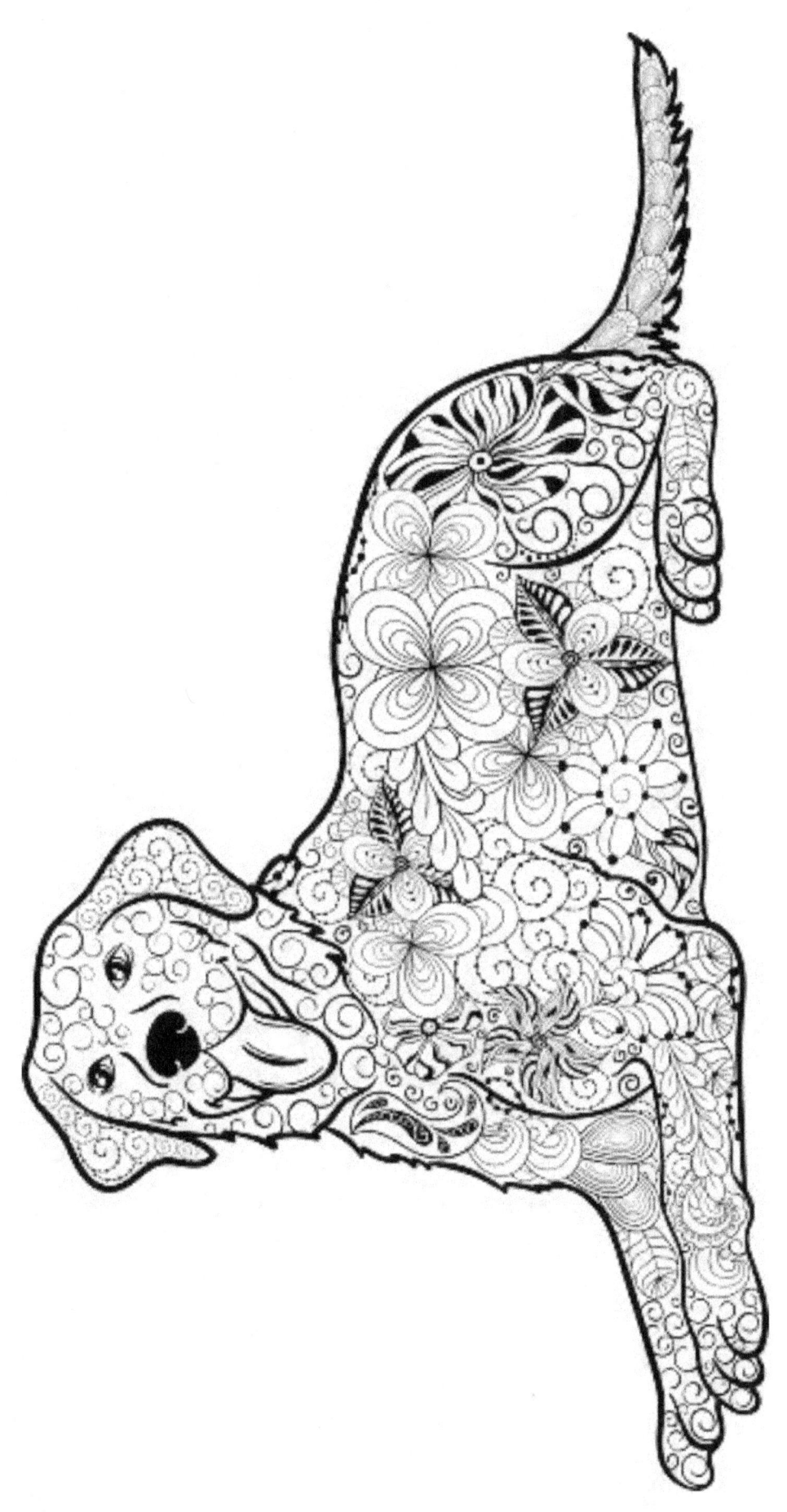

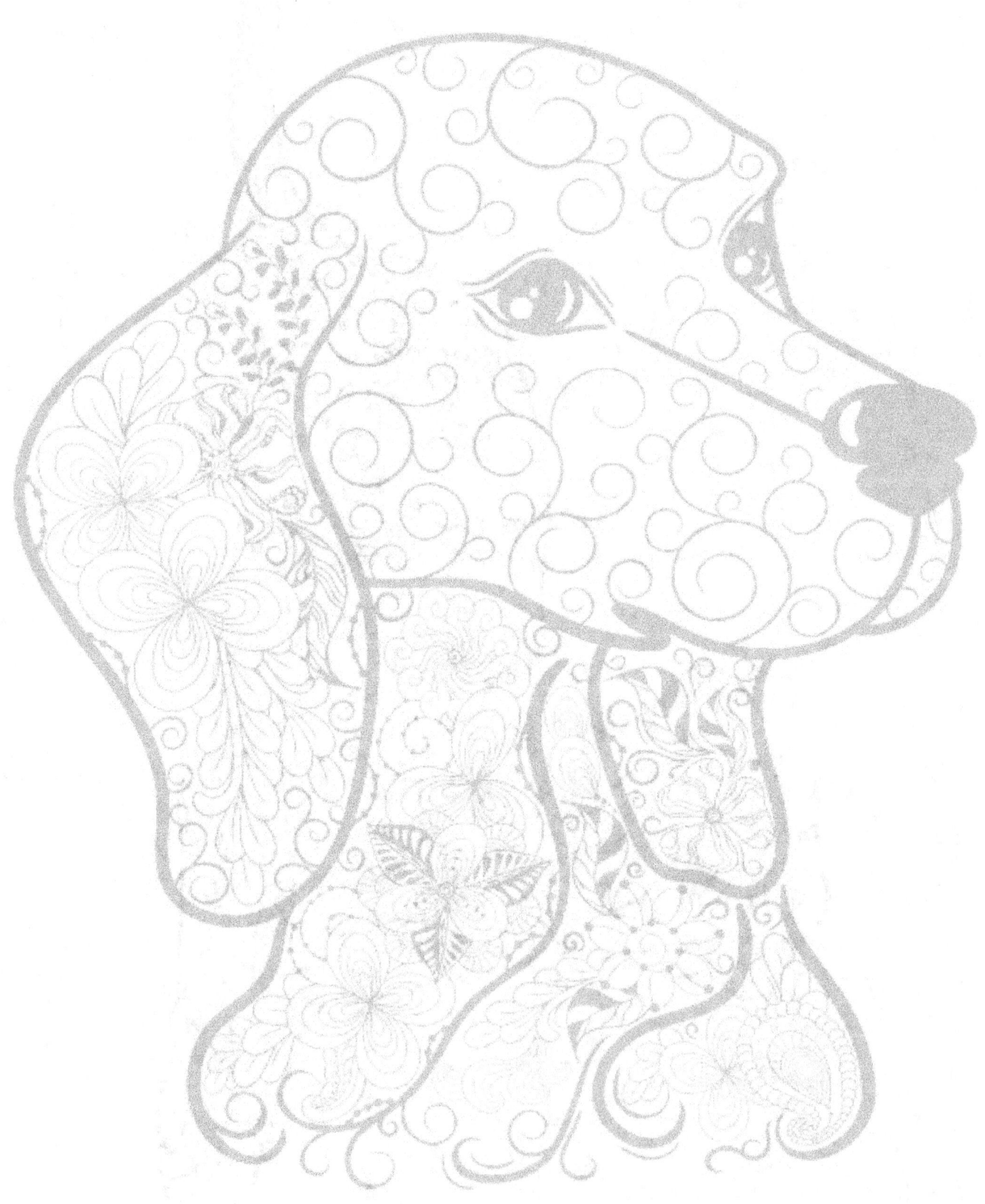

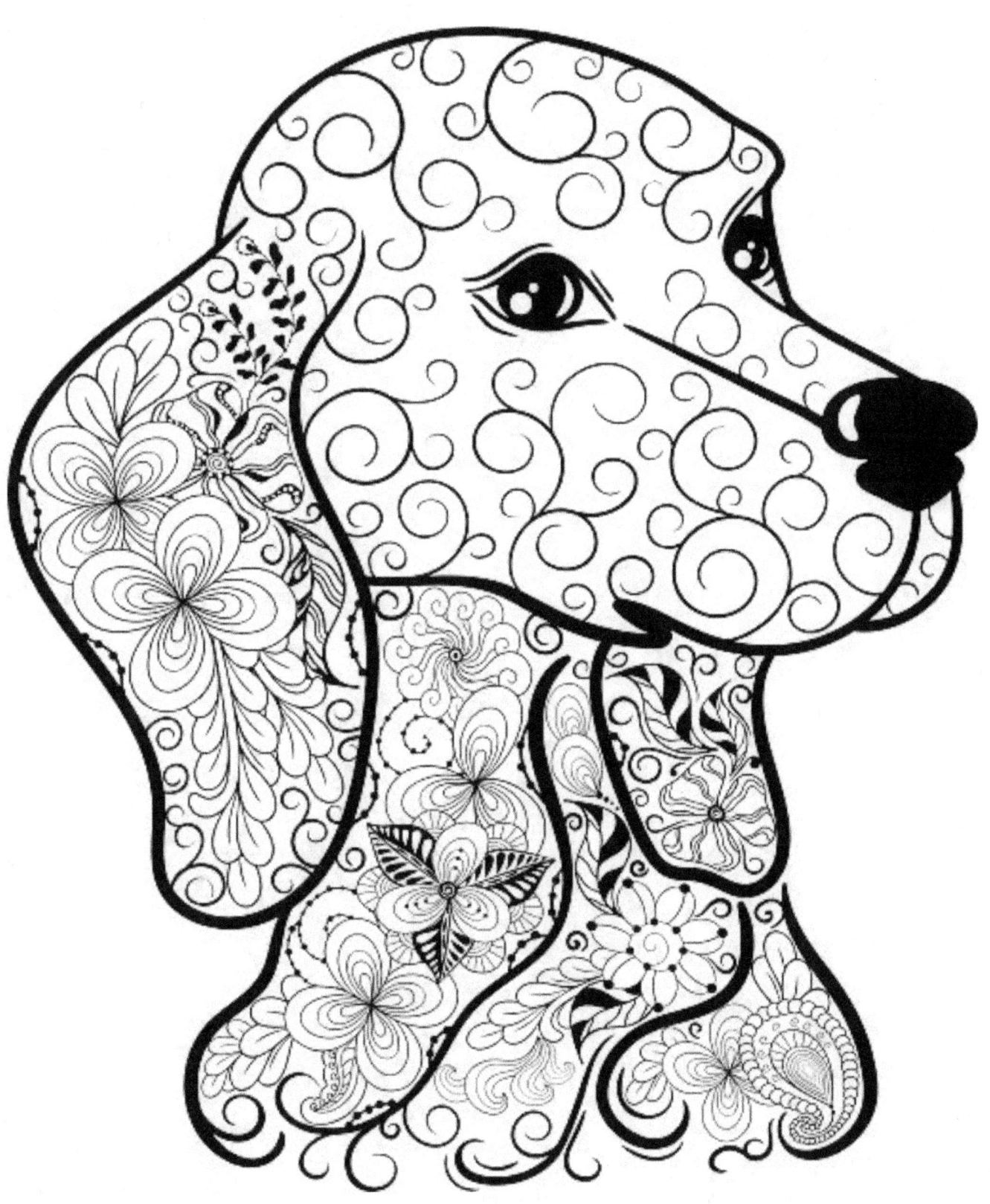

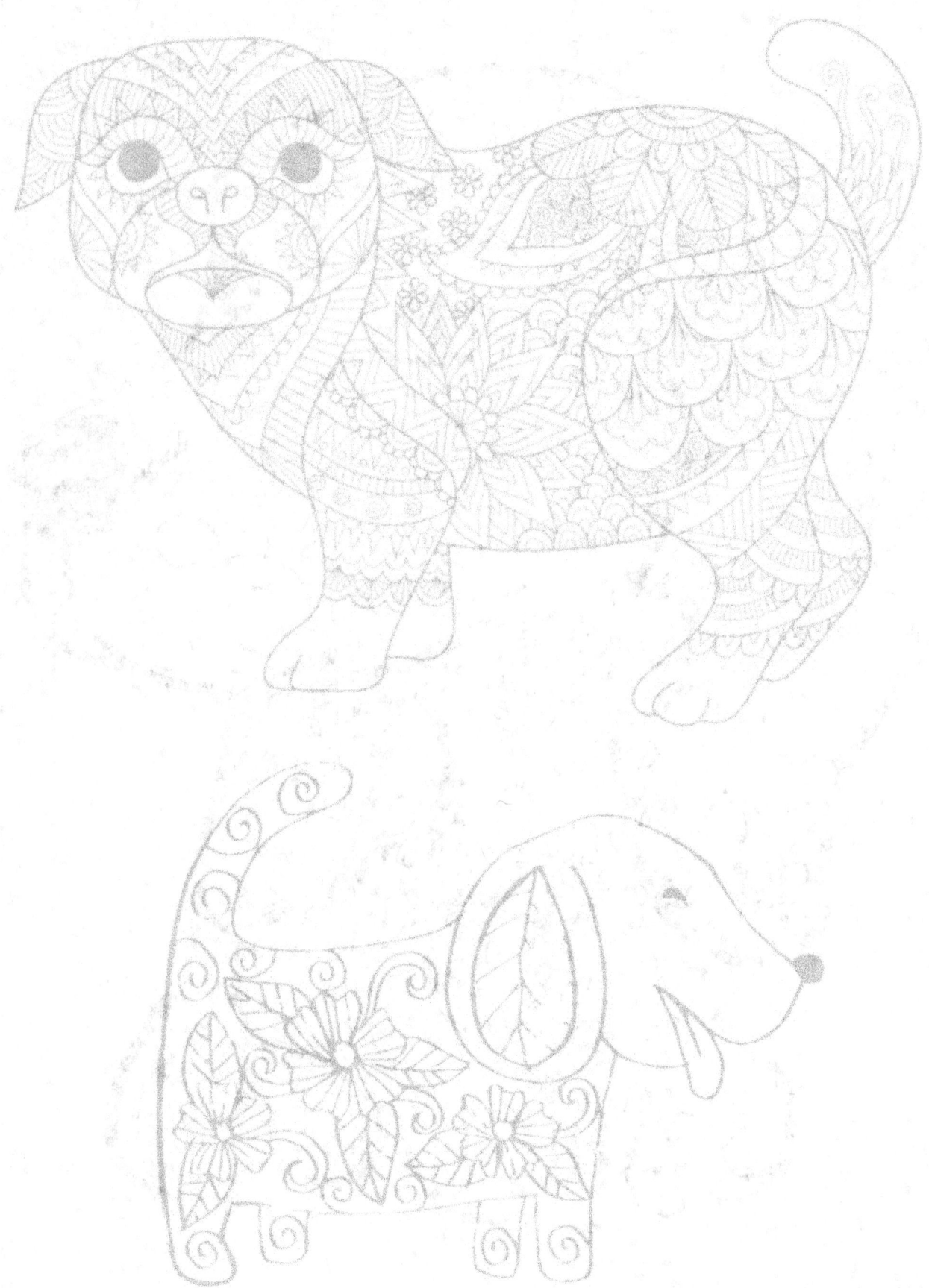

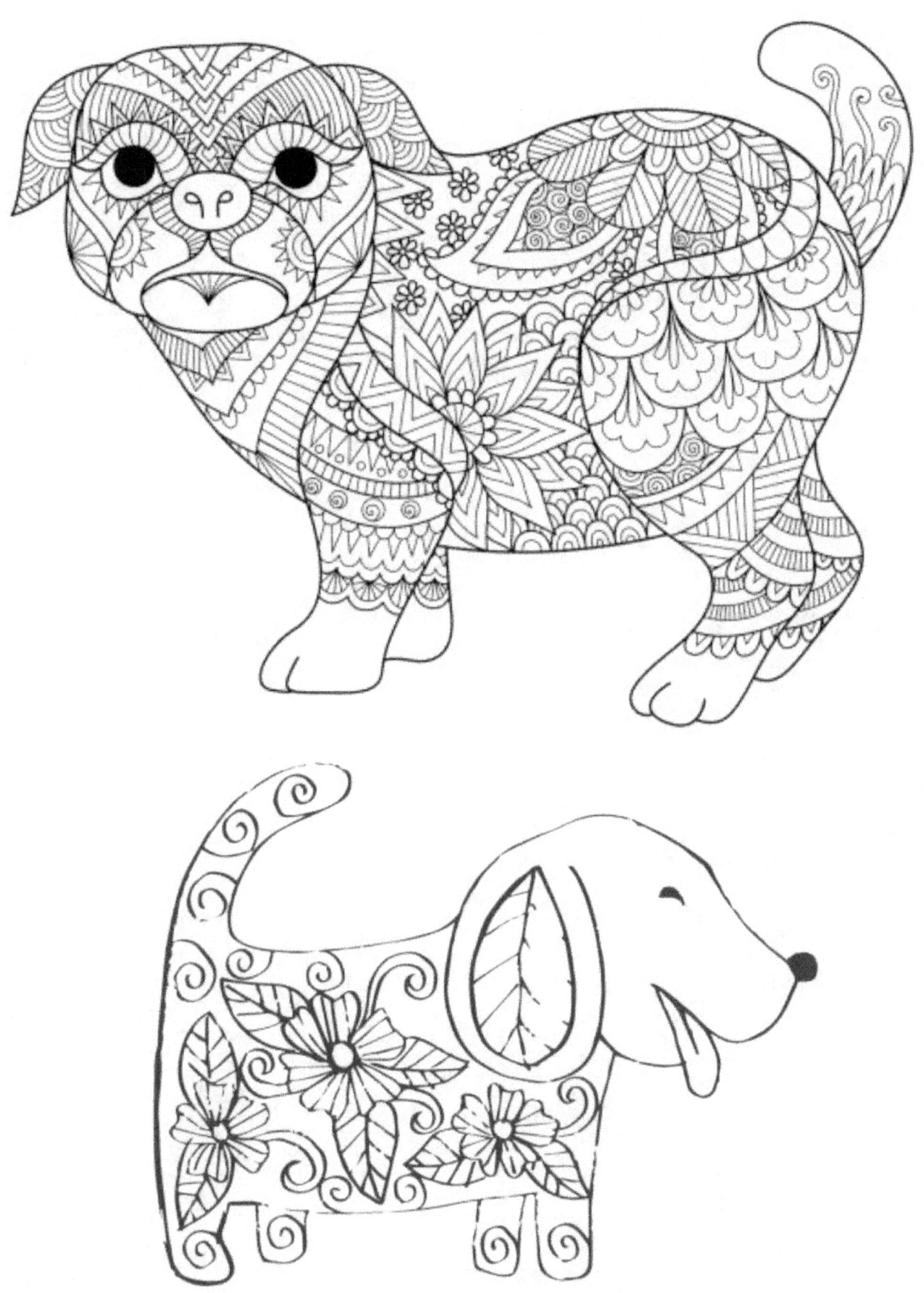

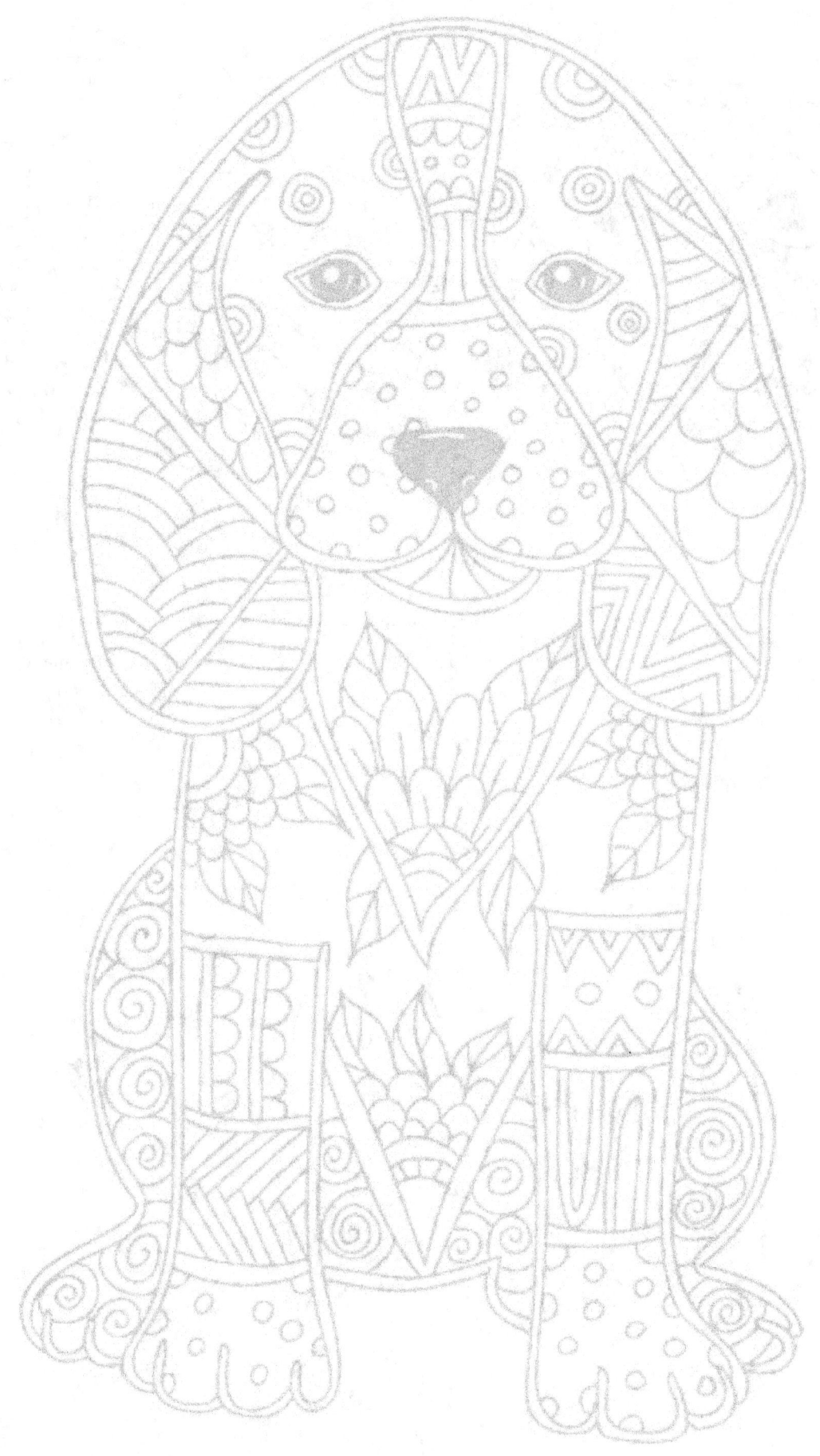

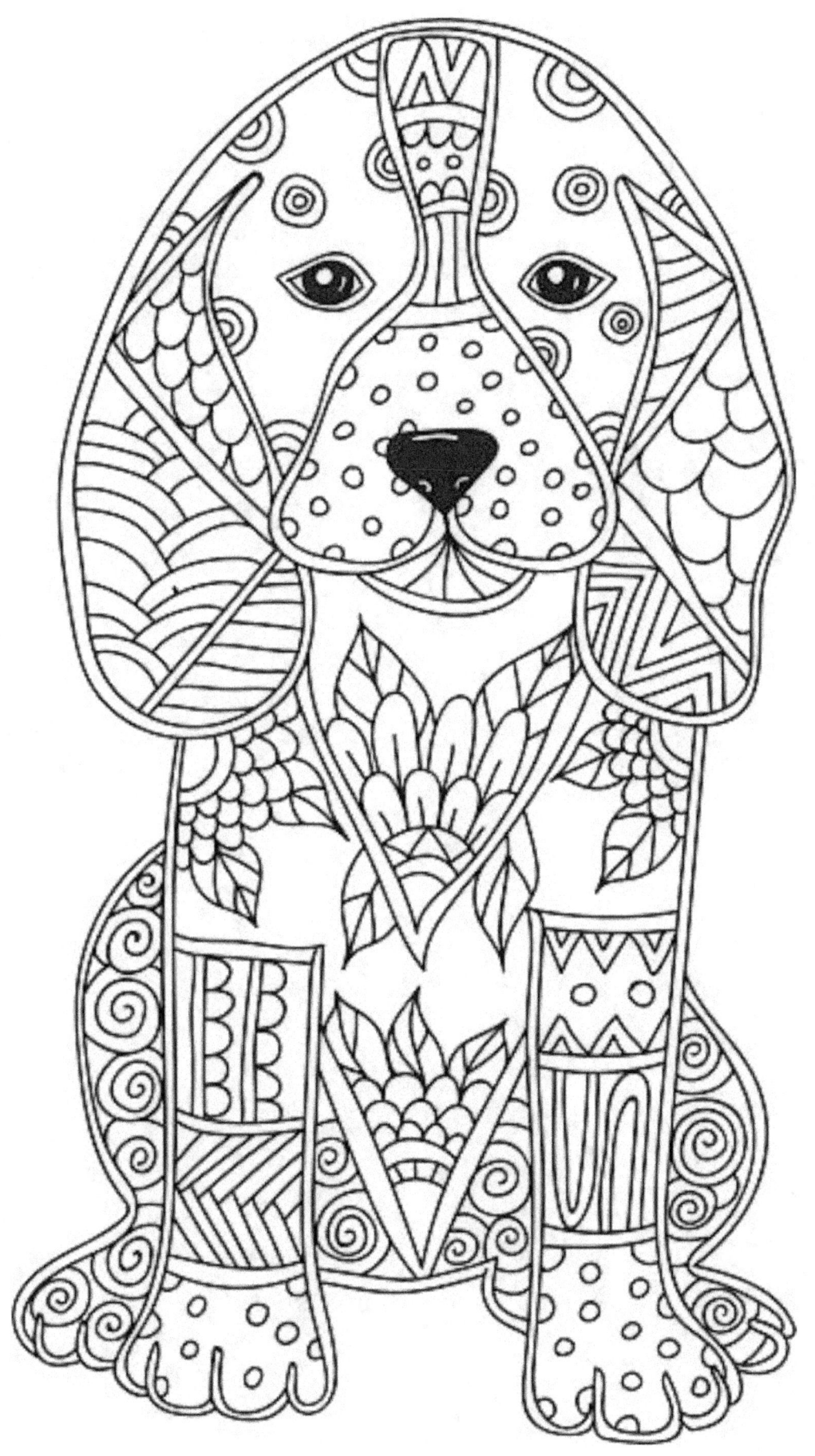

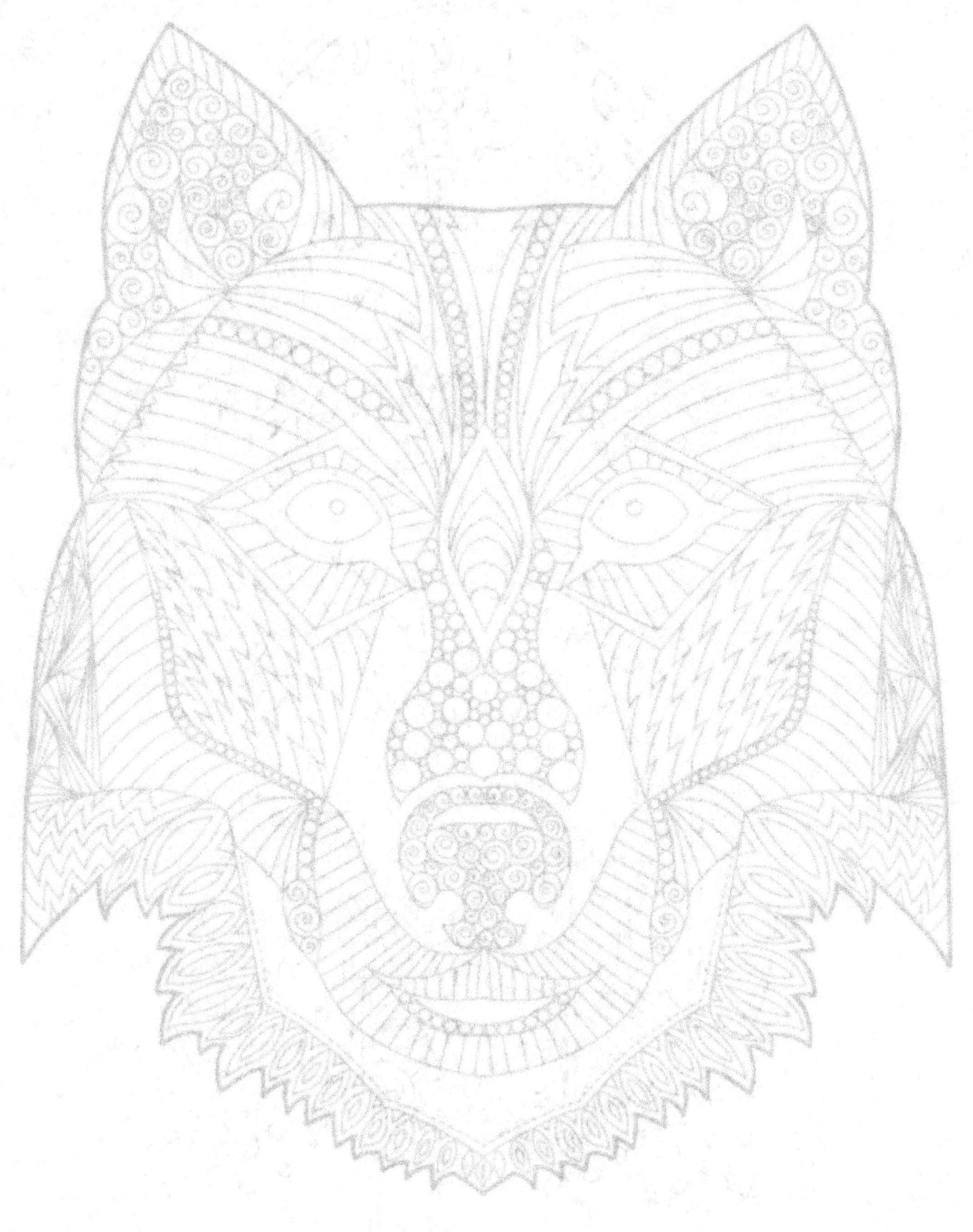

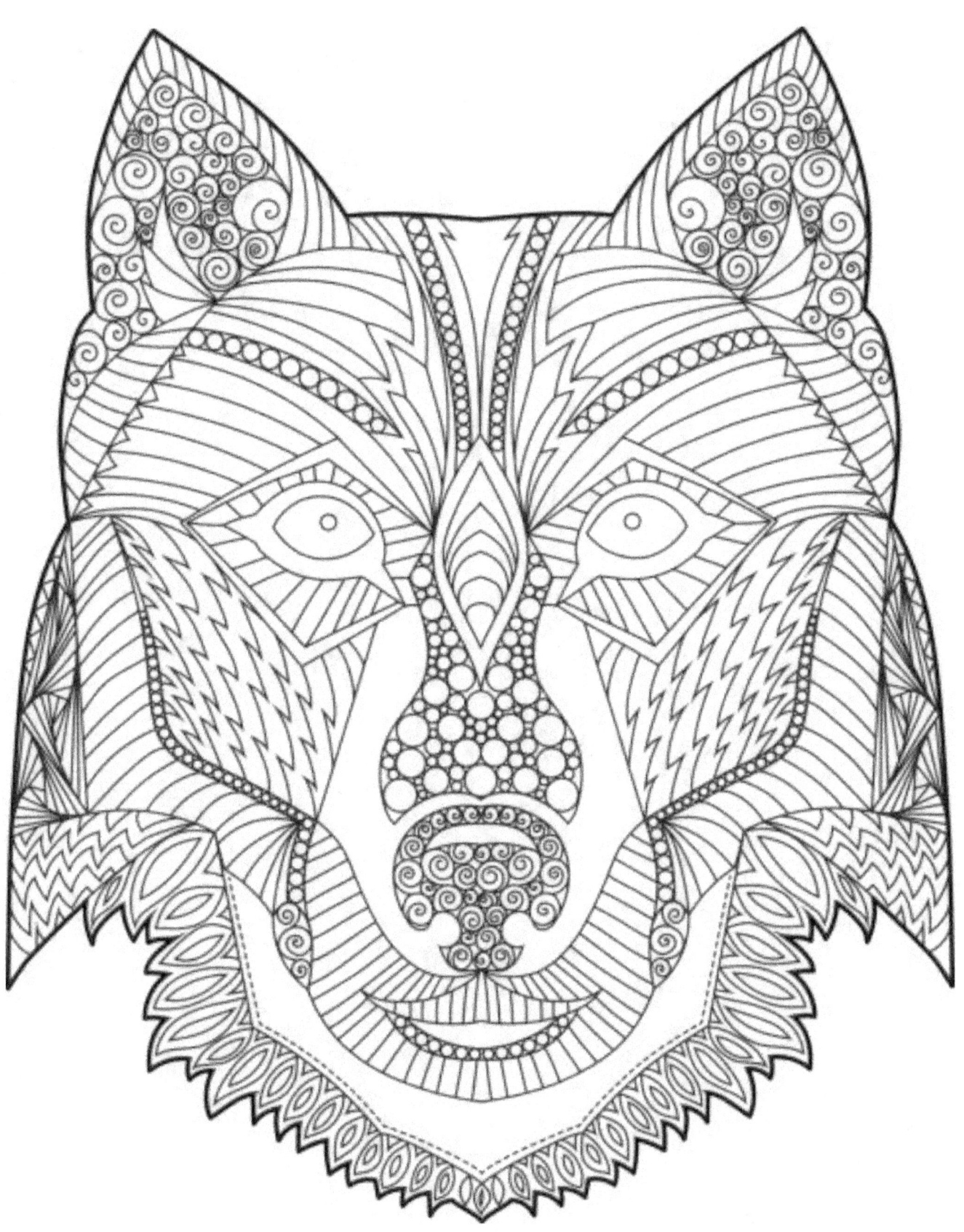

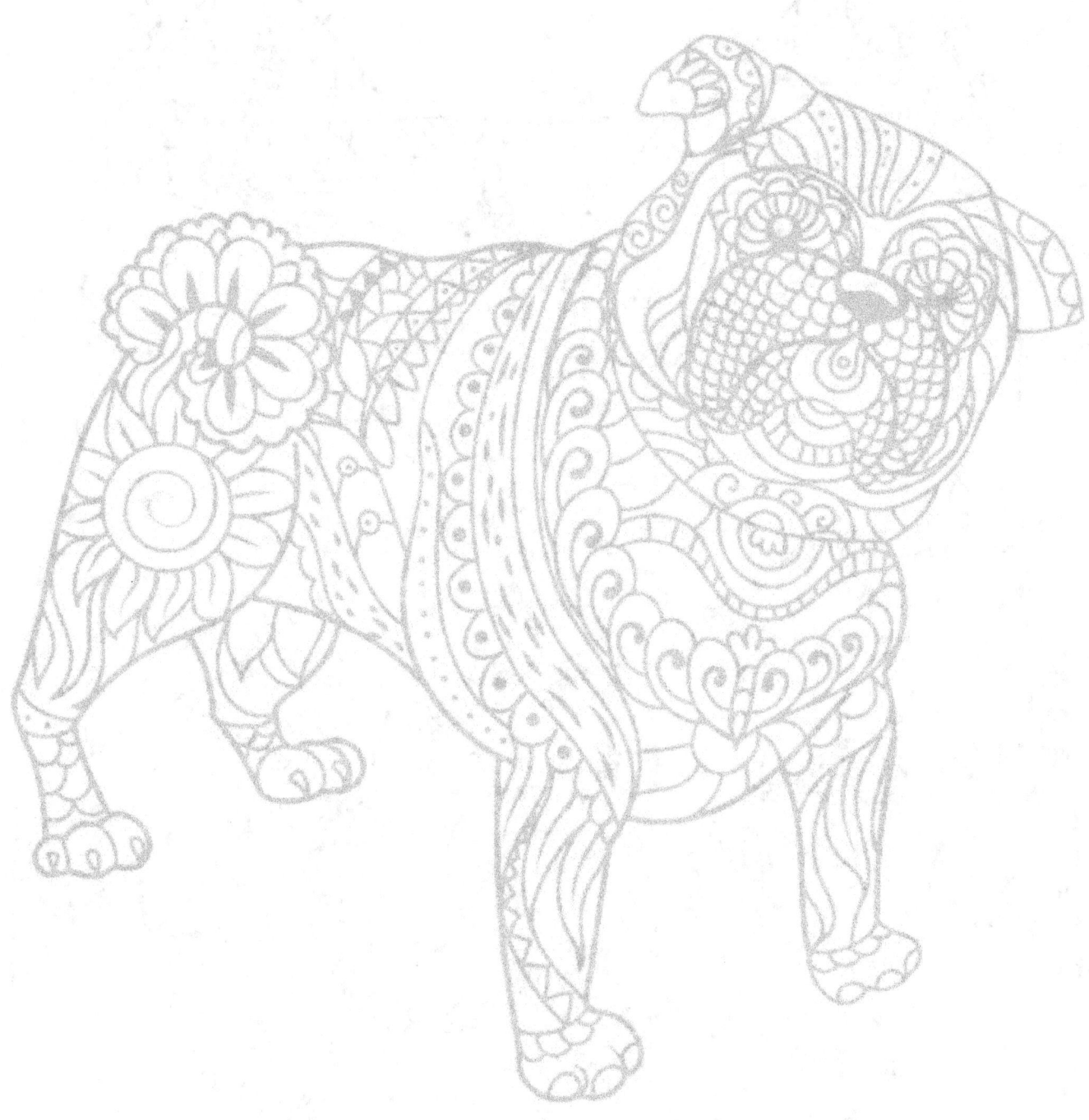

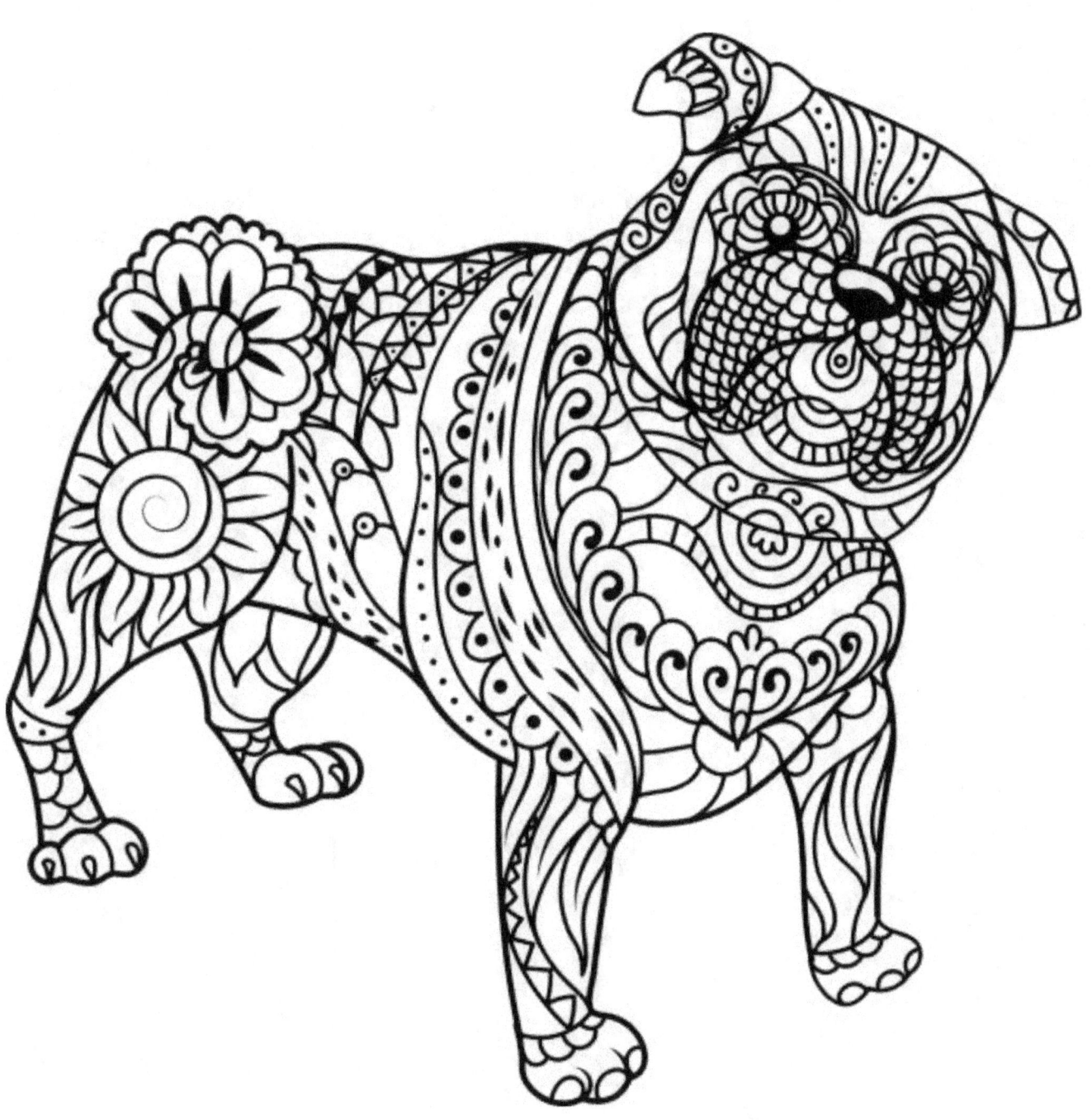

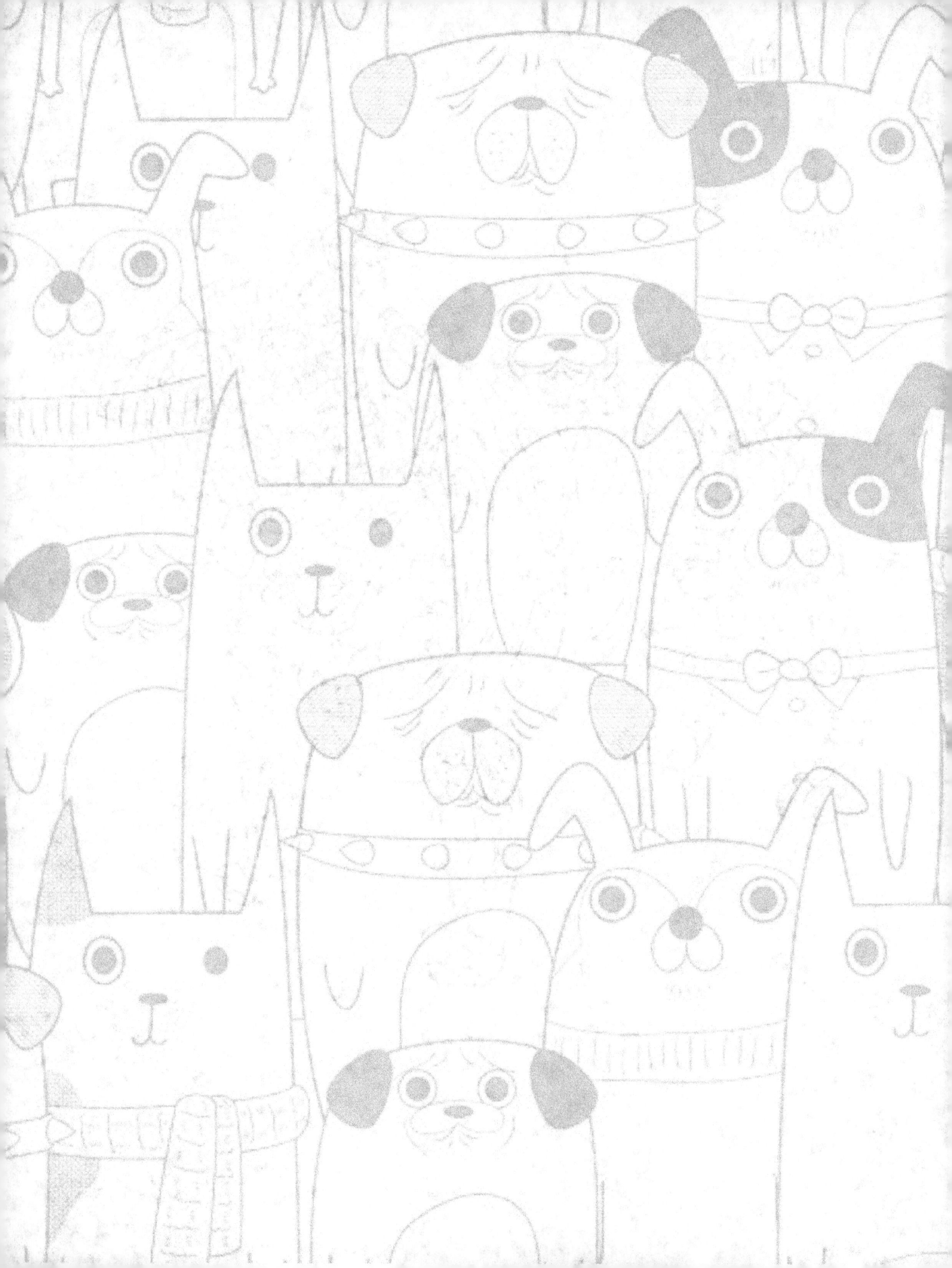

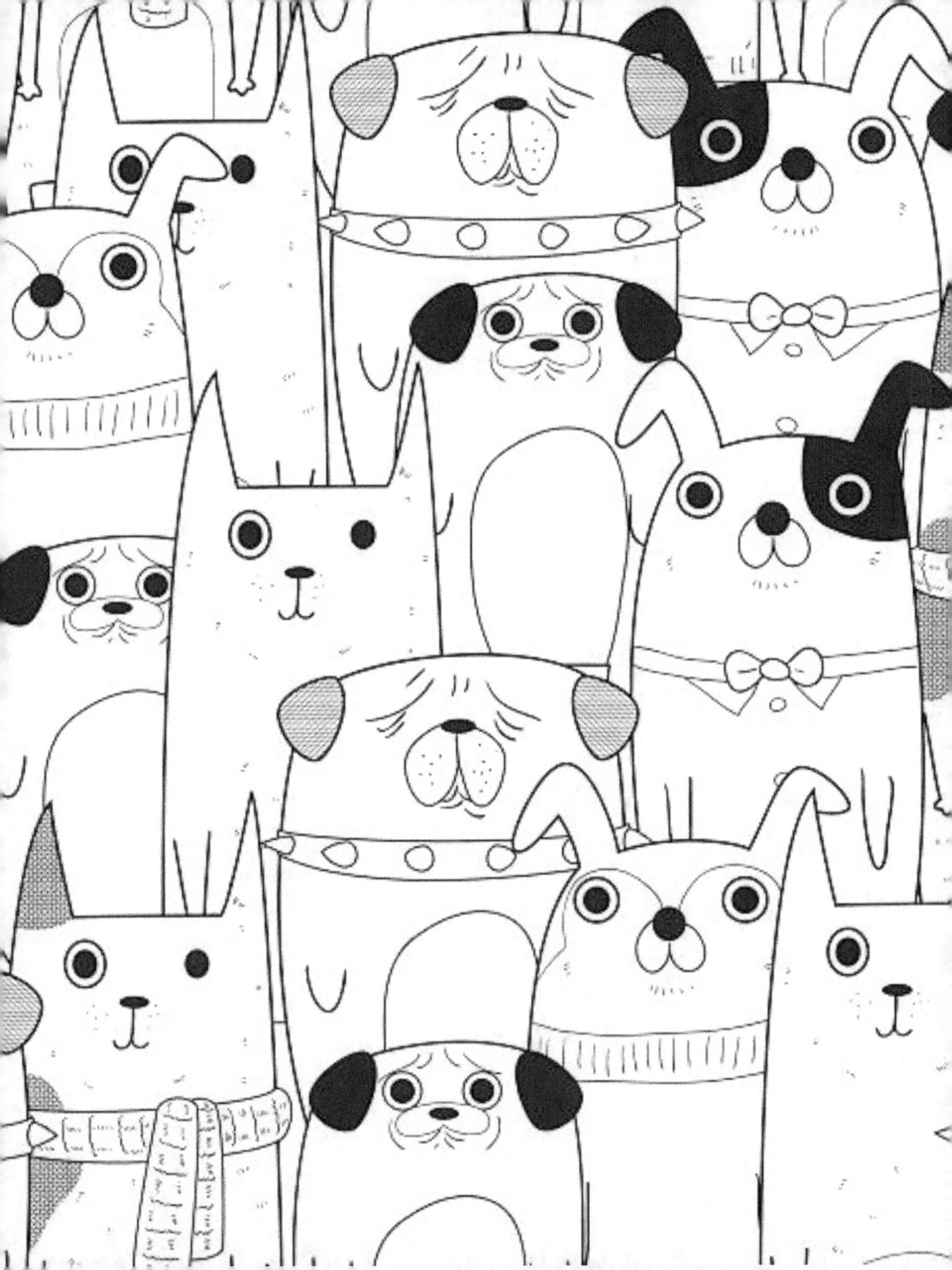

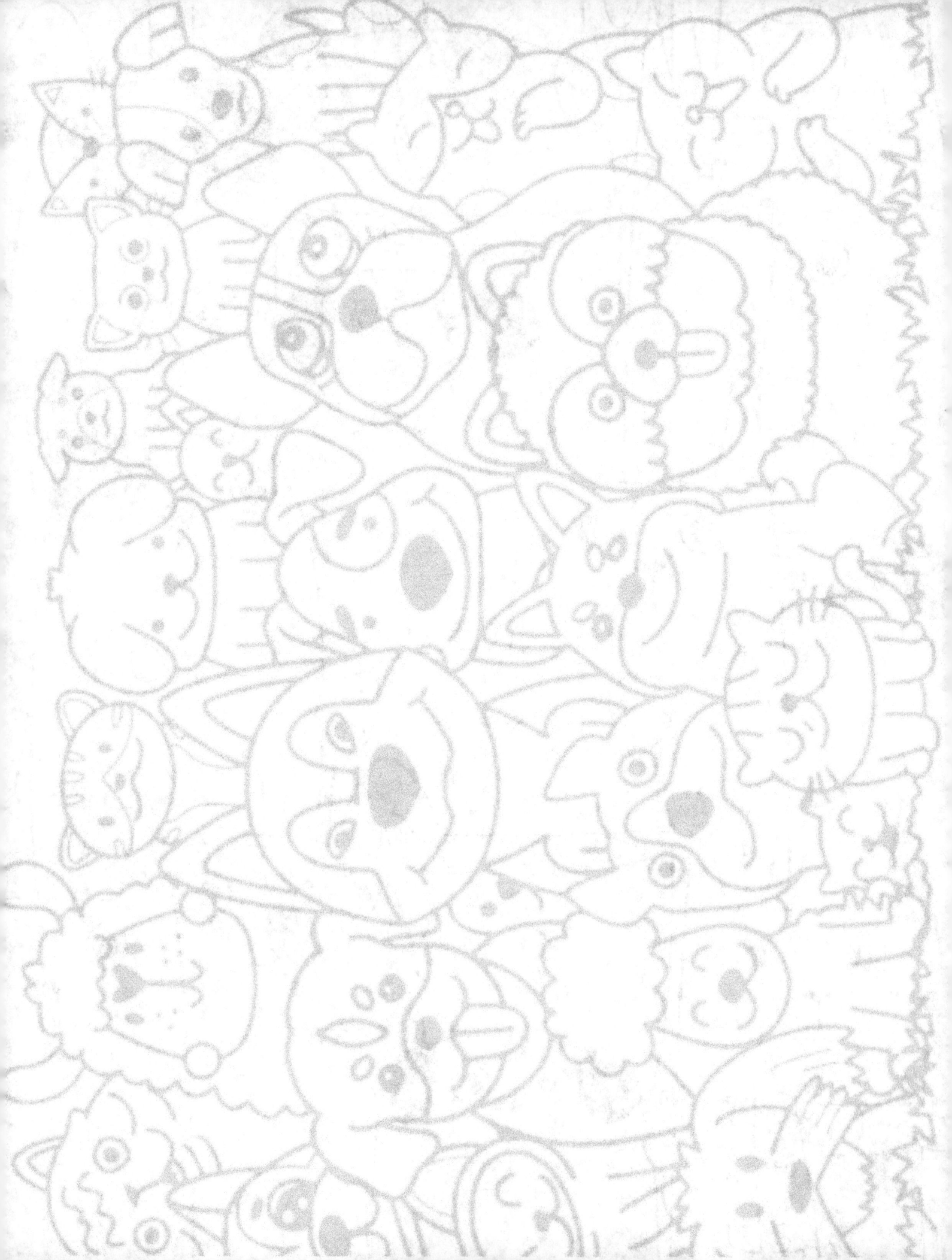

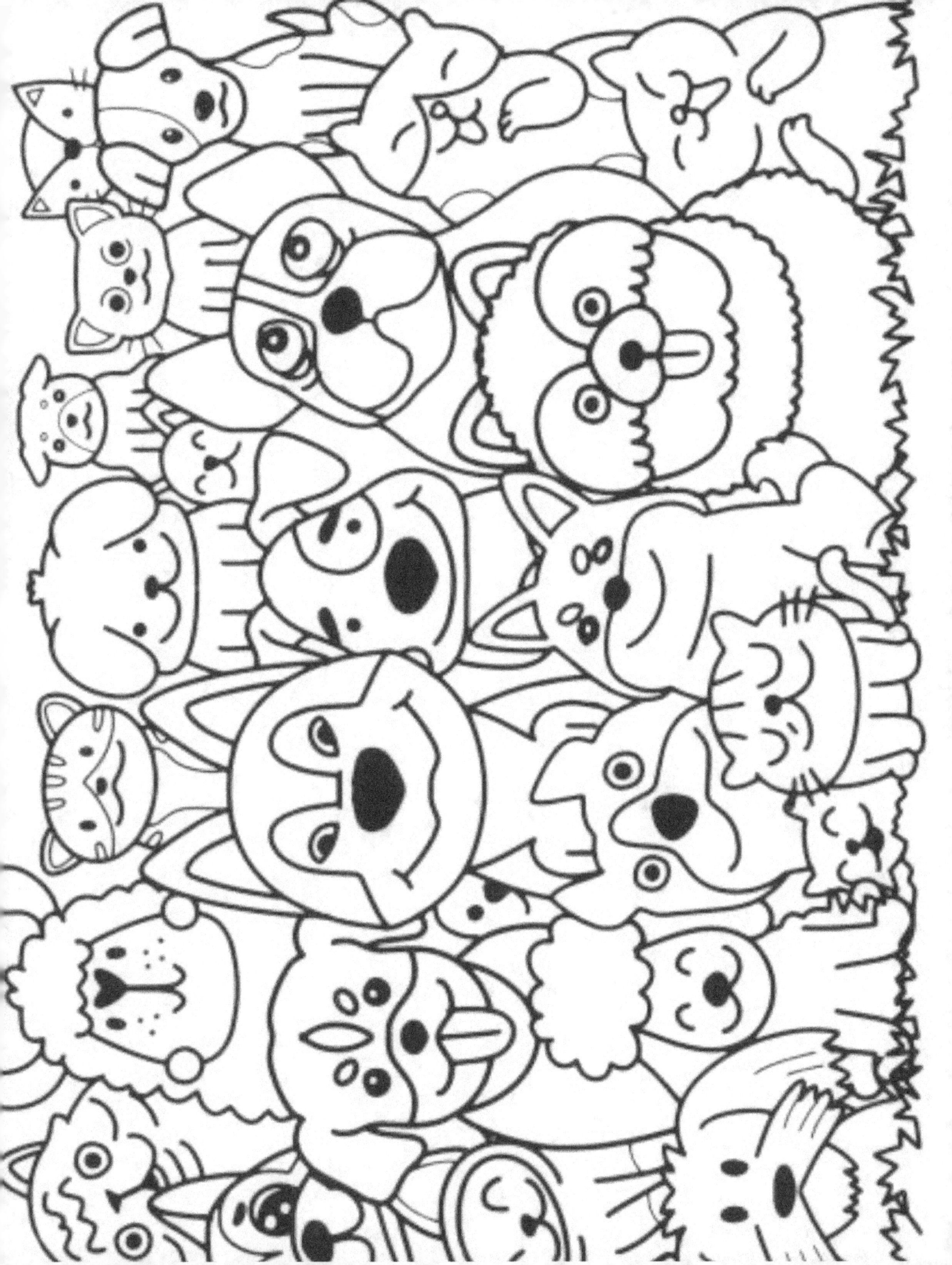

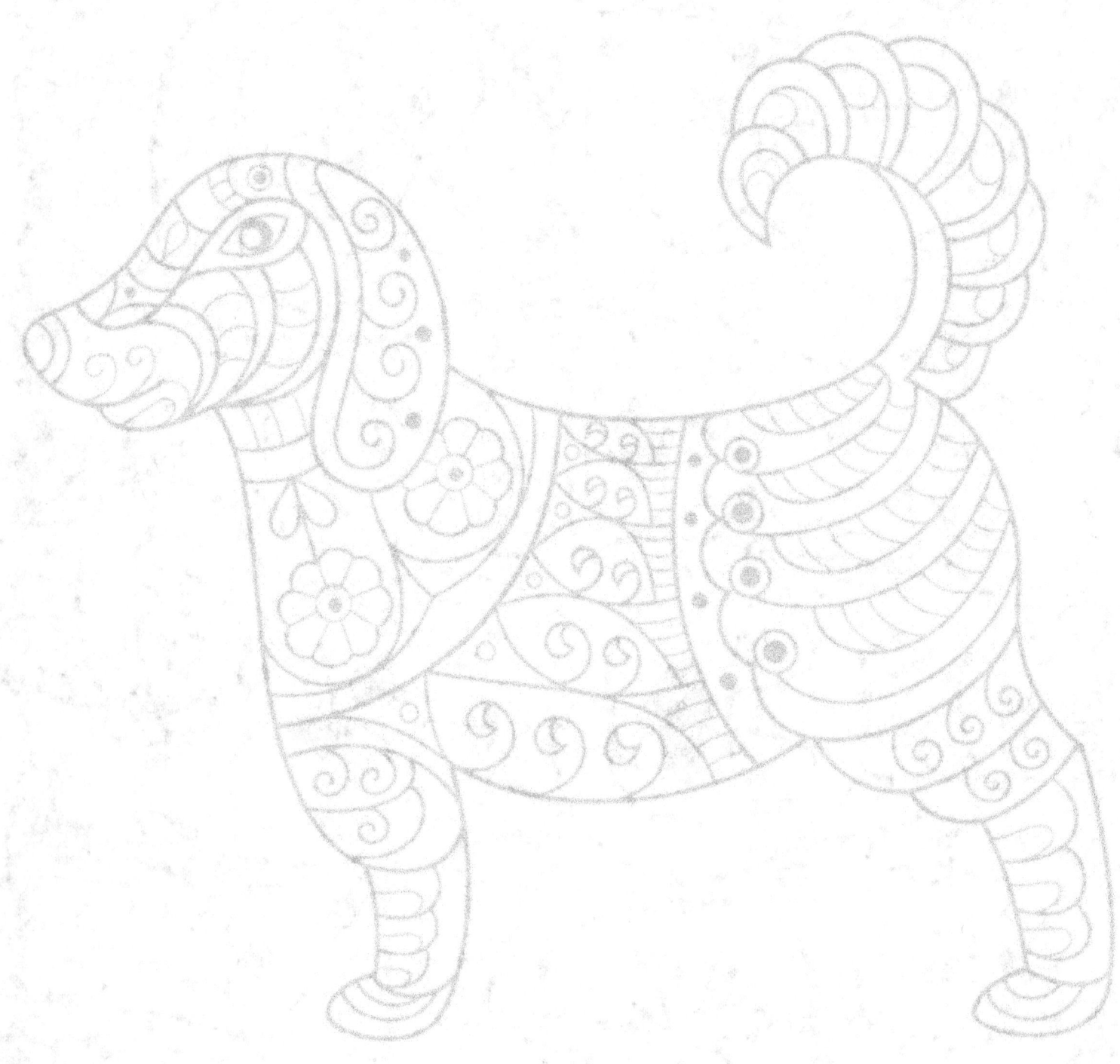

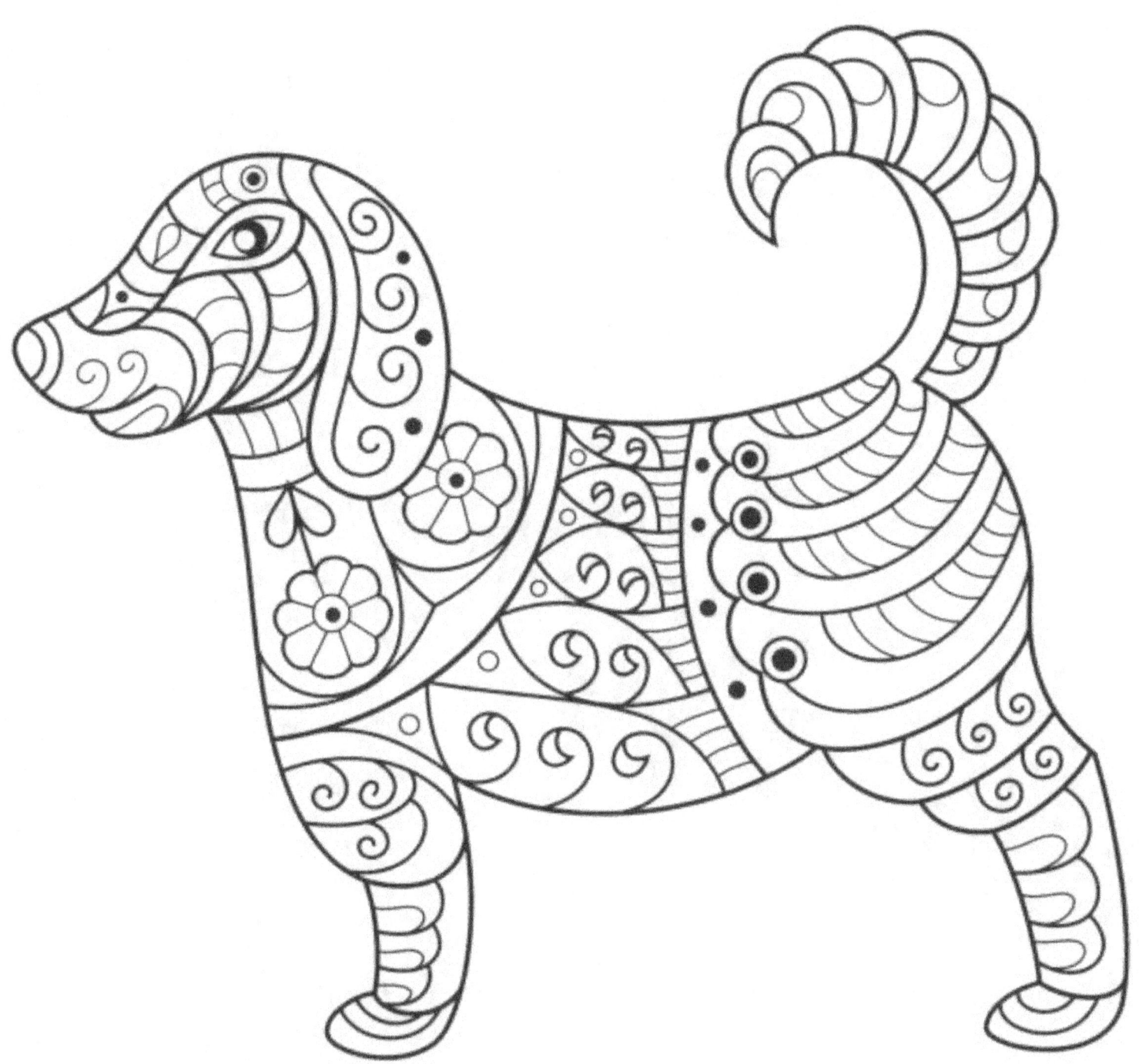

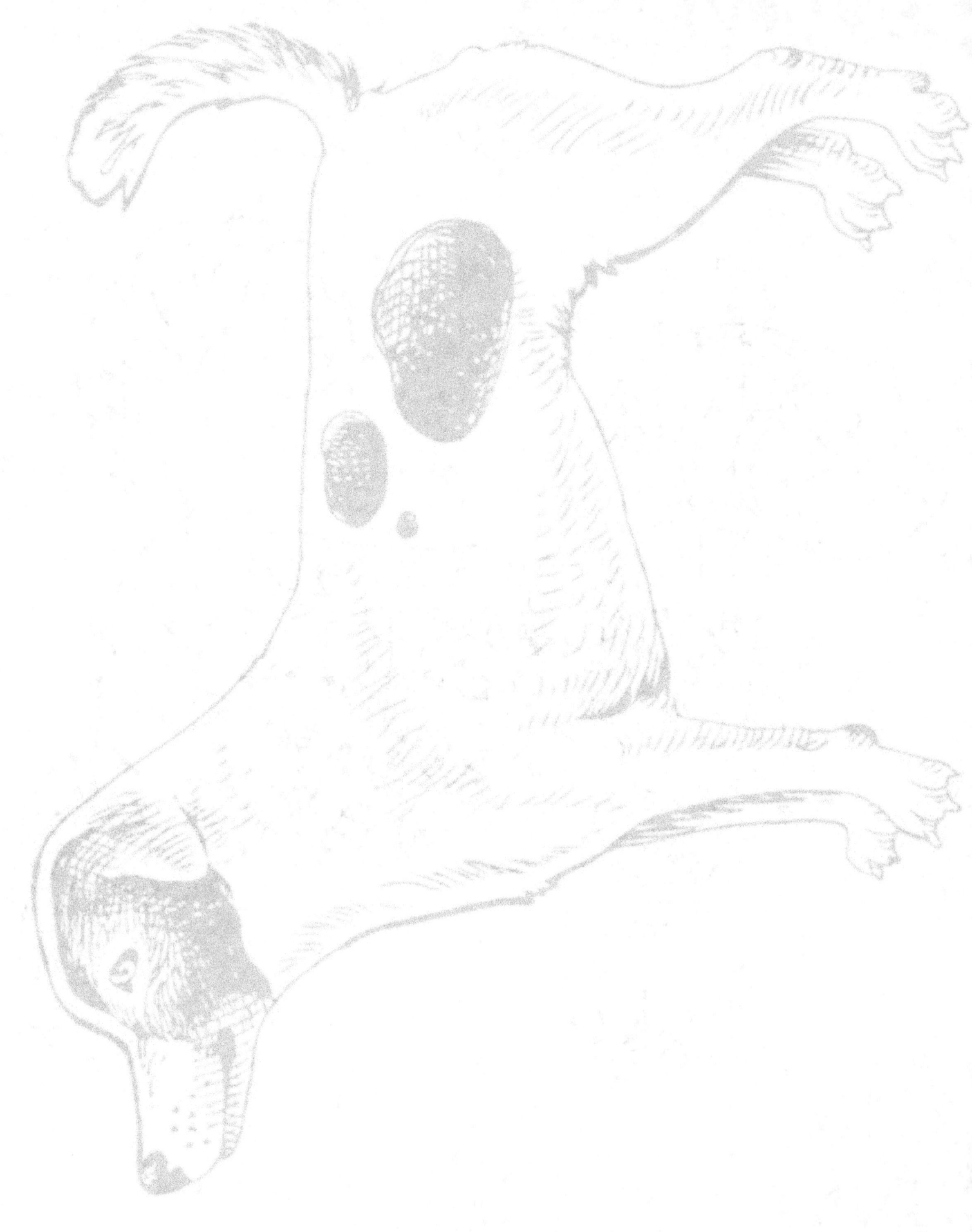

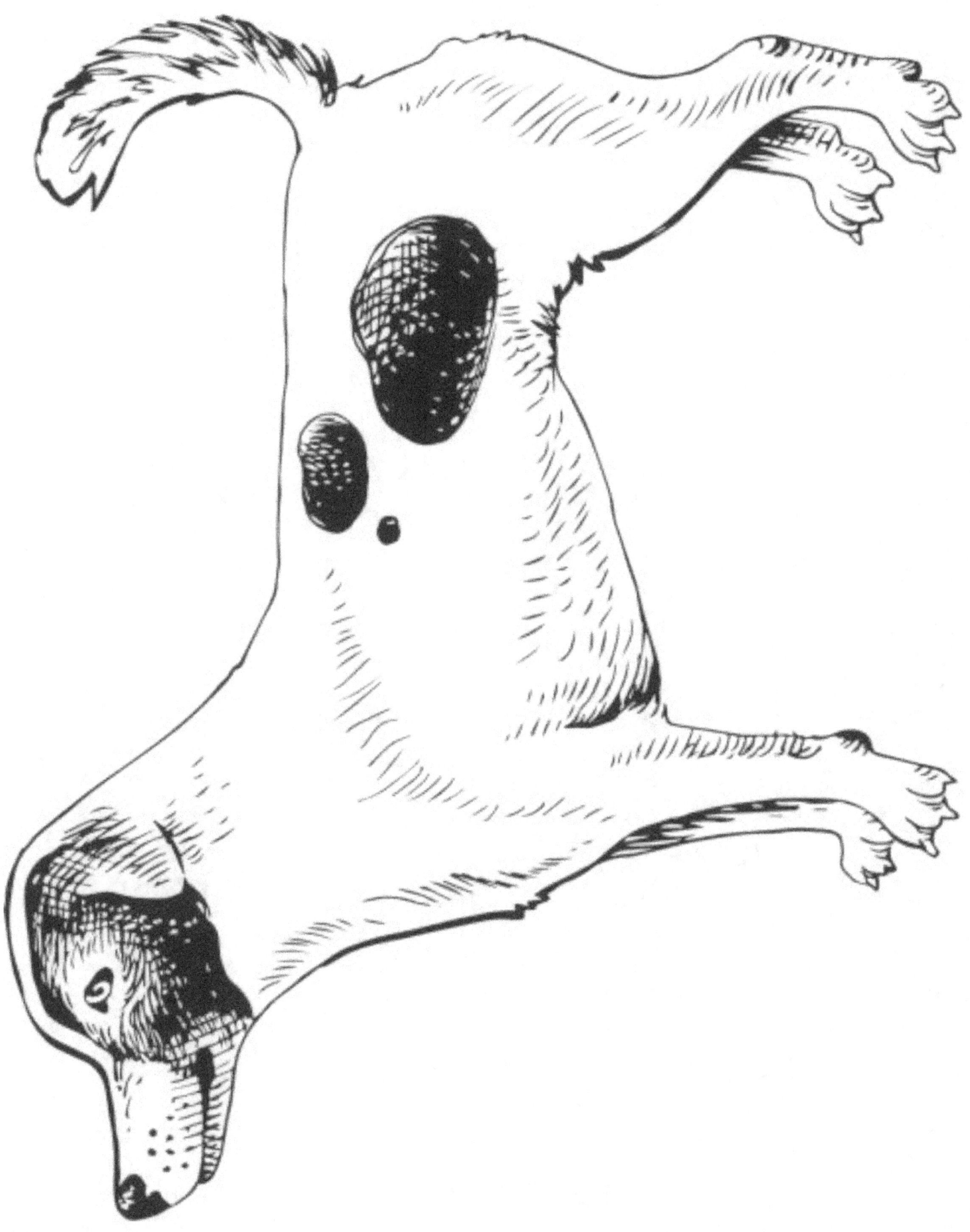

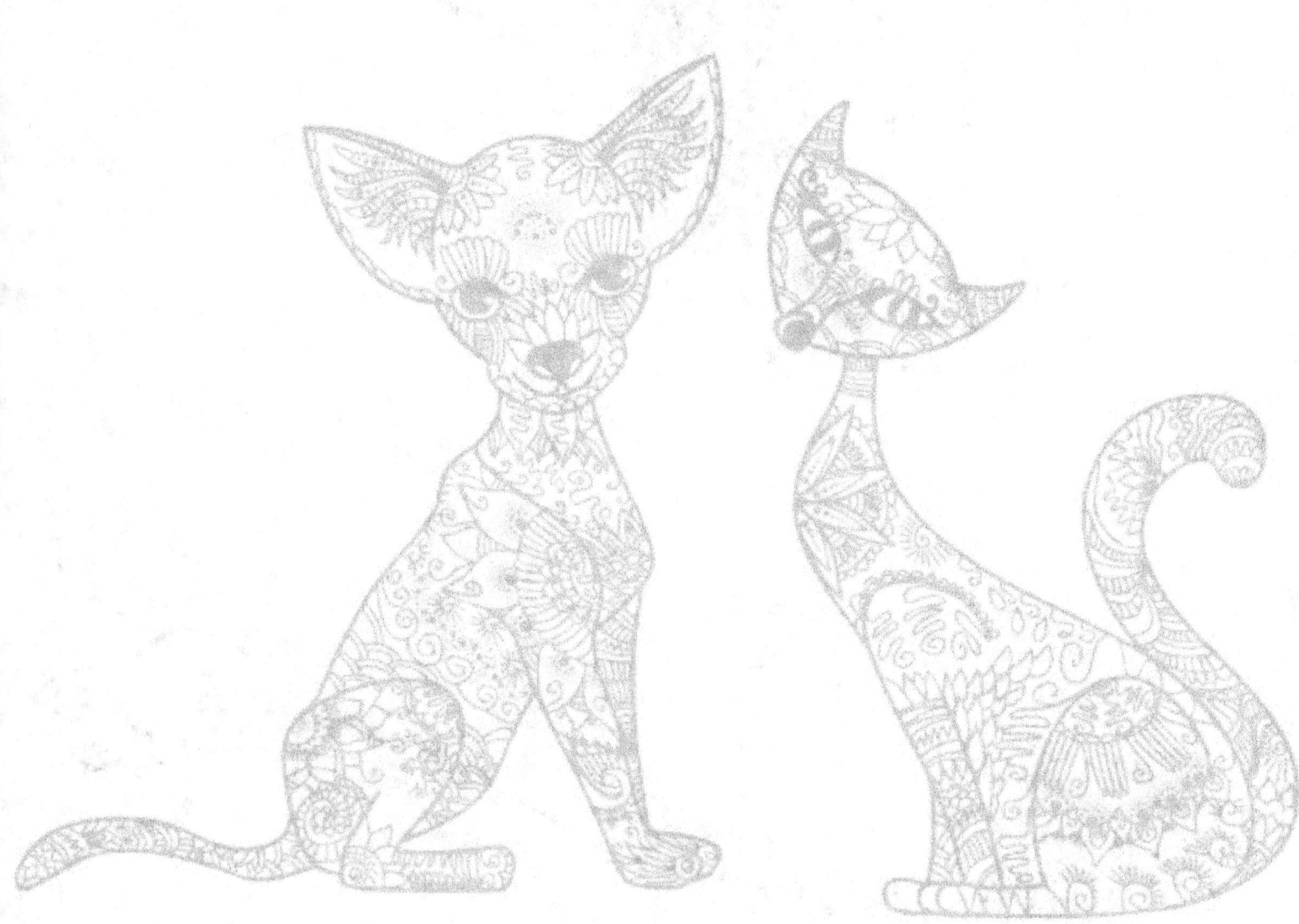

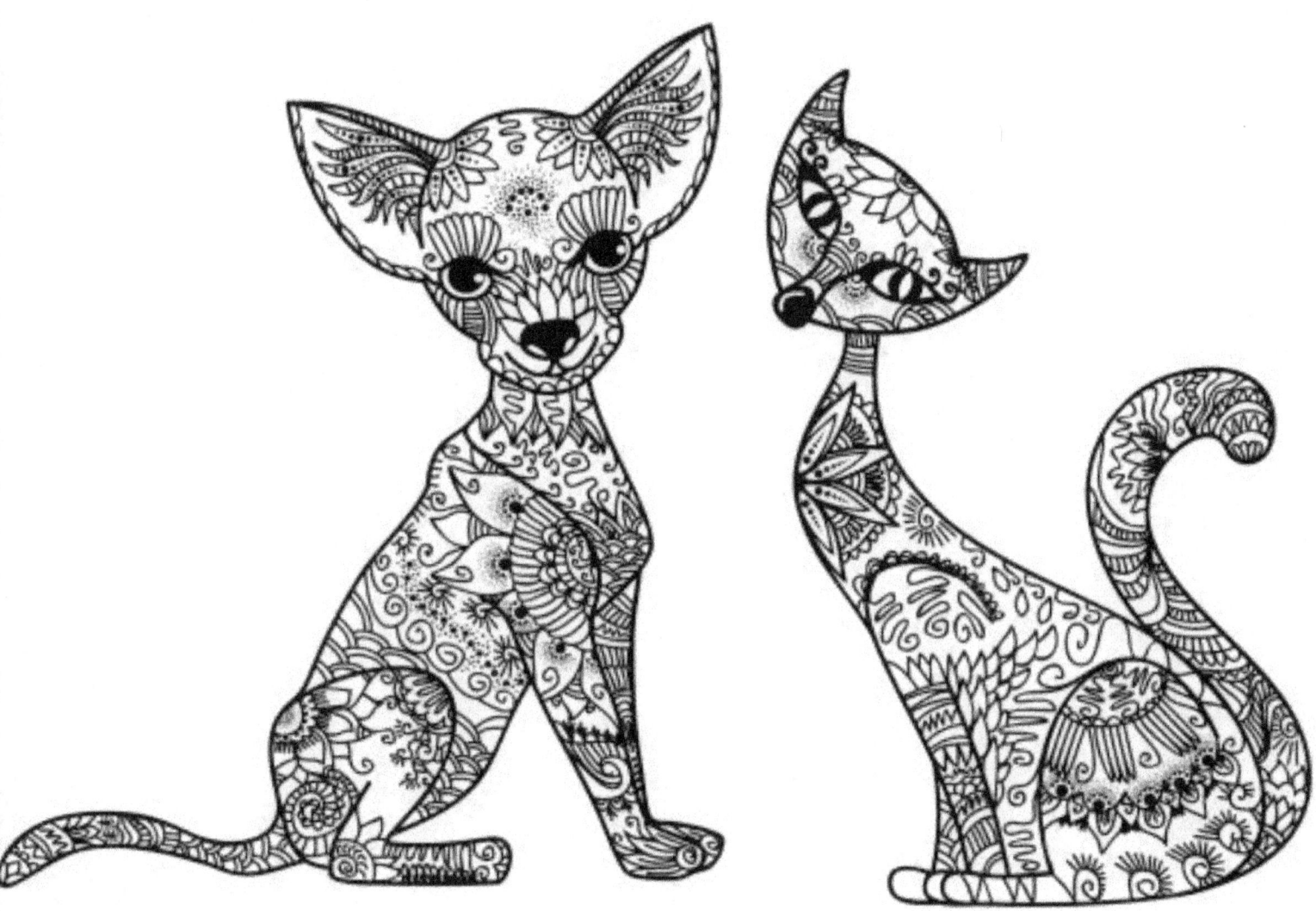

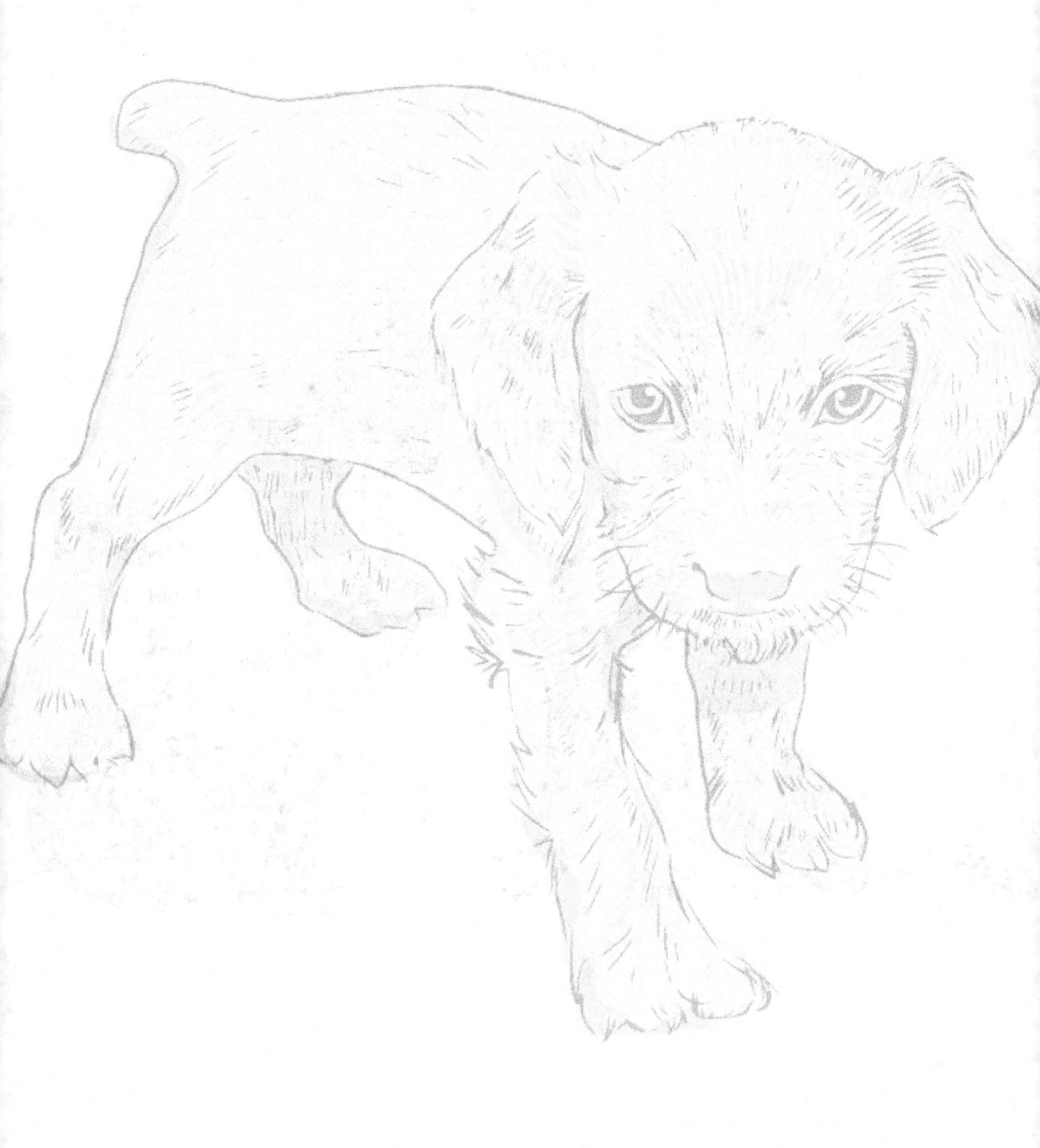

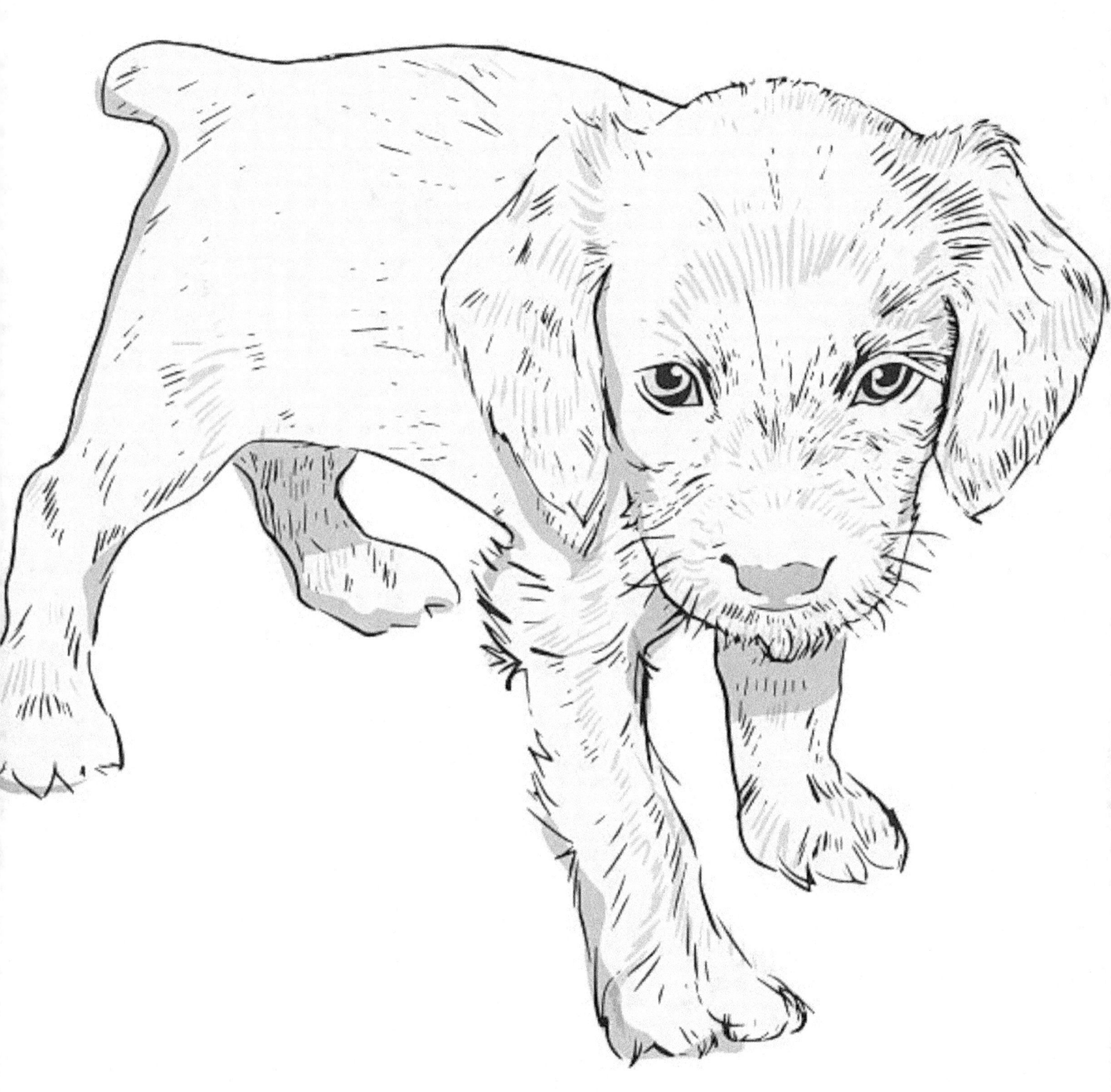

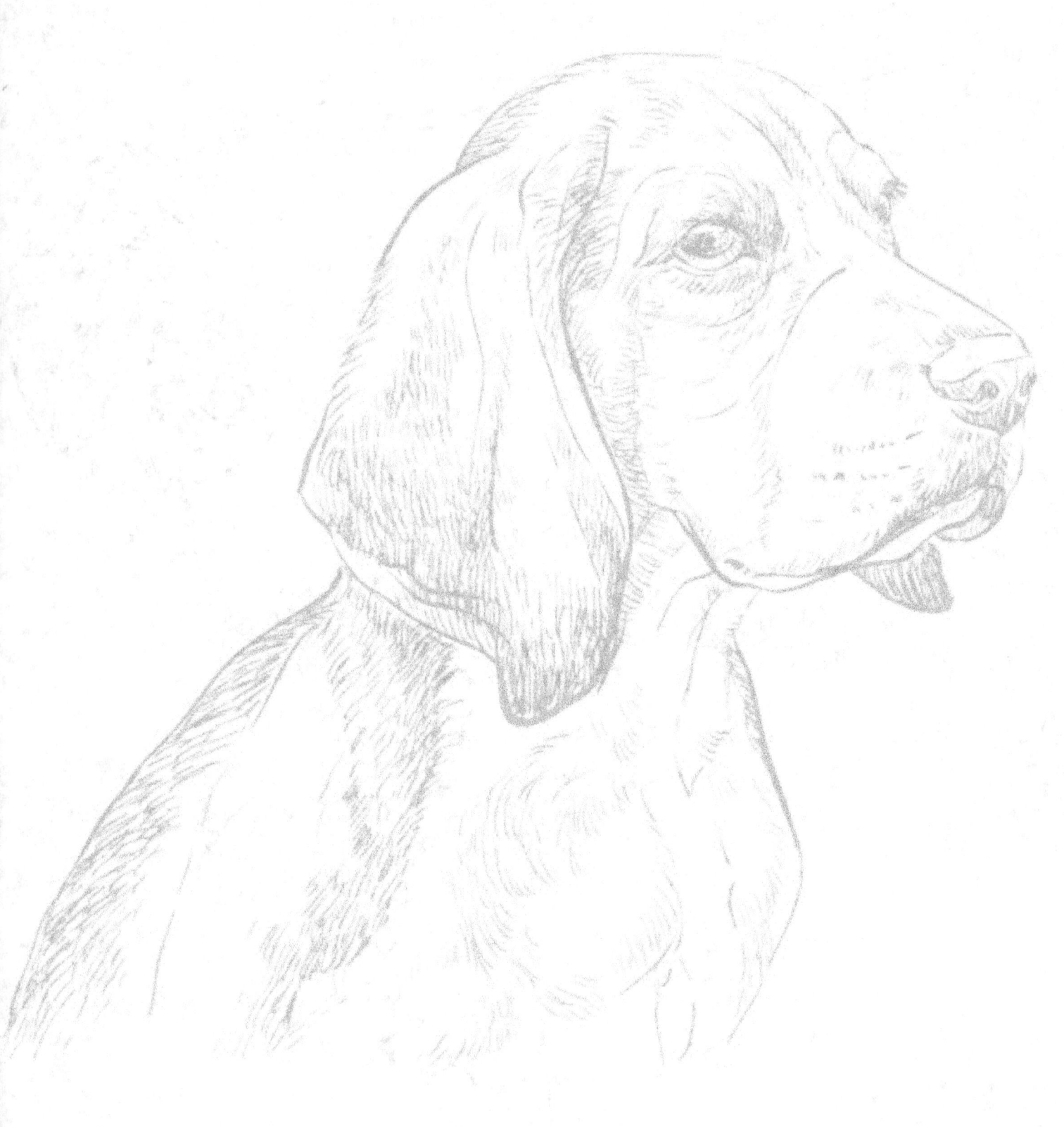

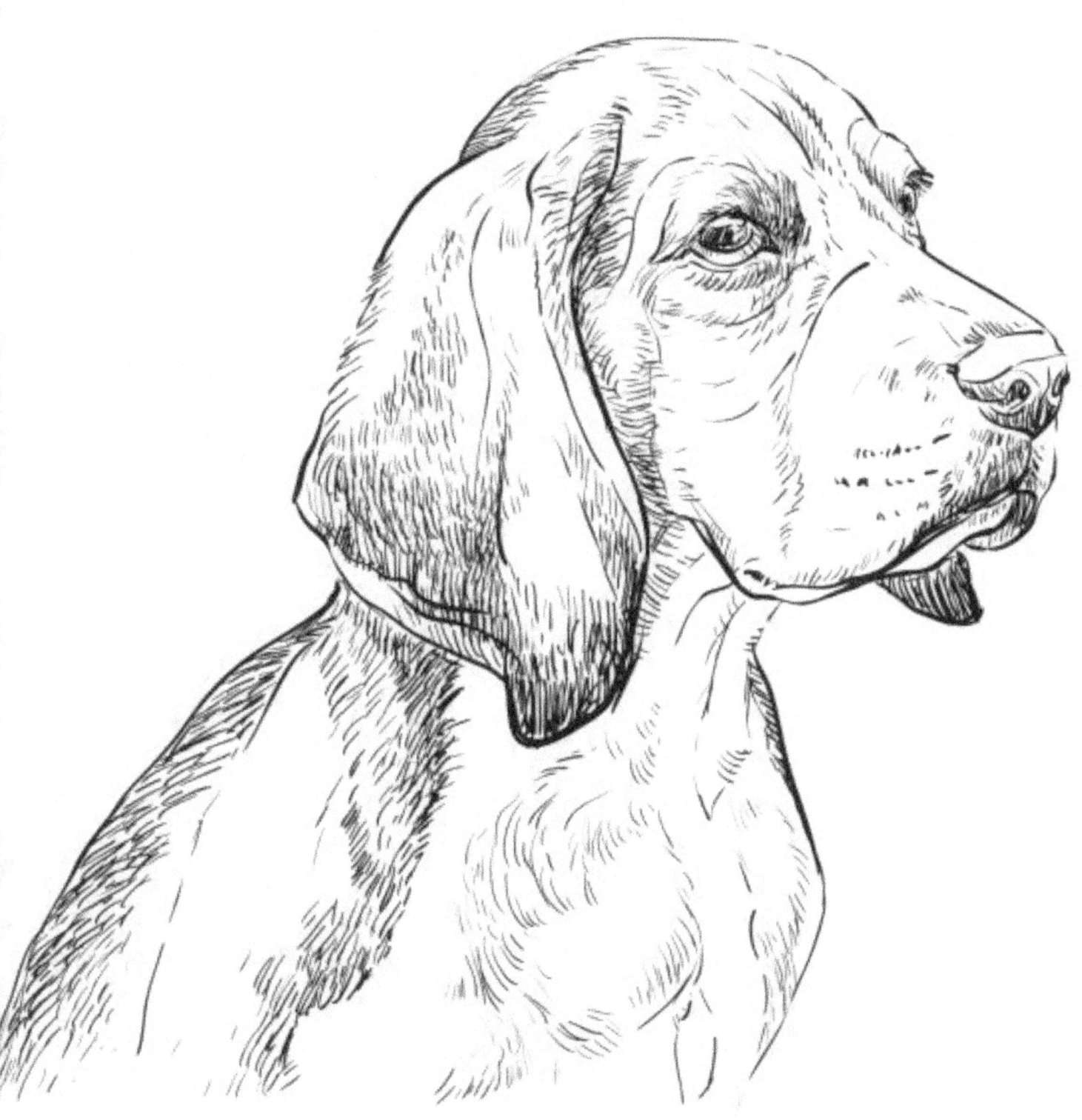

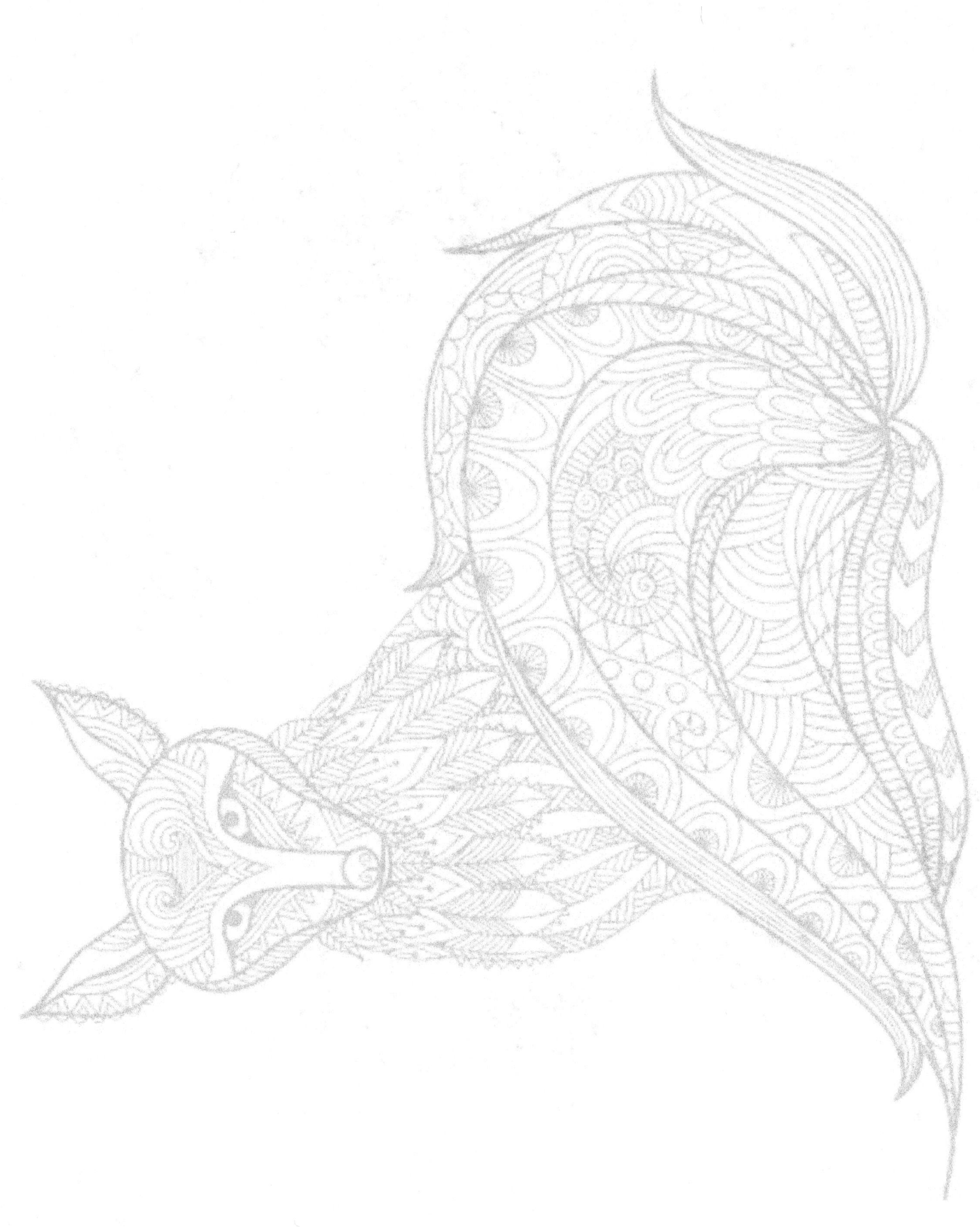

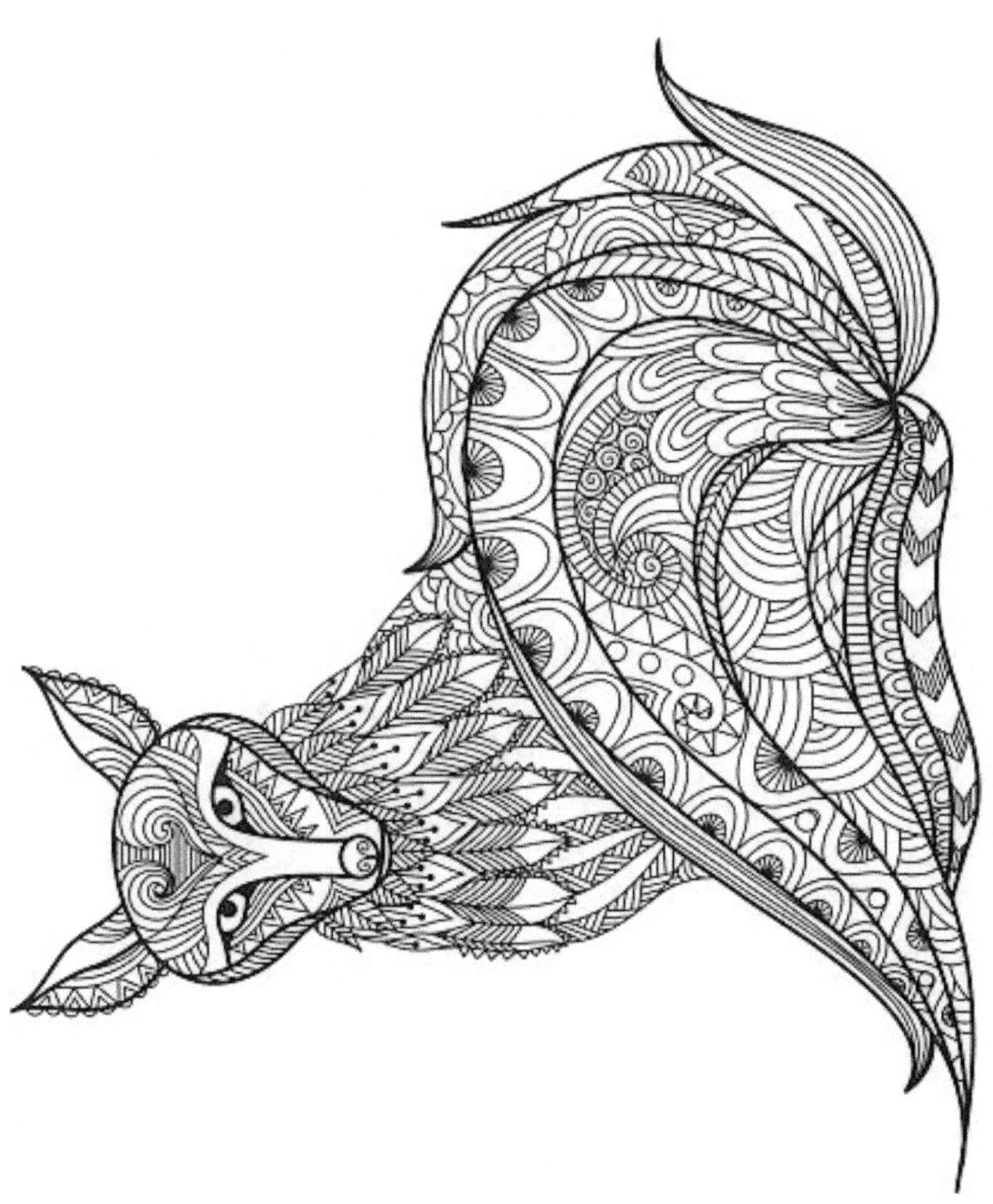

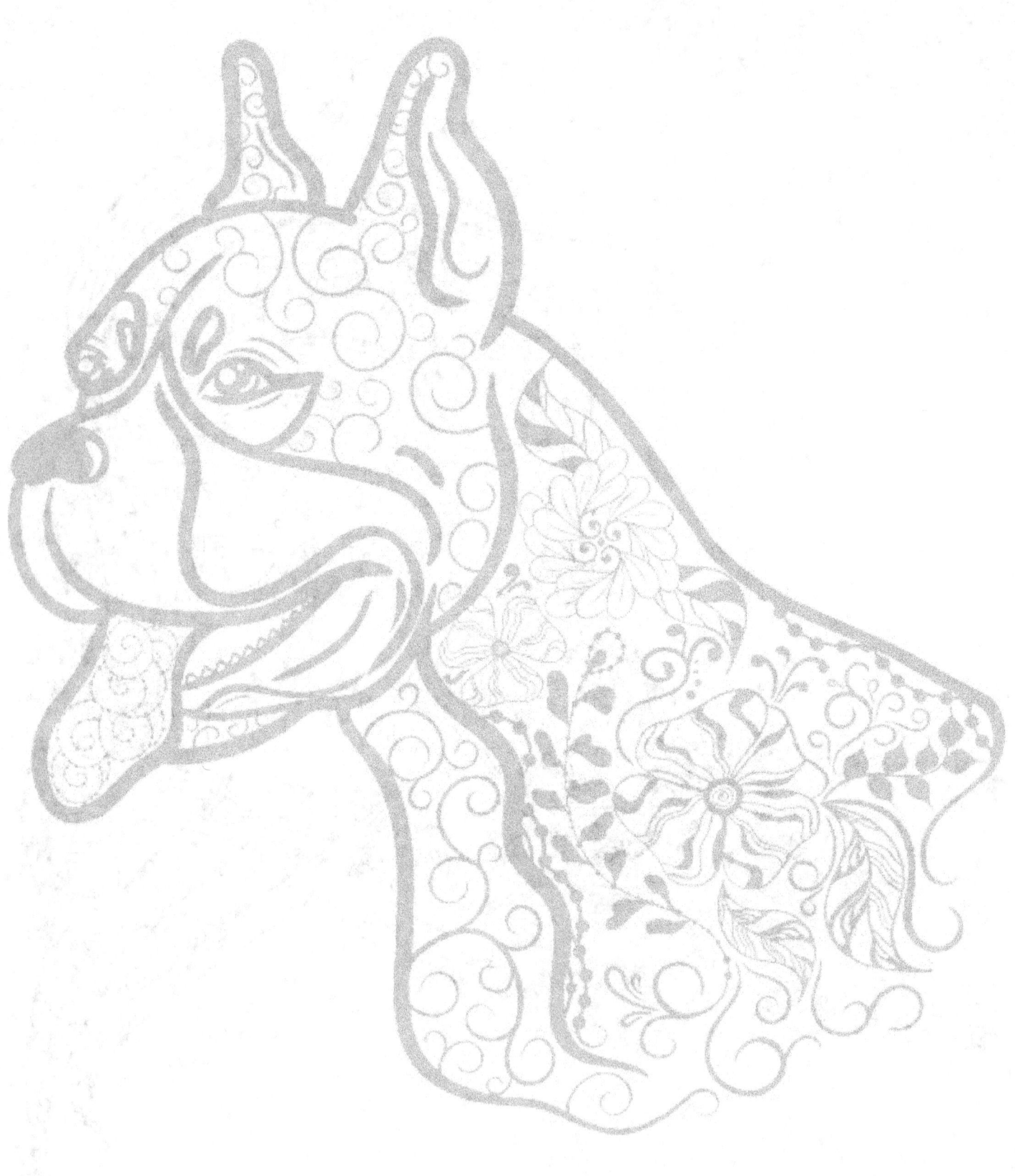

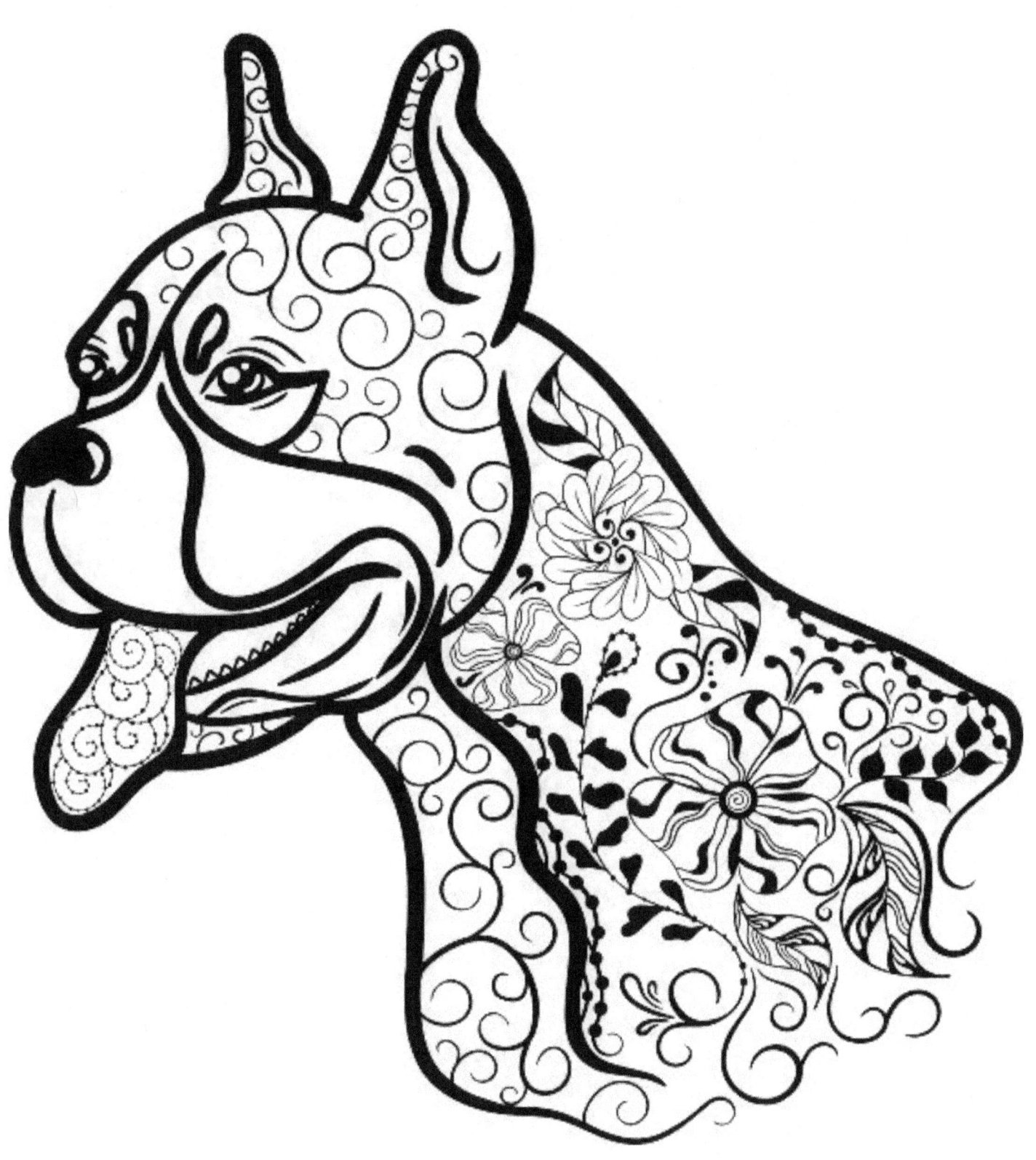

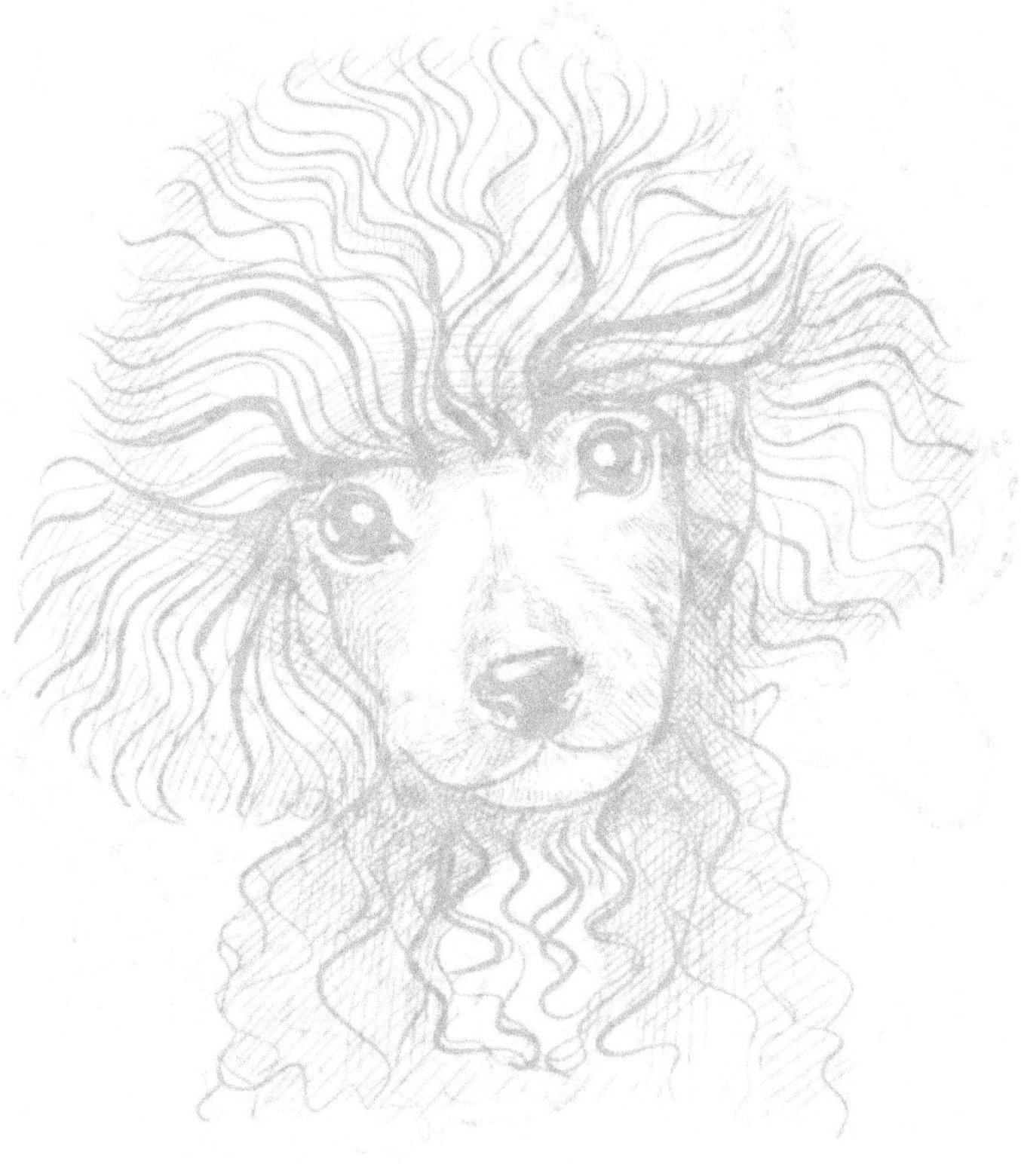

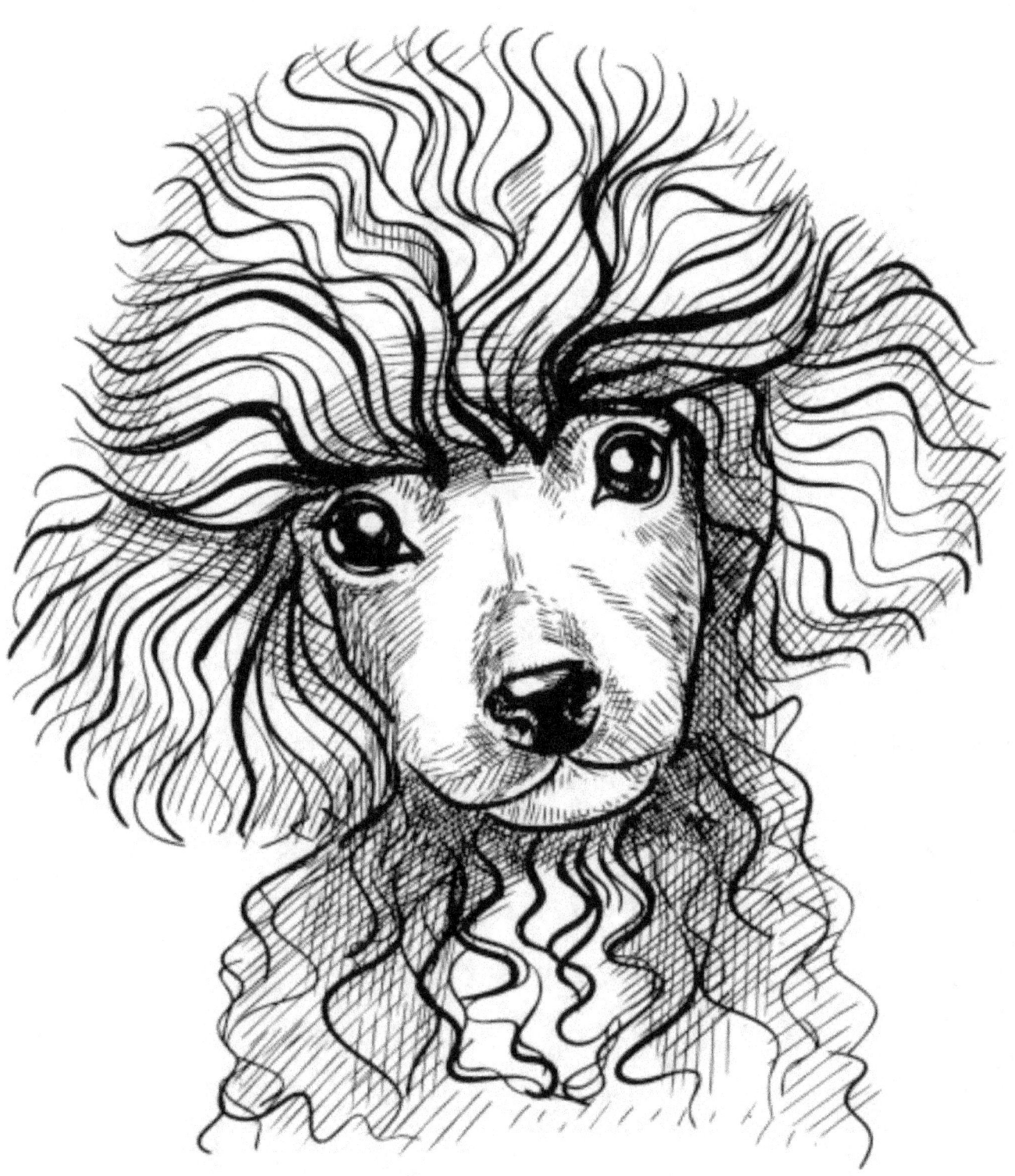

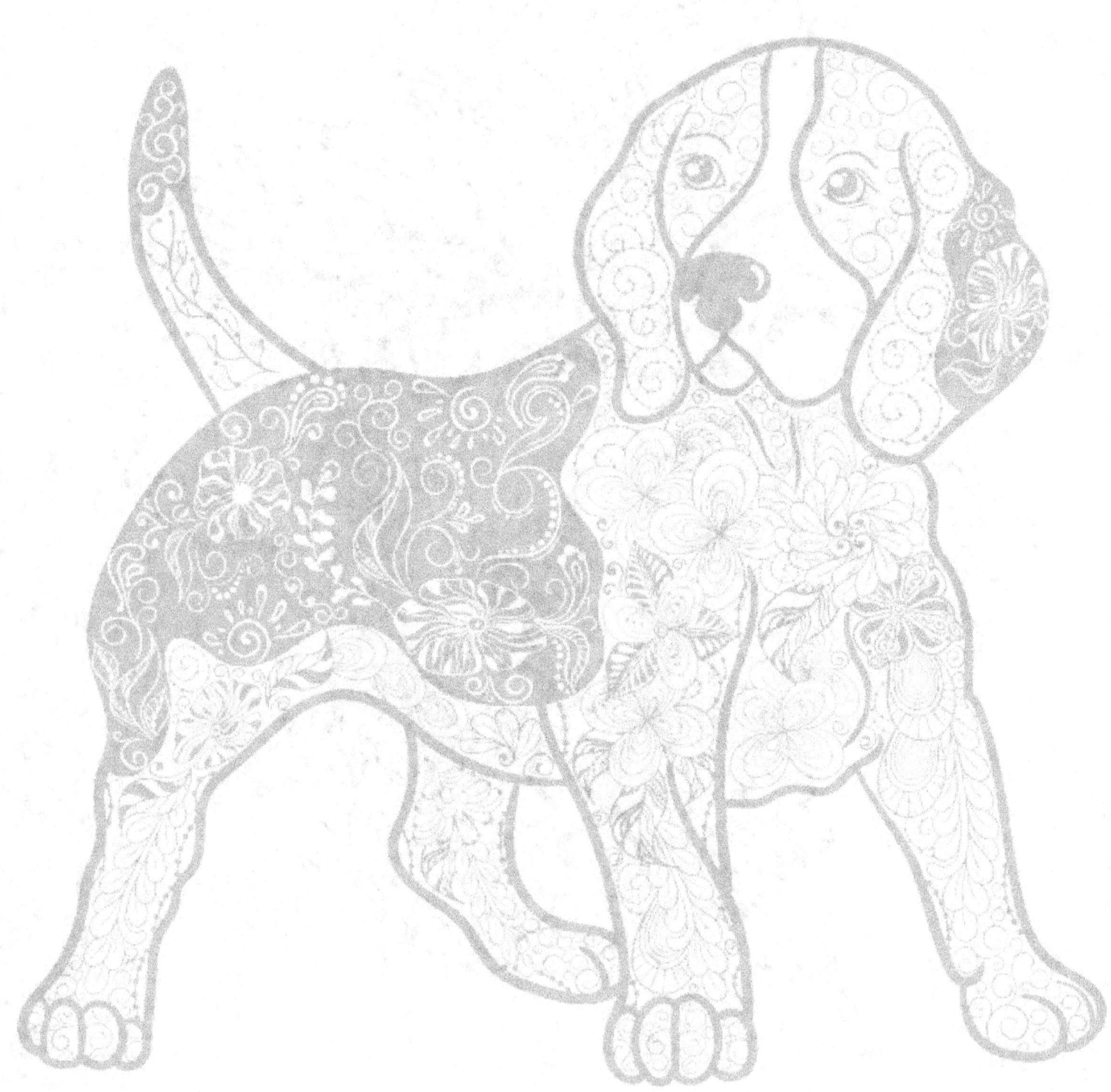

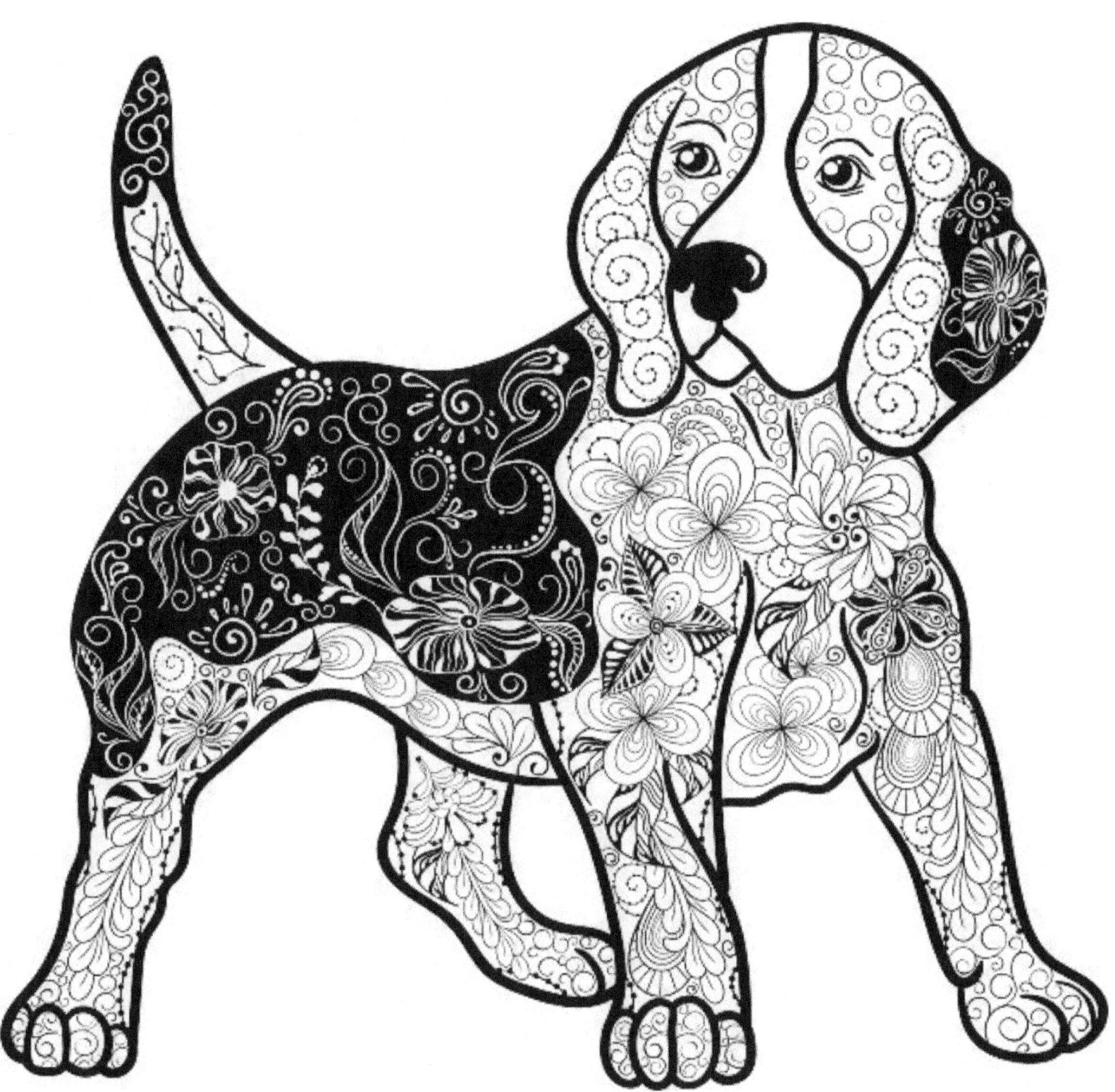

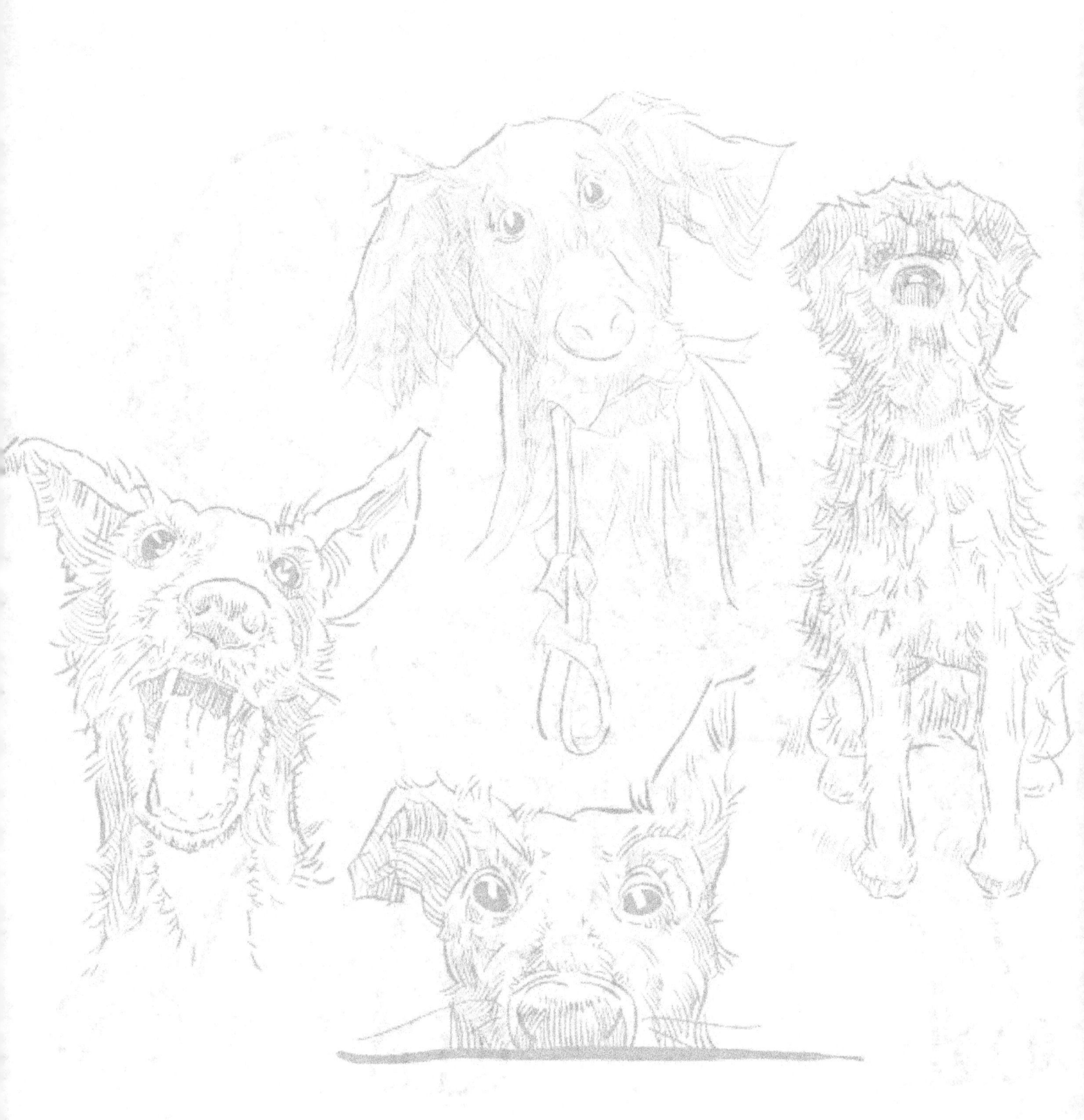

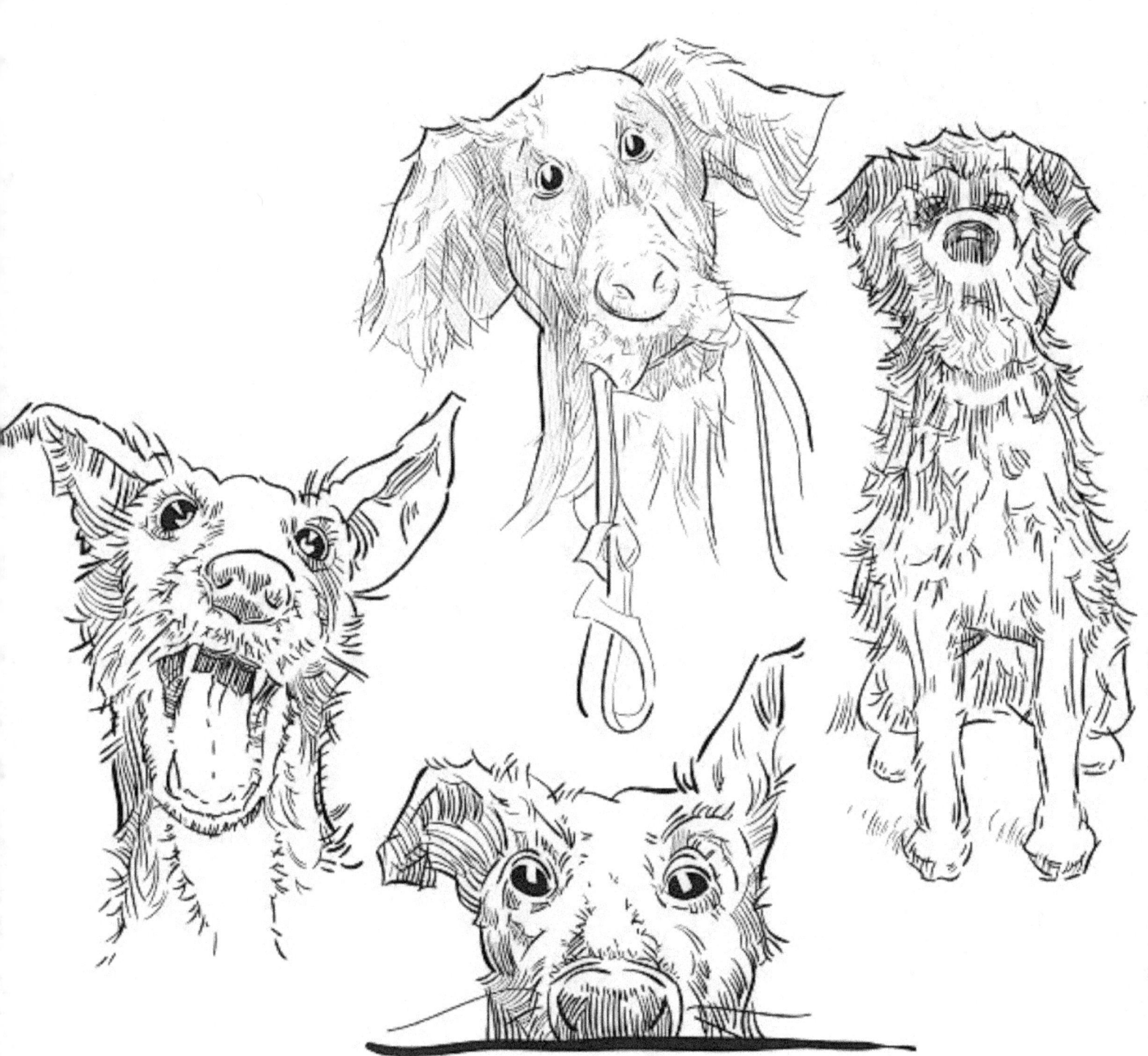

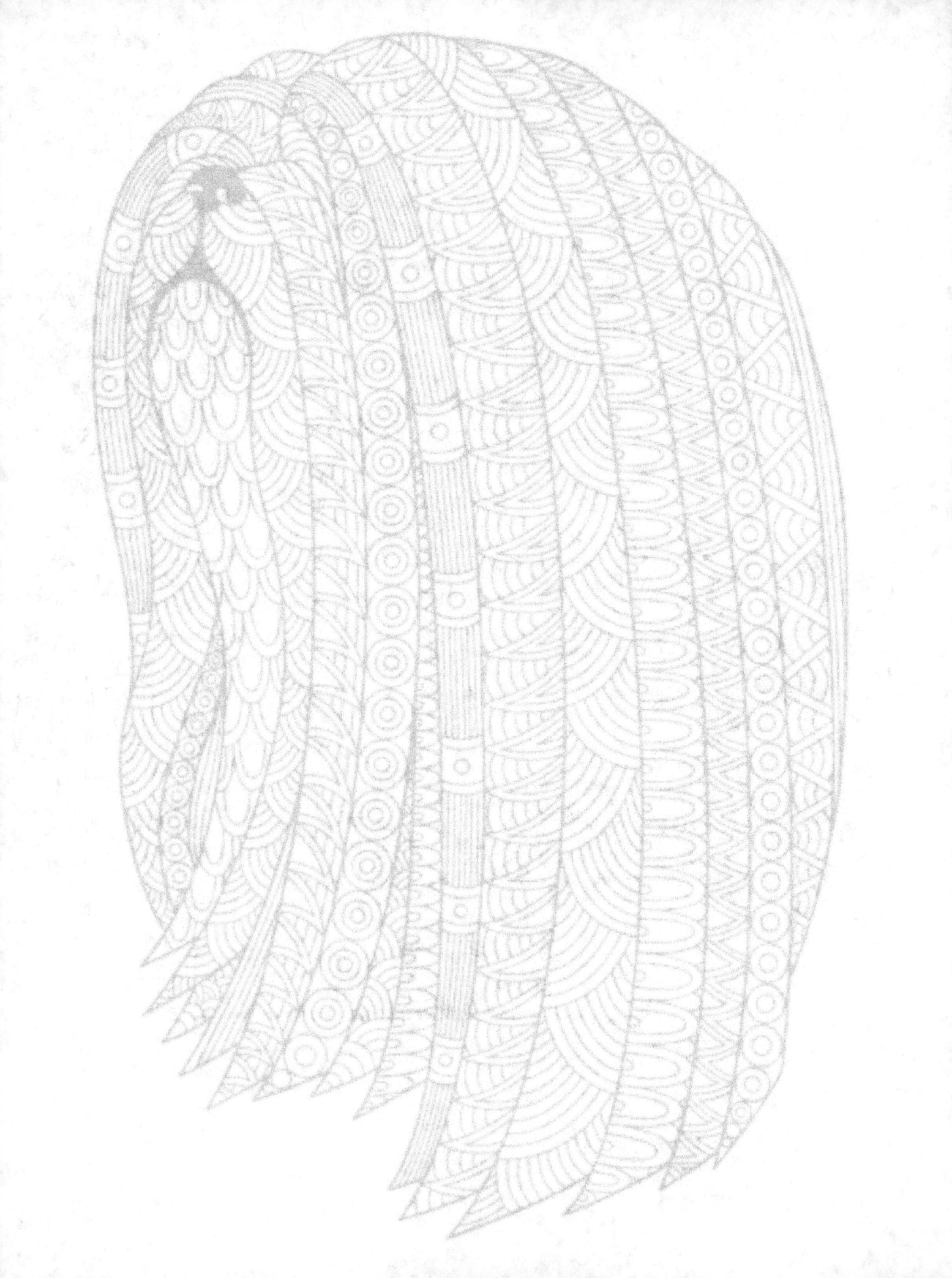

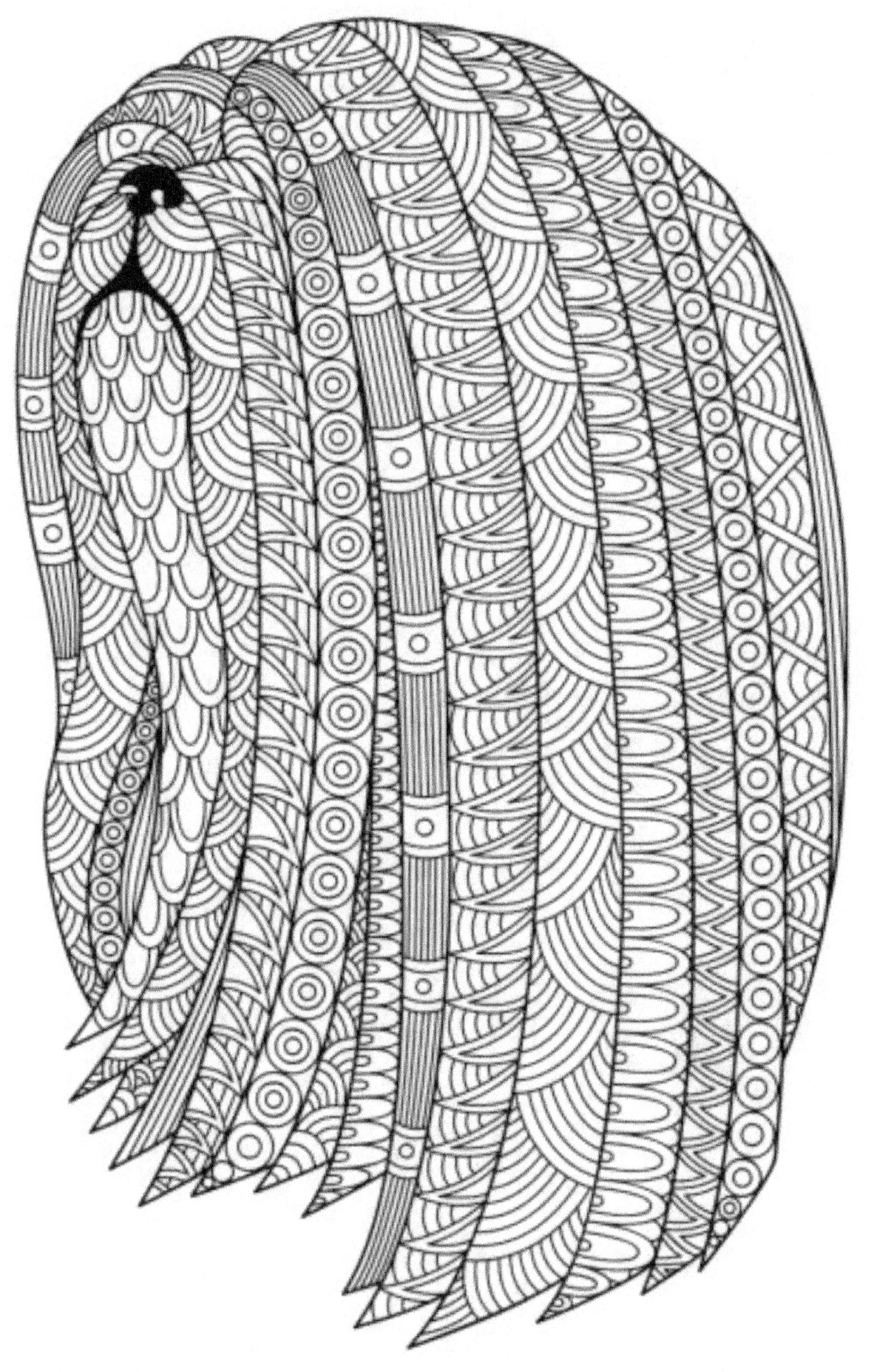

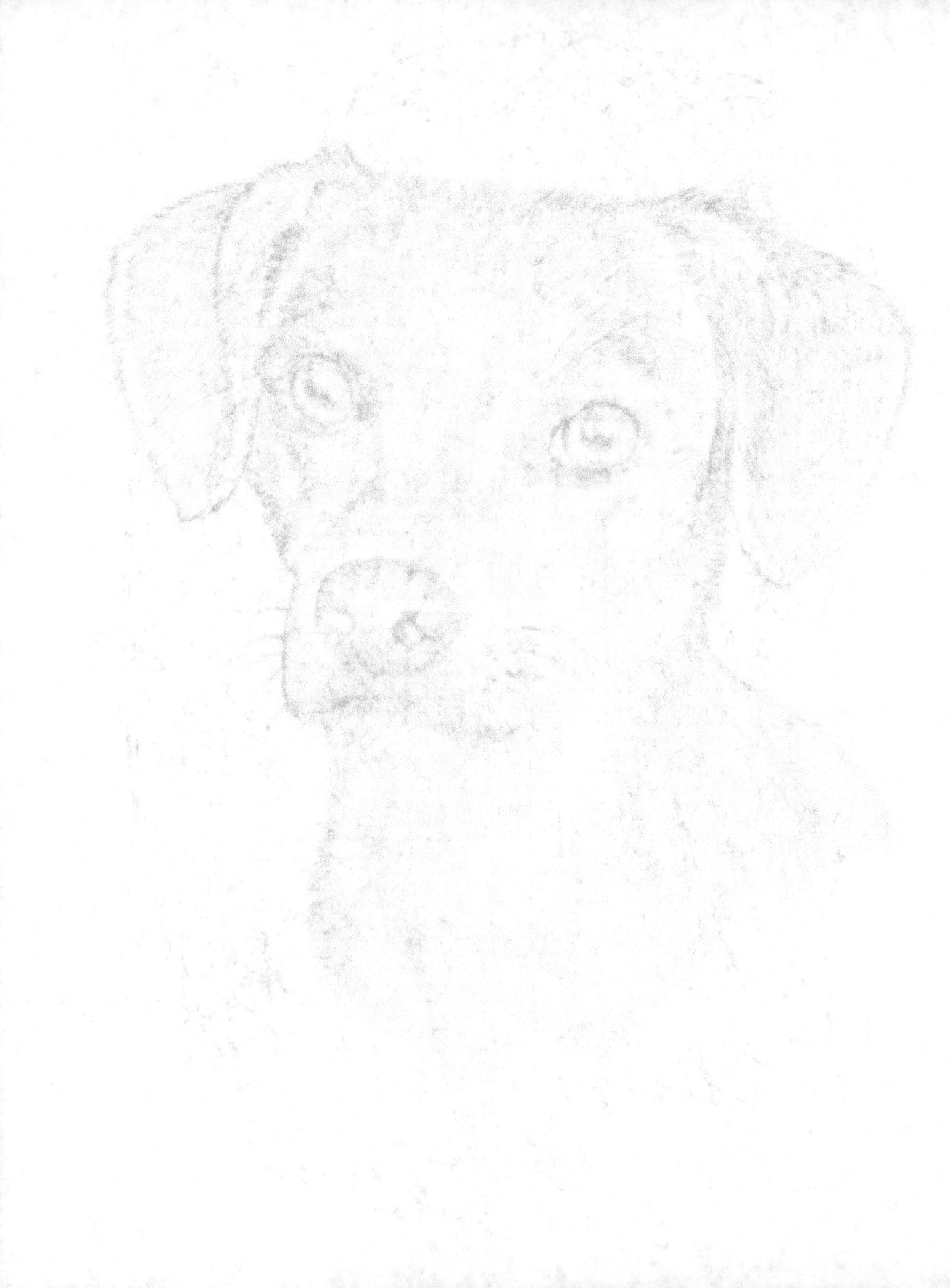

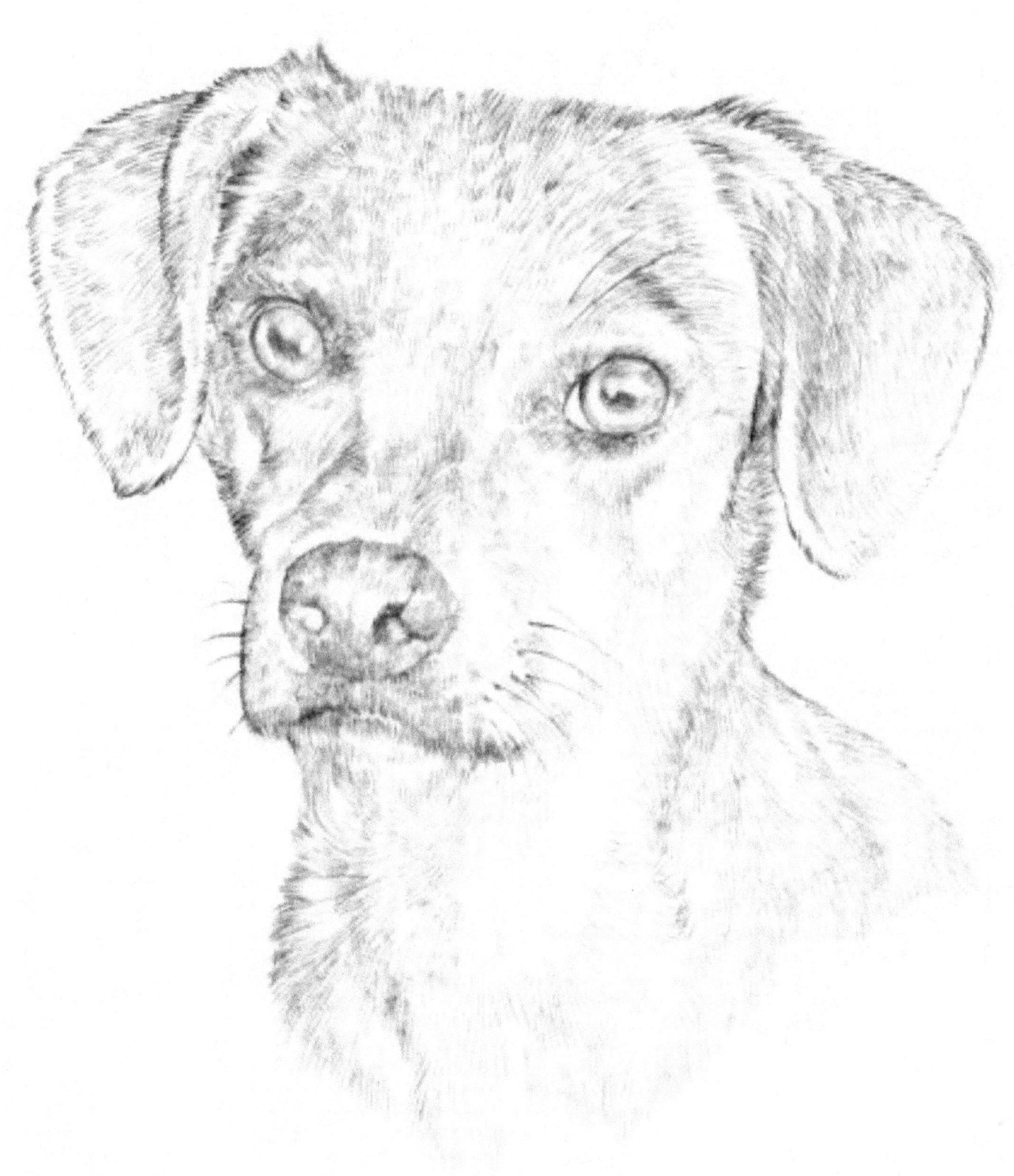

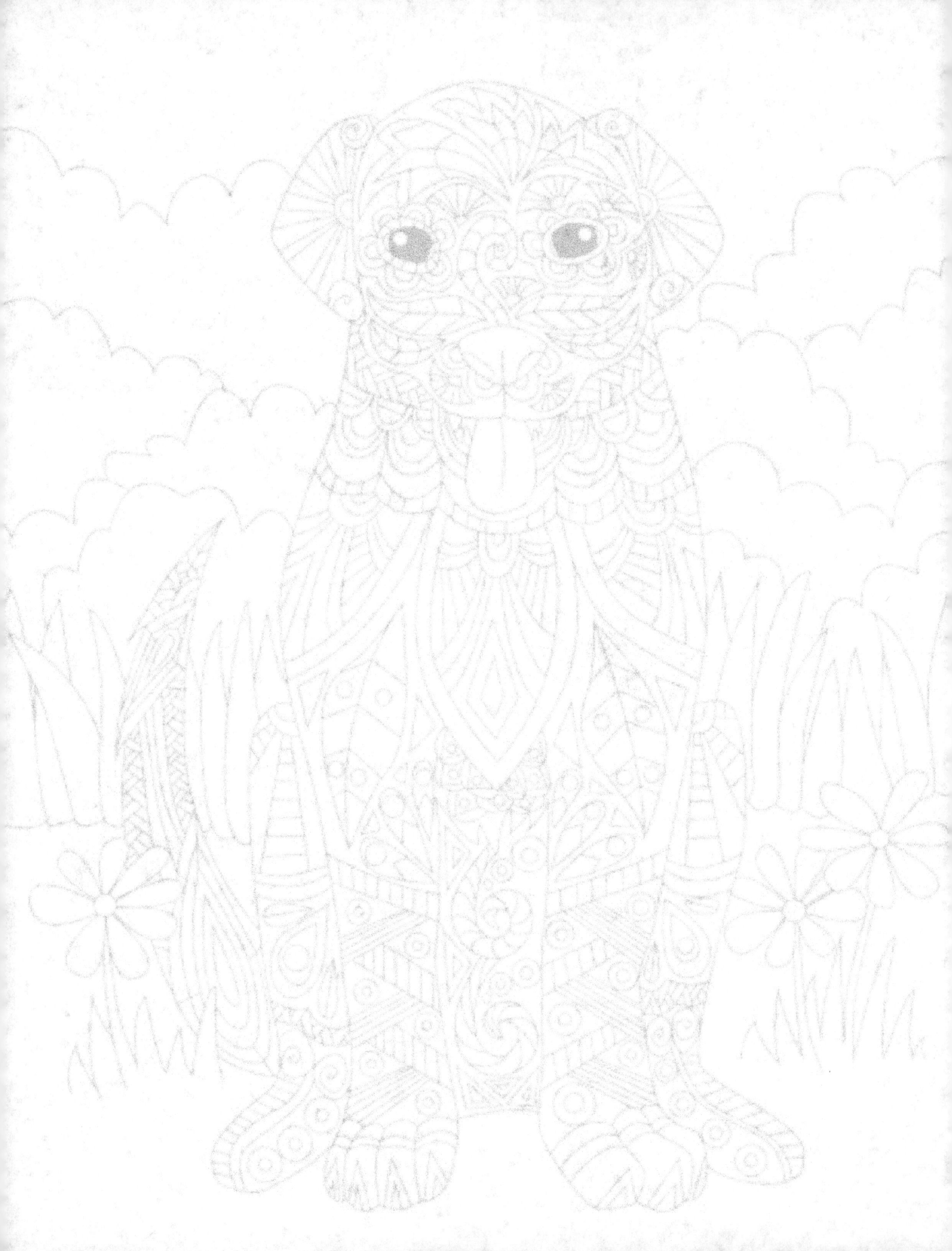

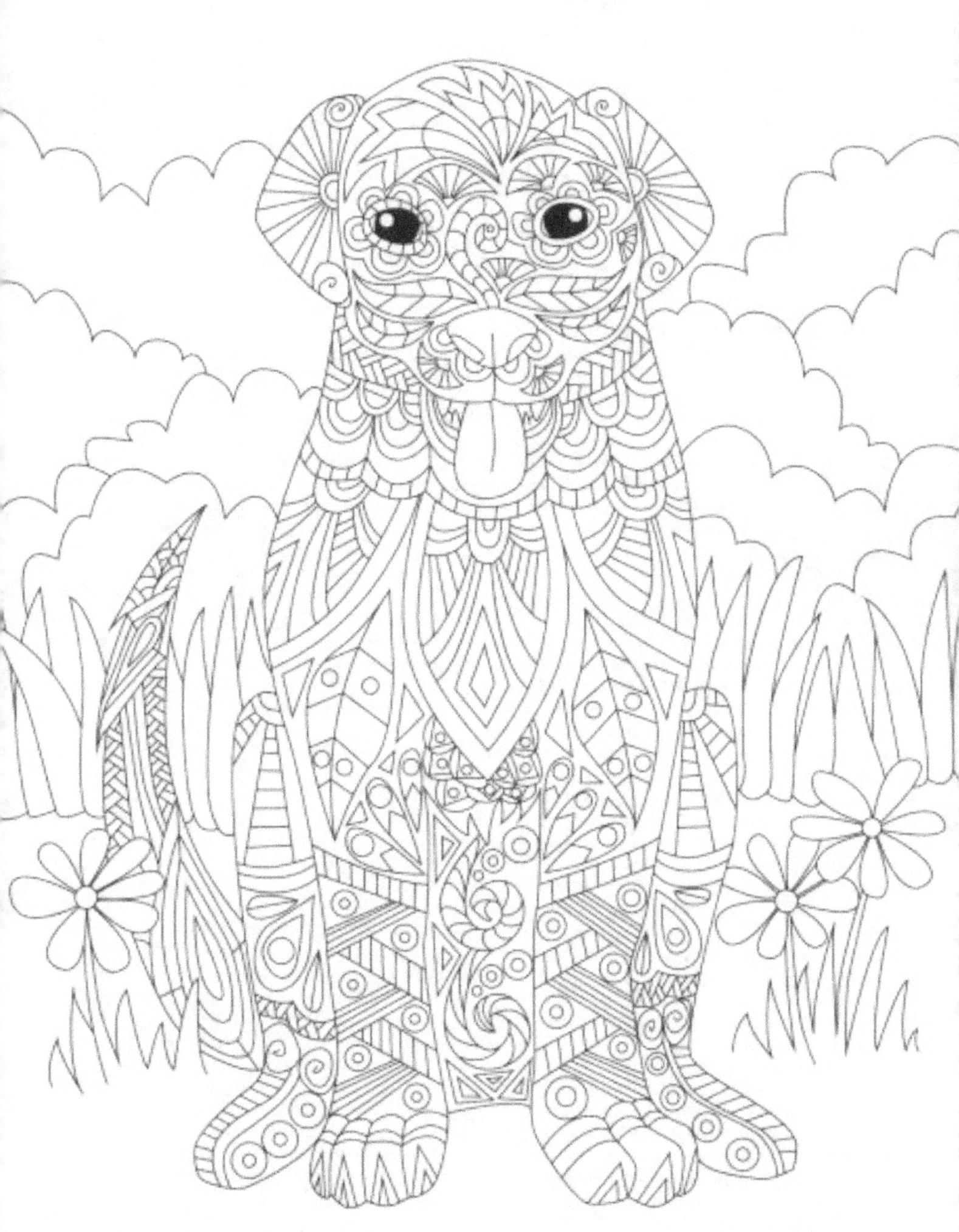

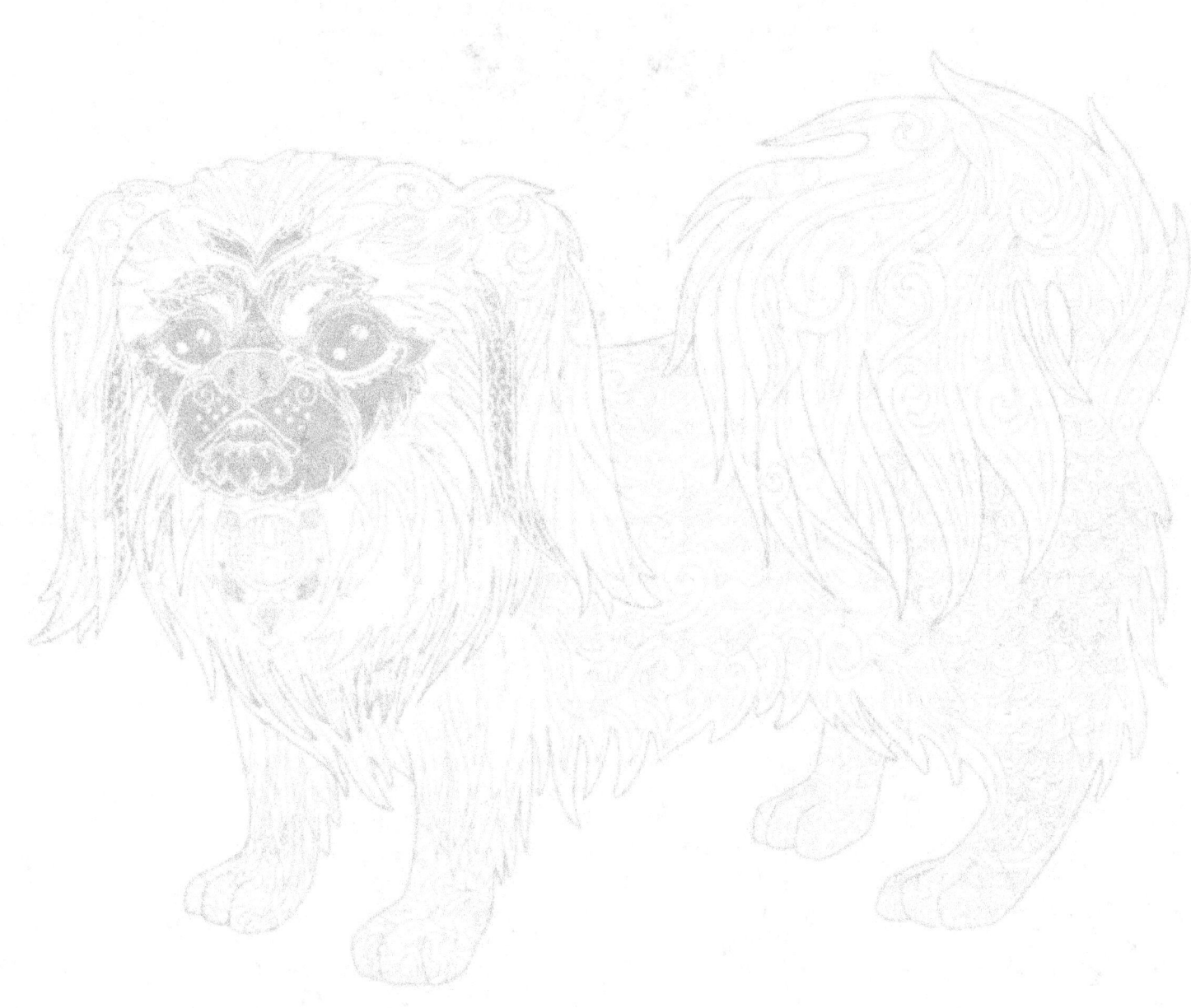

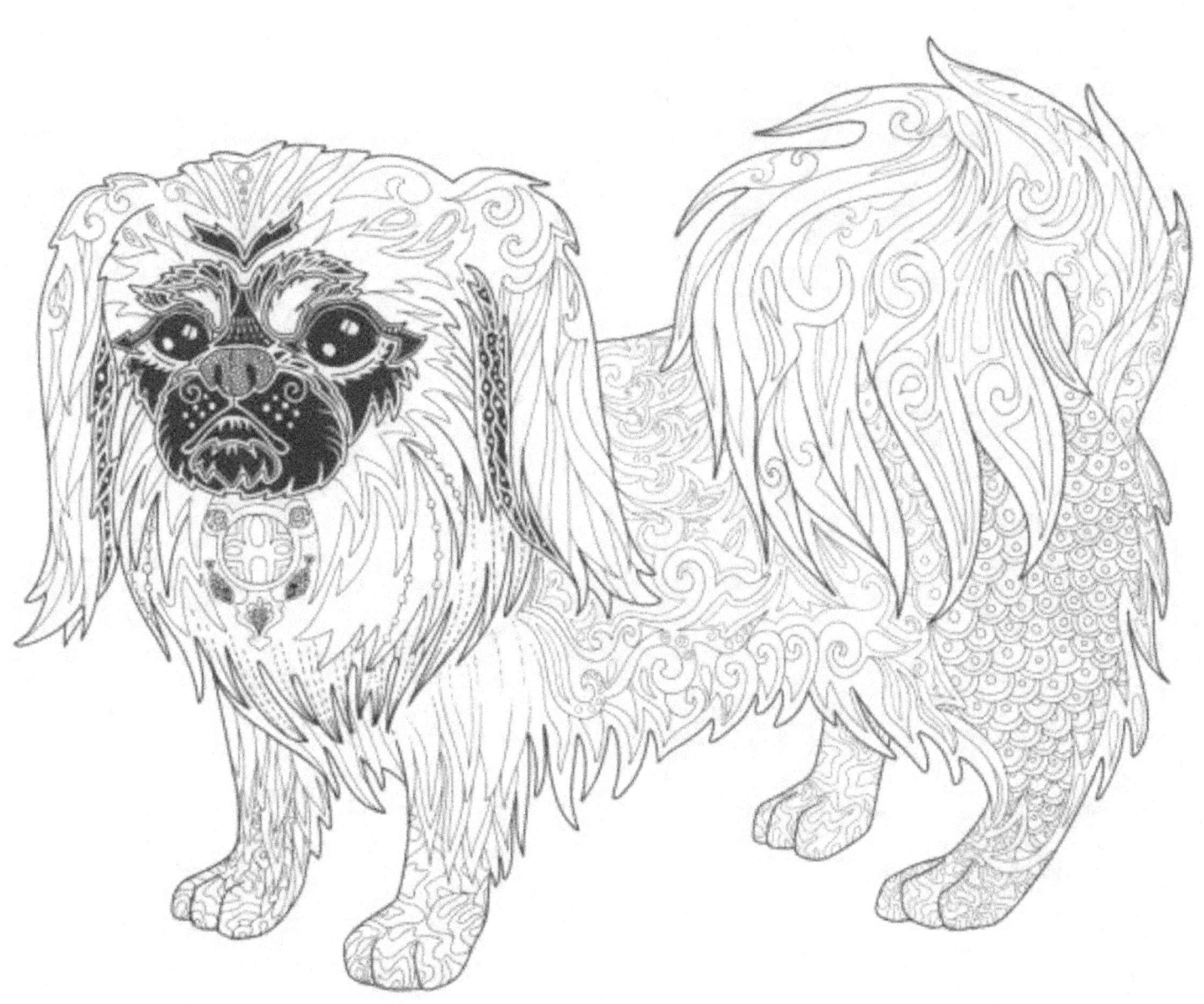

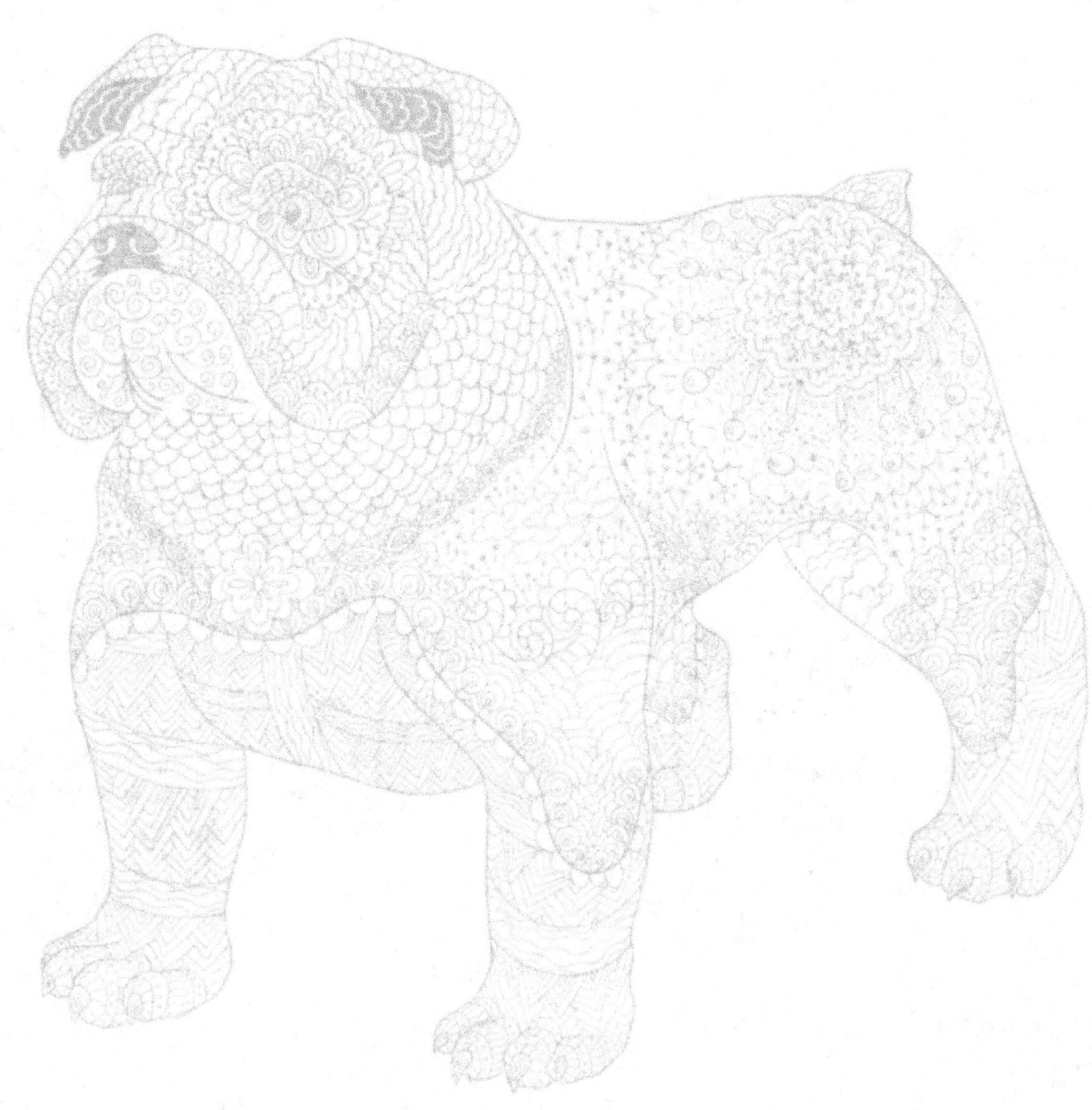

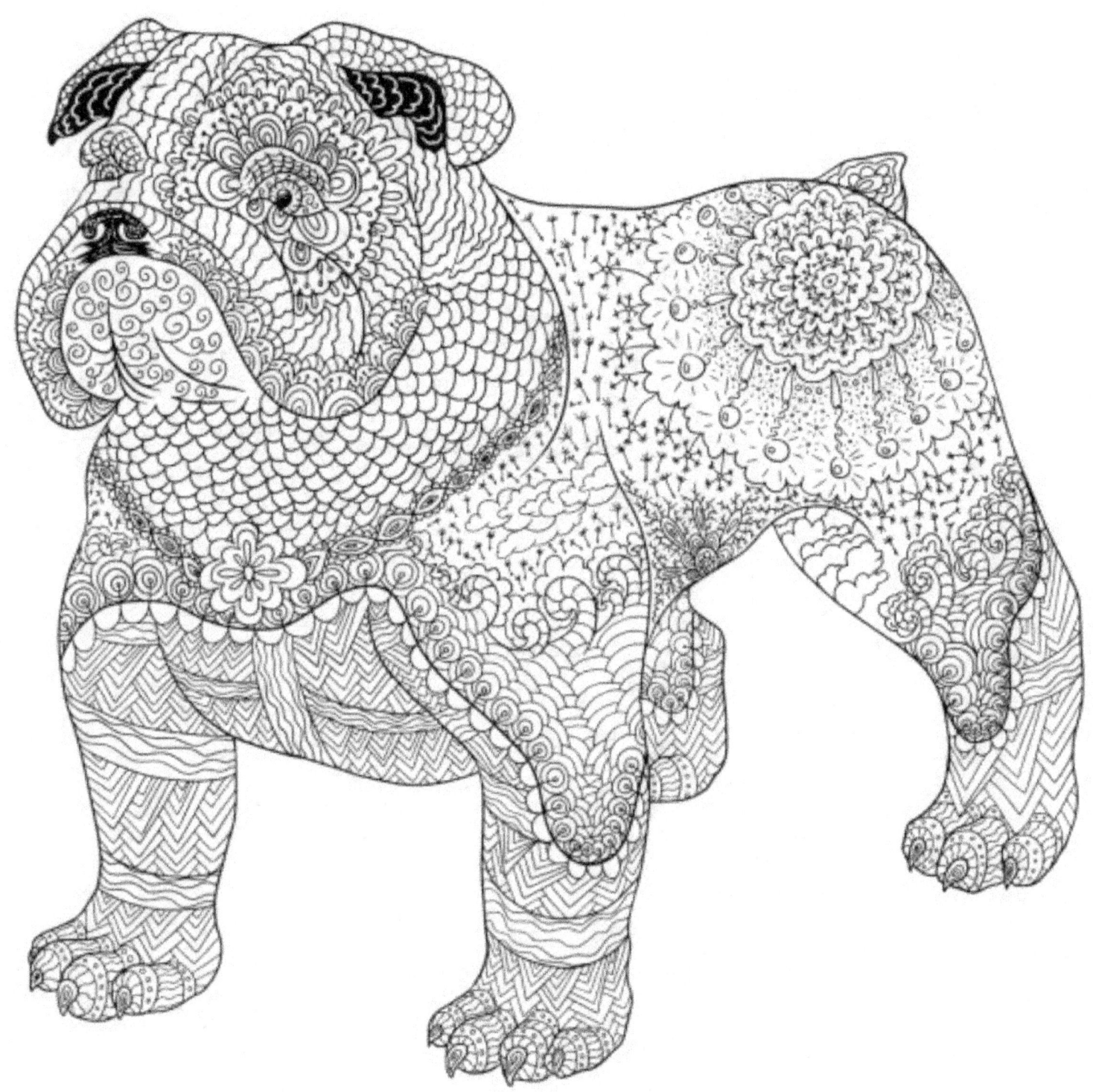

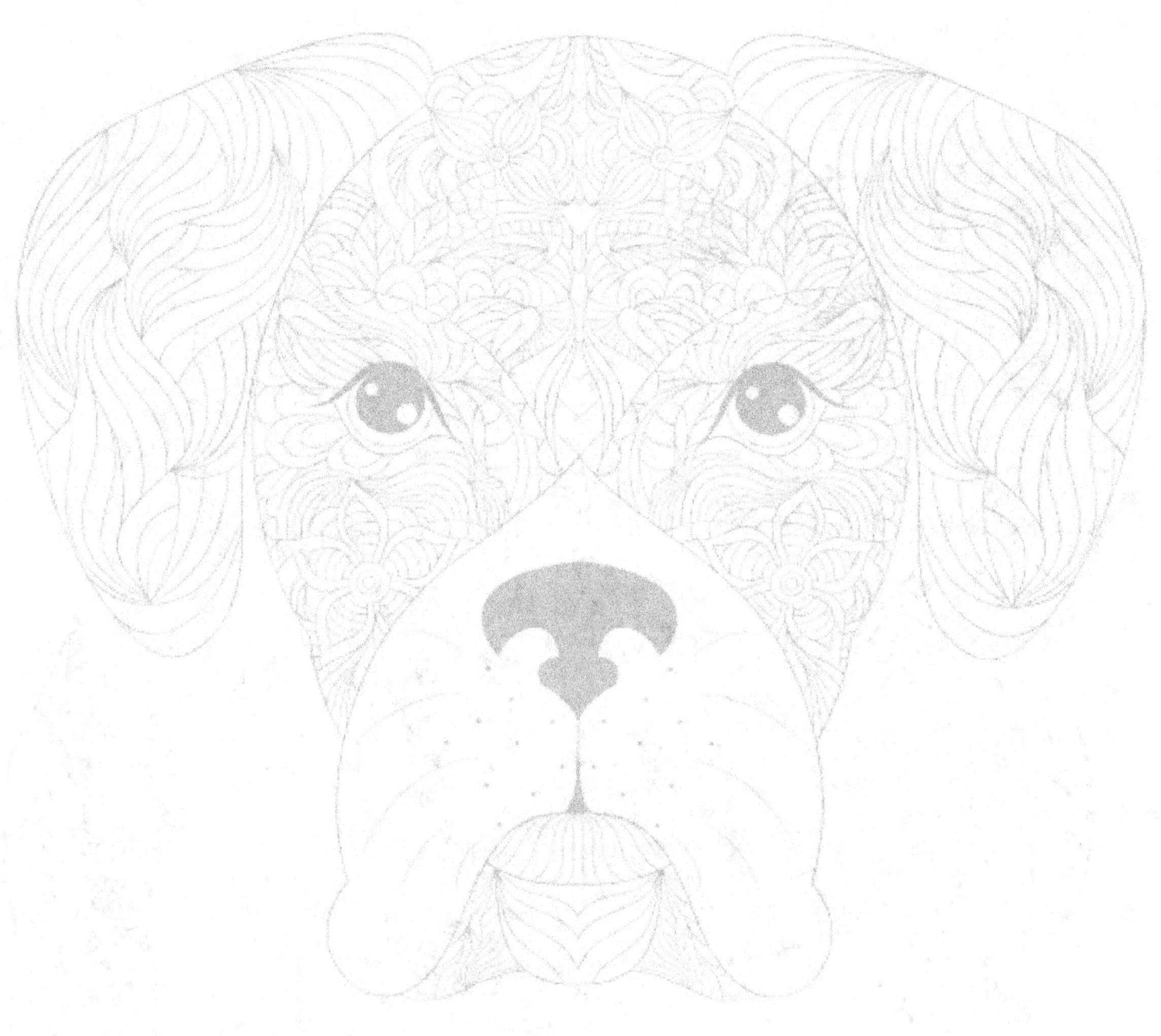

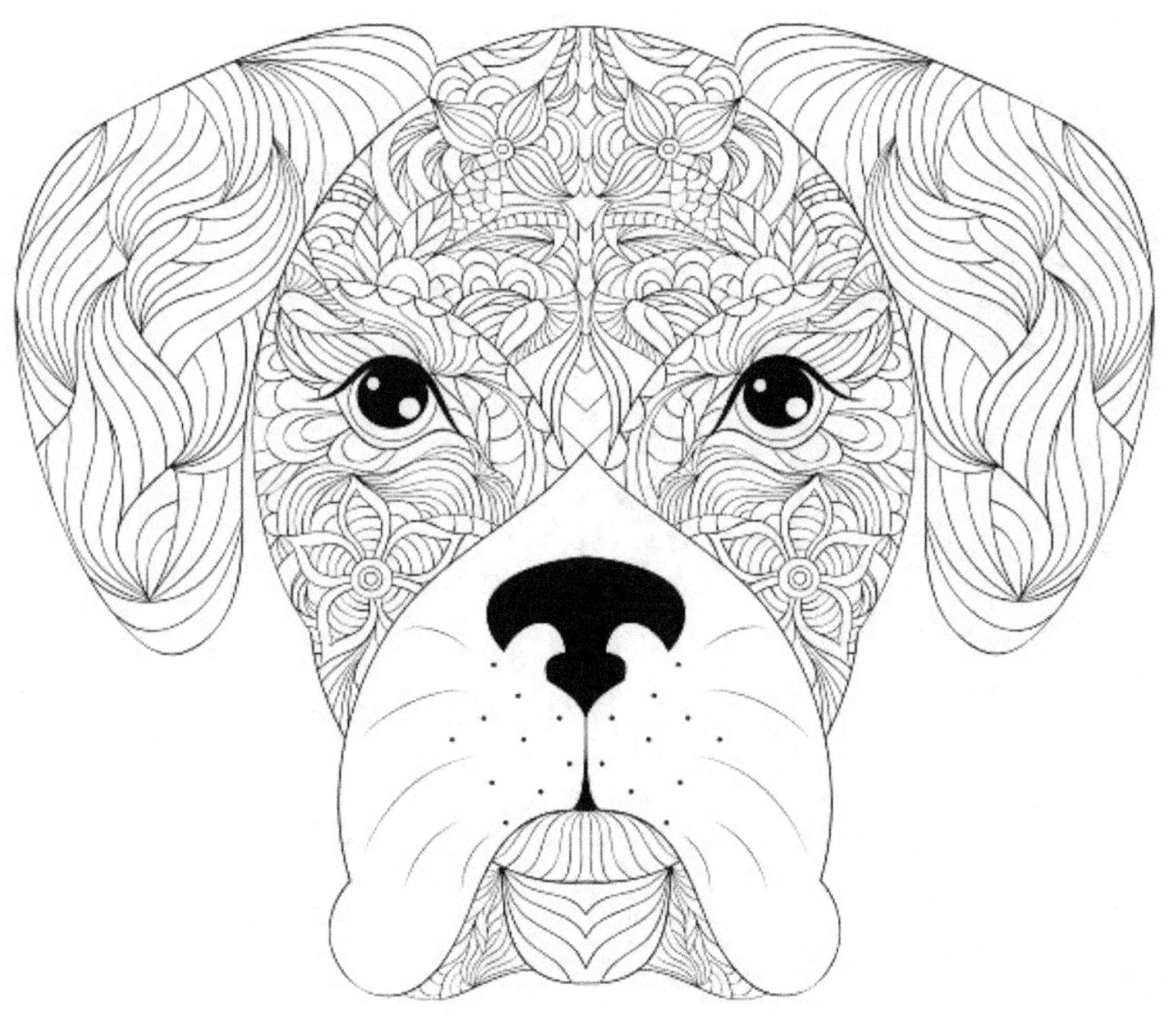

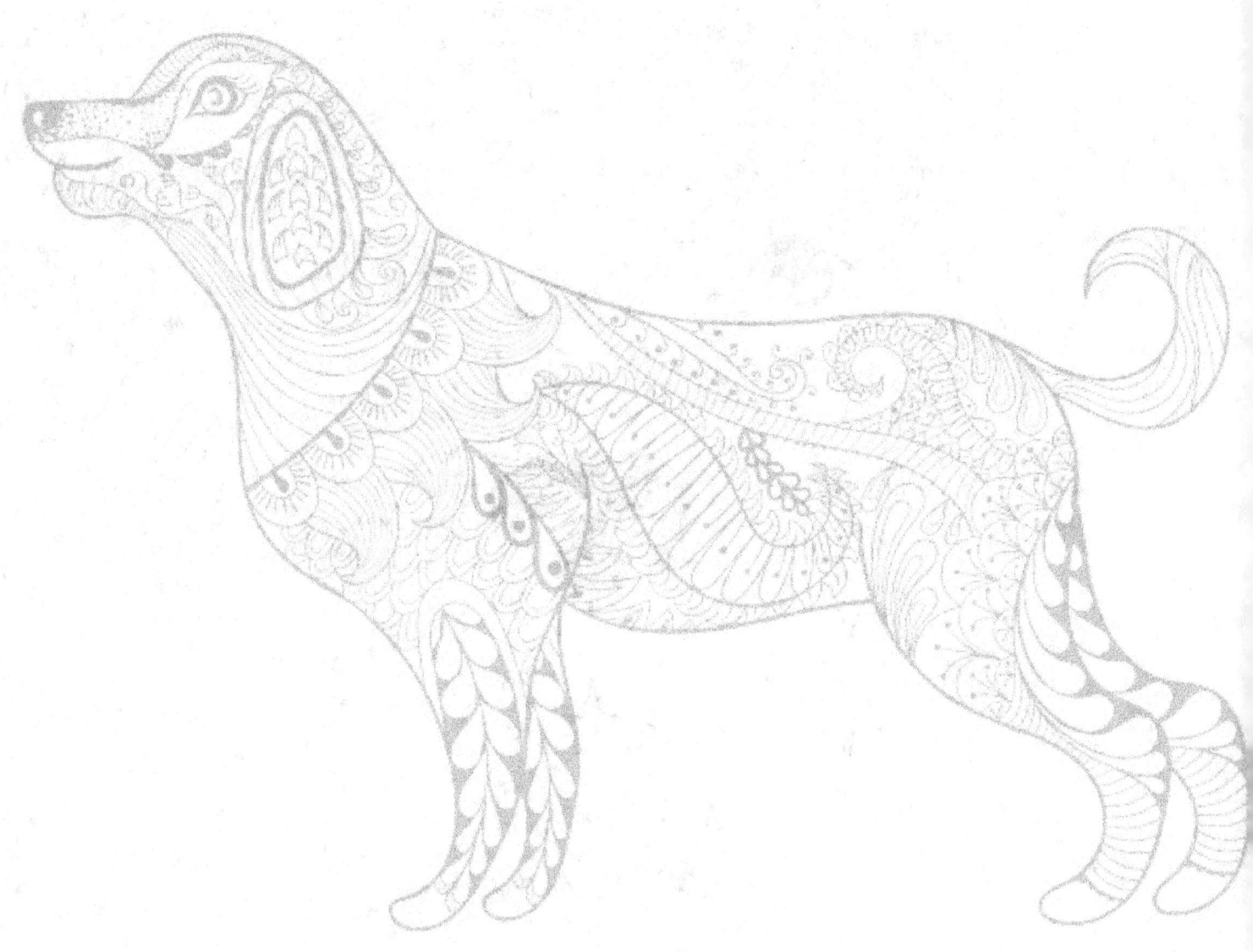

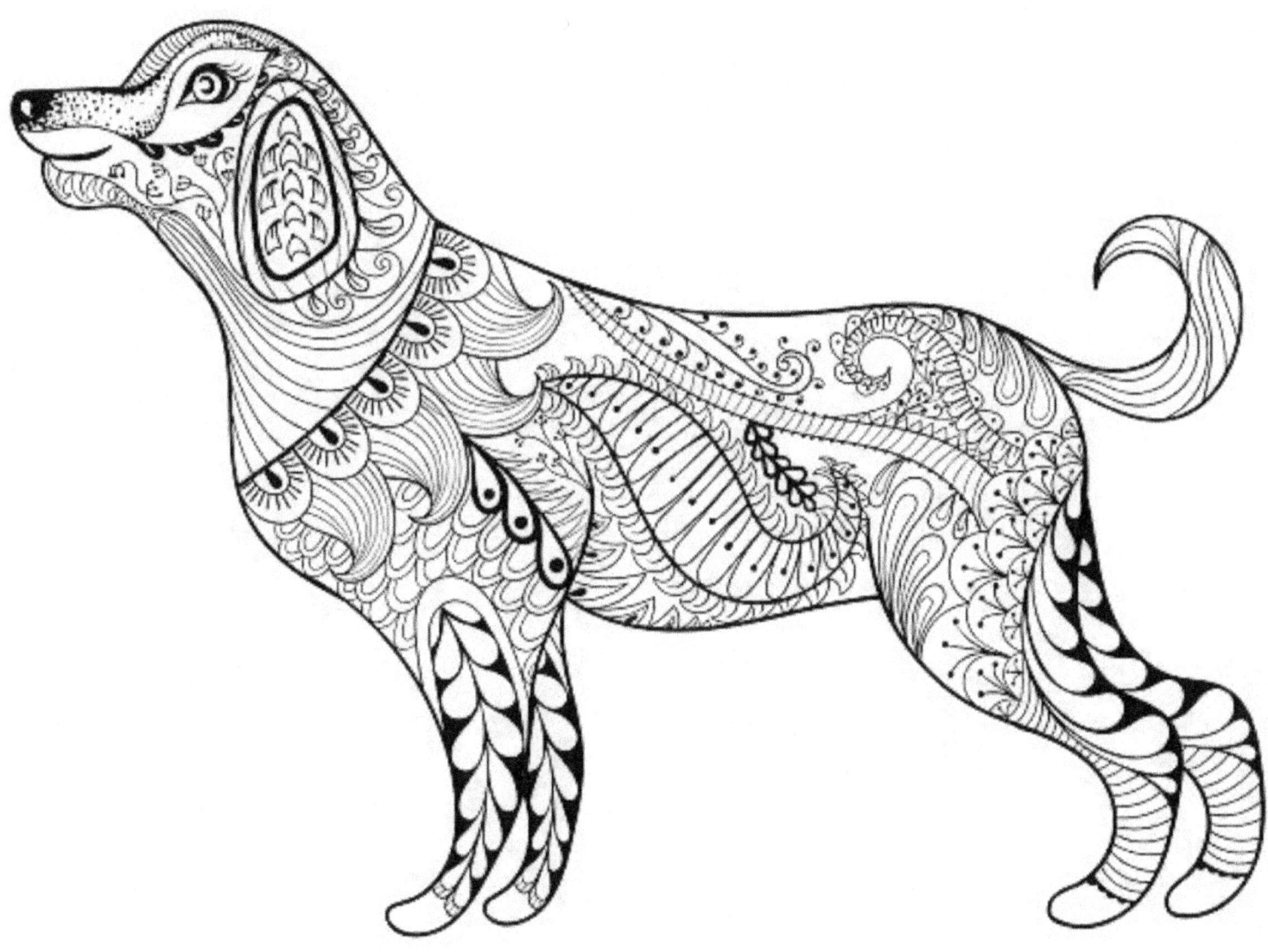

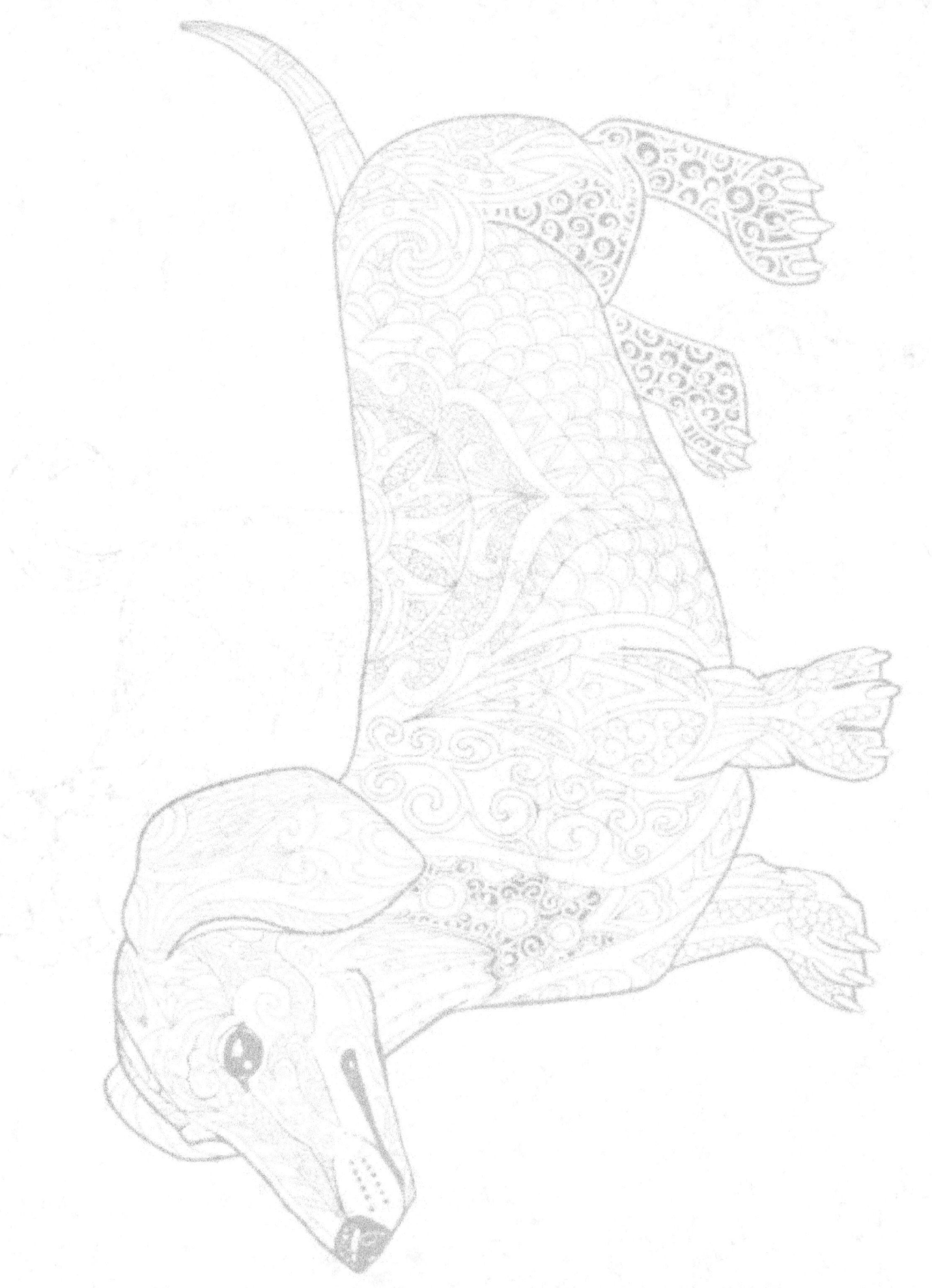

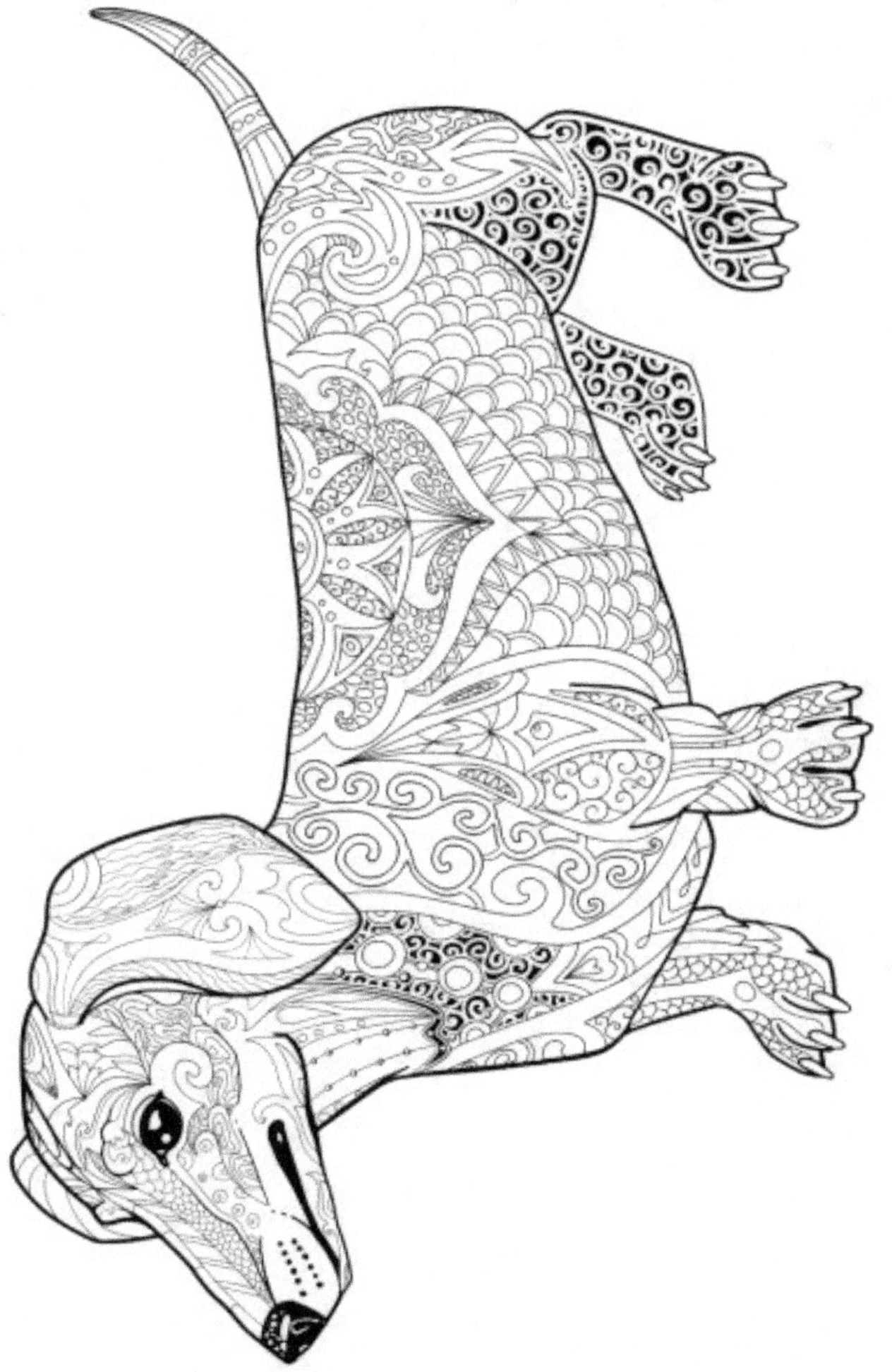

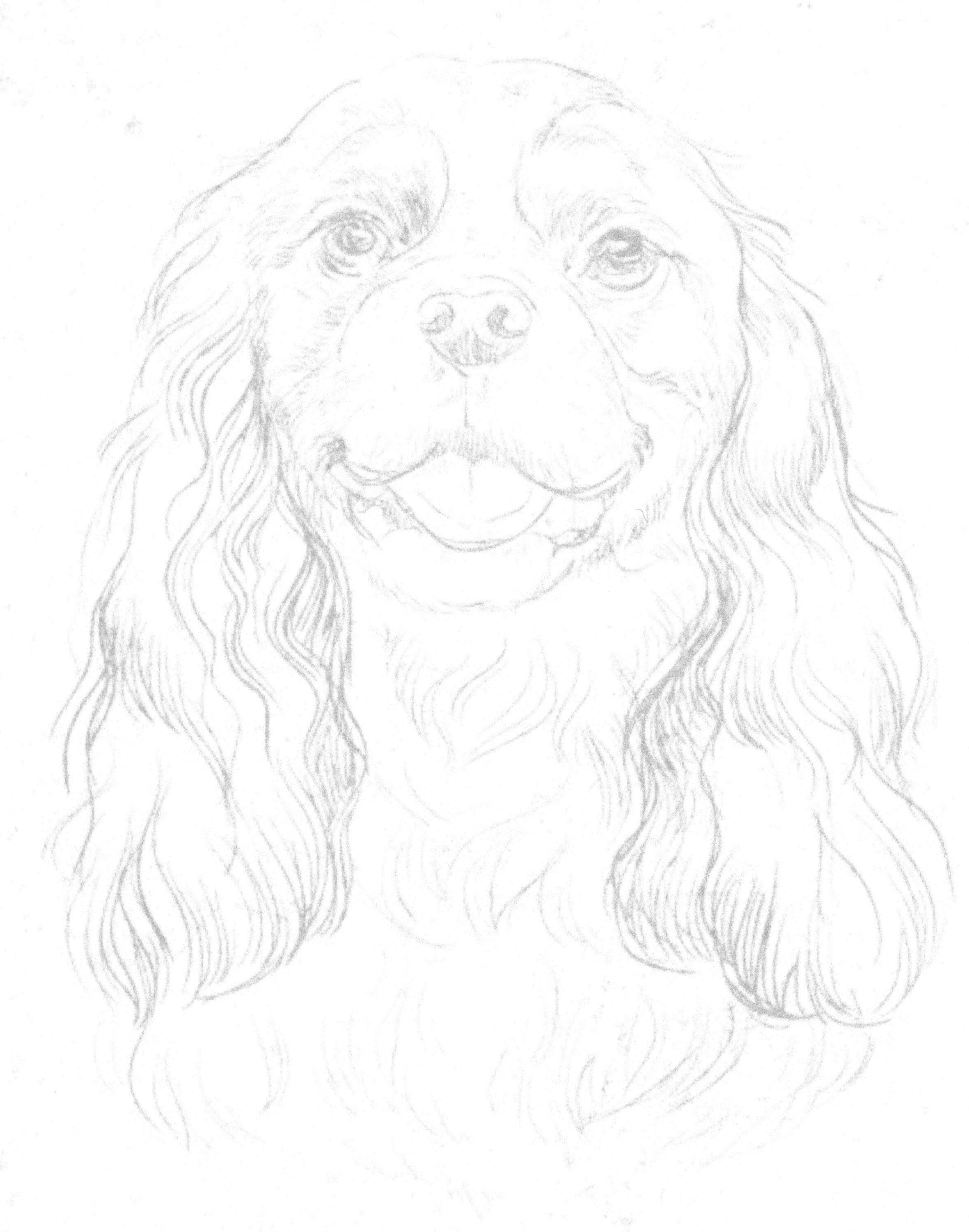

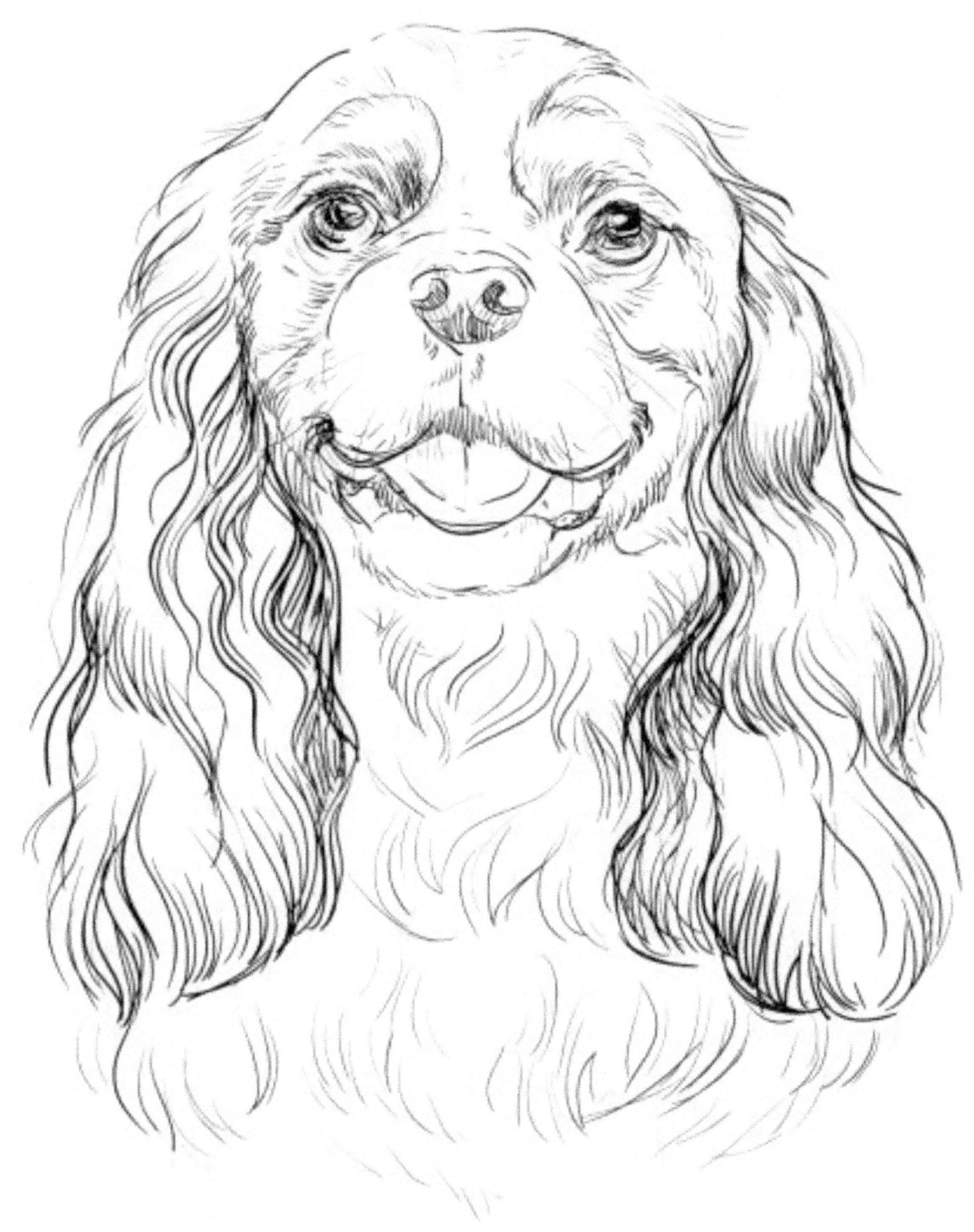

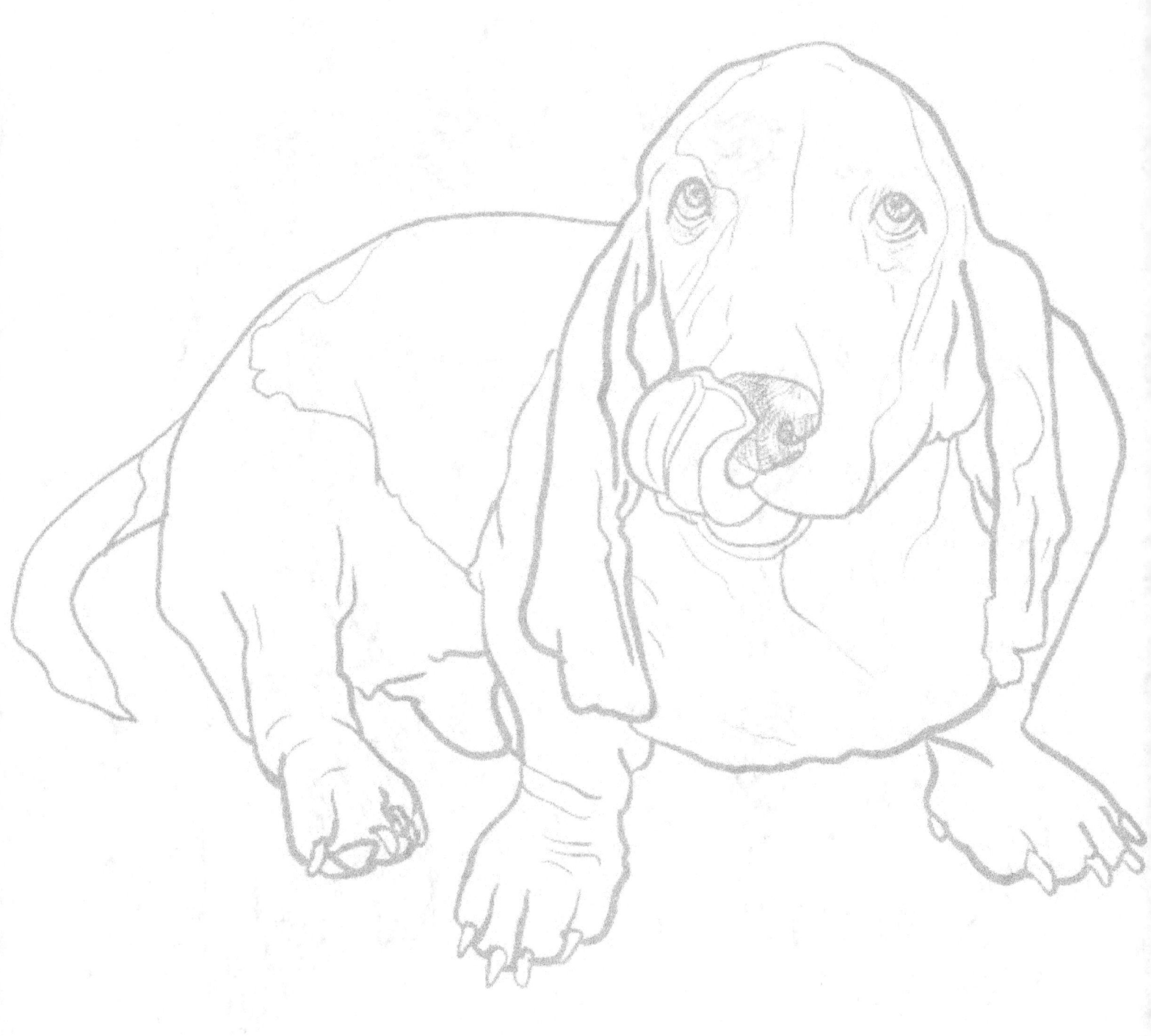

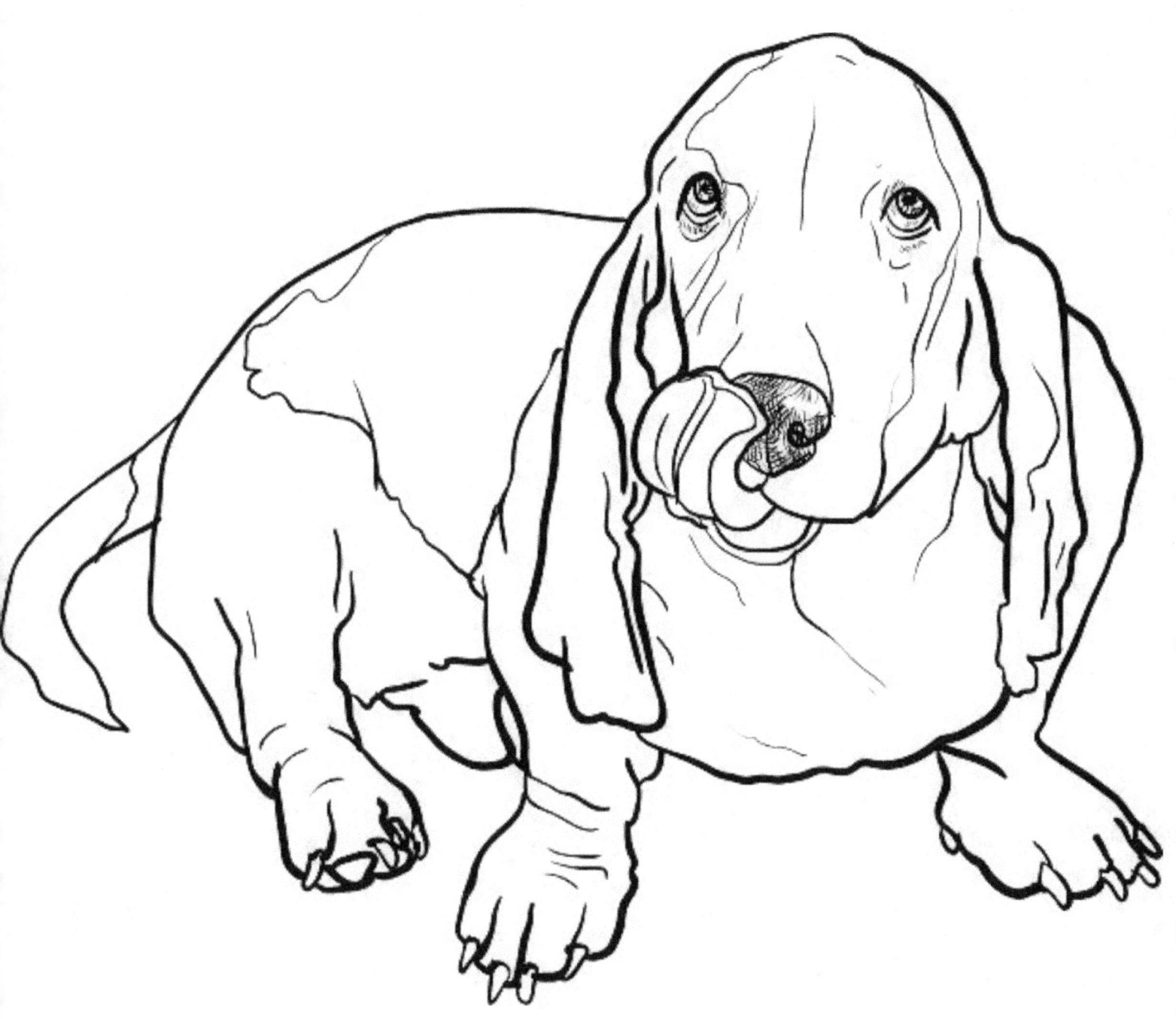

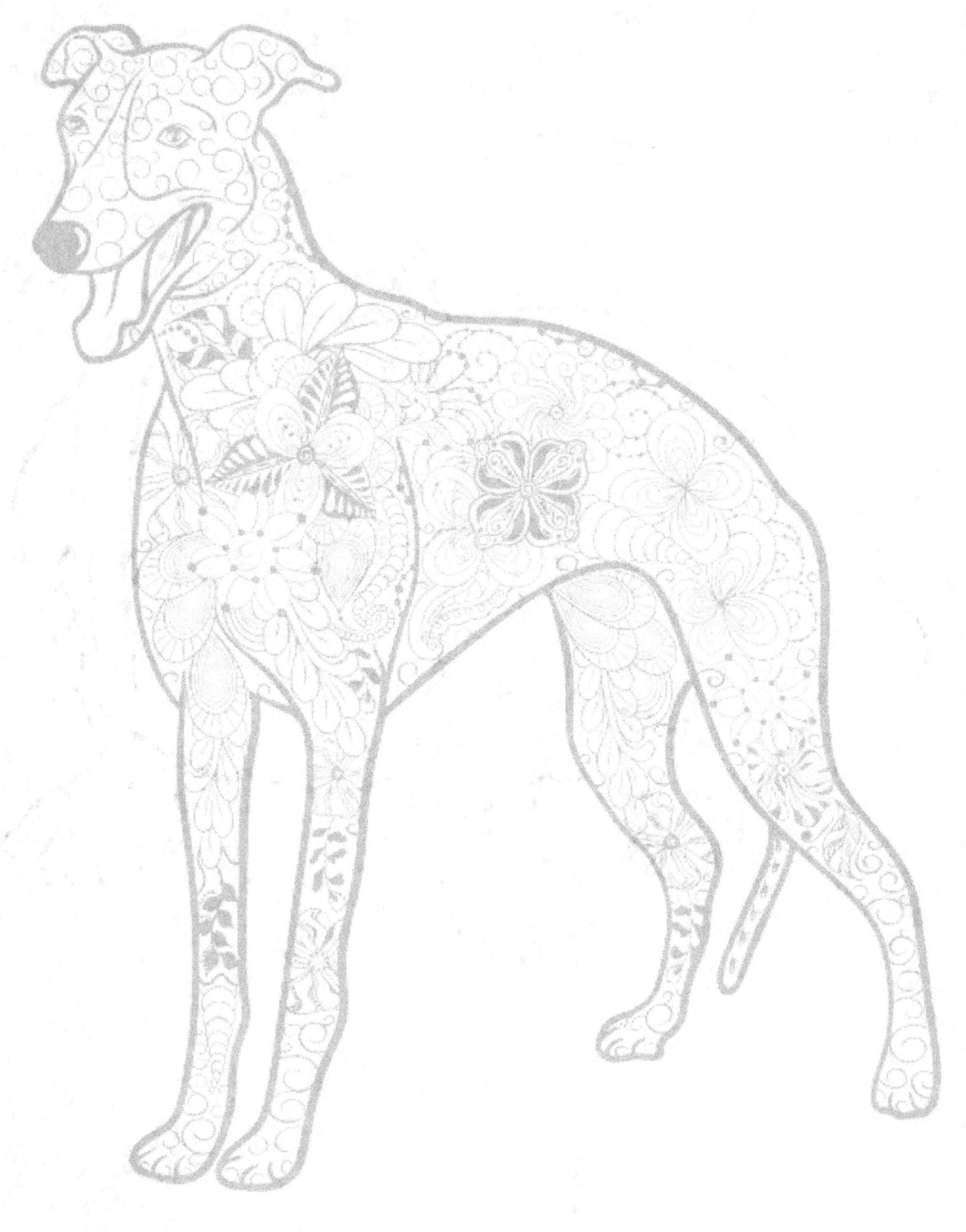

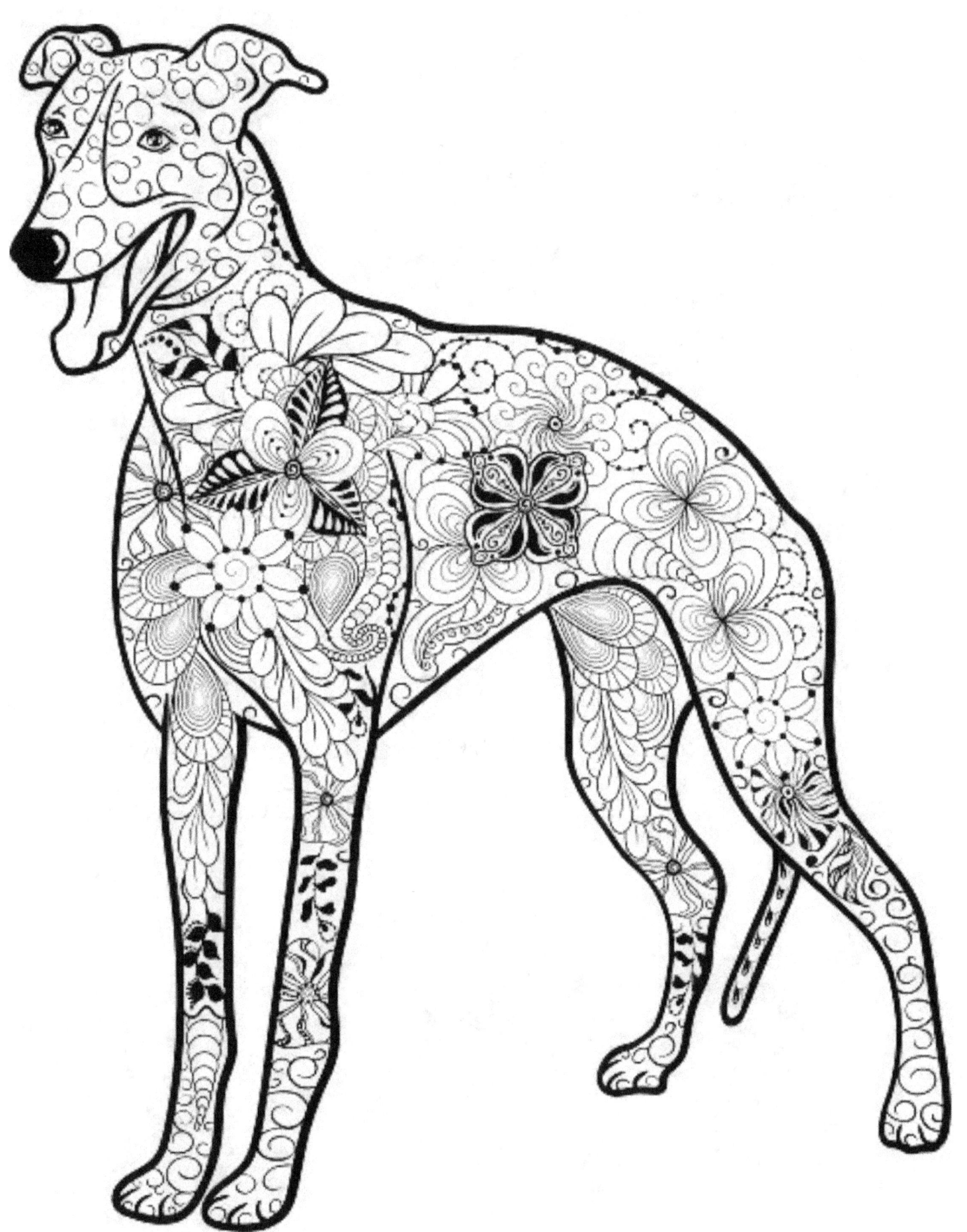

You Might Enjoy

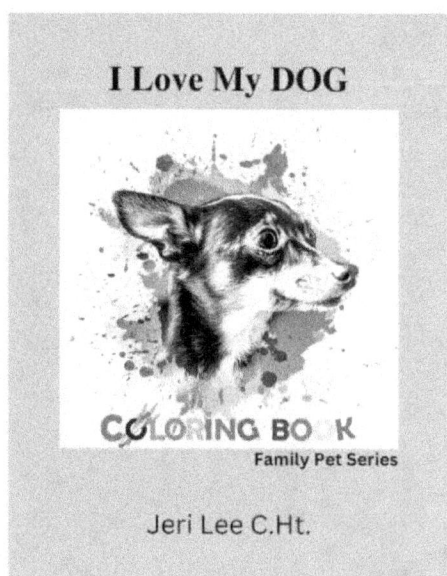
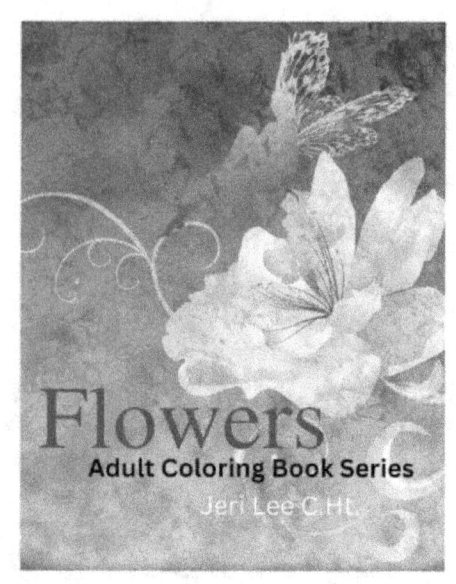
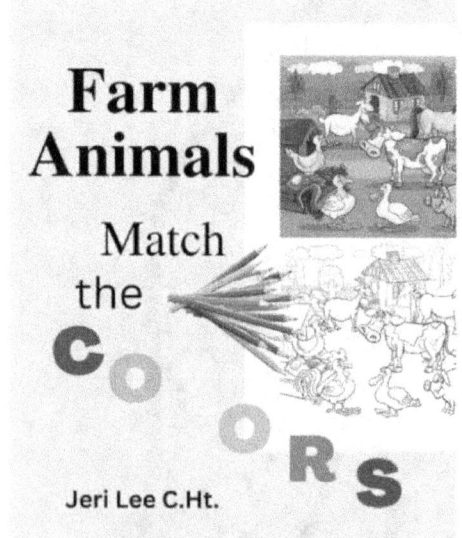

Other Coloring Books

Save the Planet Series
Family Pets Series
Match the Colors Series
Fantasy Series
Flowers & Birds Series
Adult Coloring Book Series

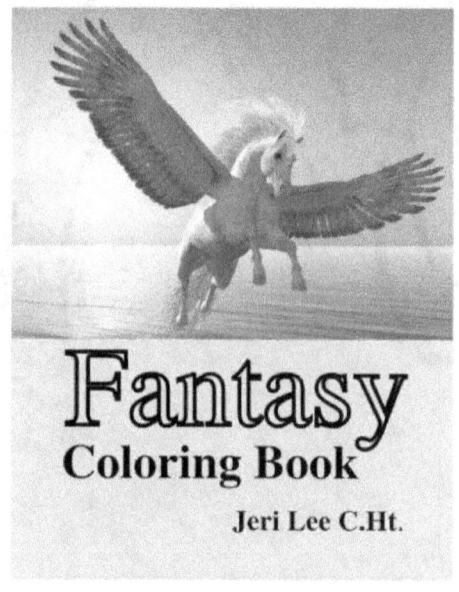
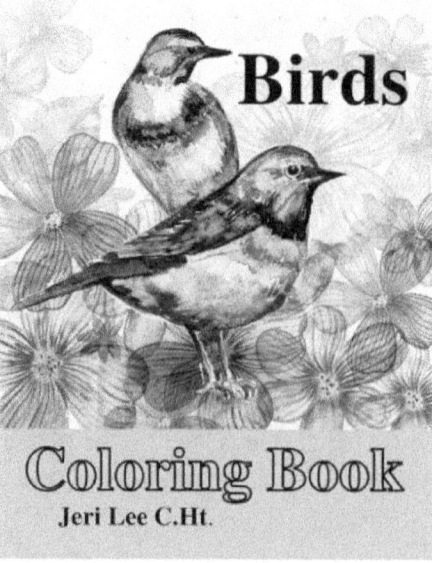
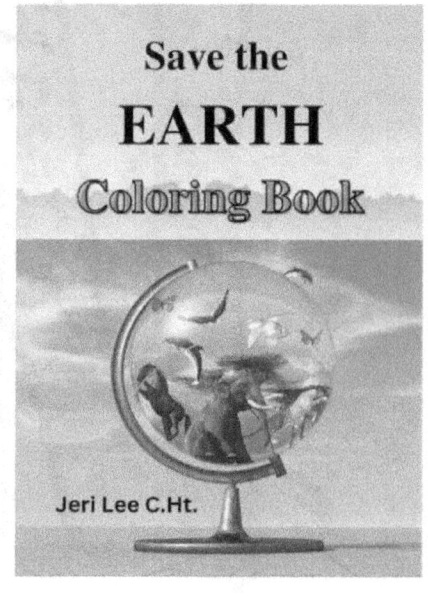

Author and Artist
Jeri LeeC.Ht.

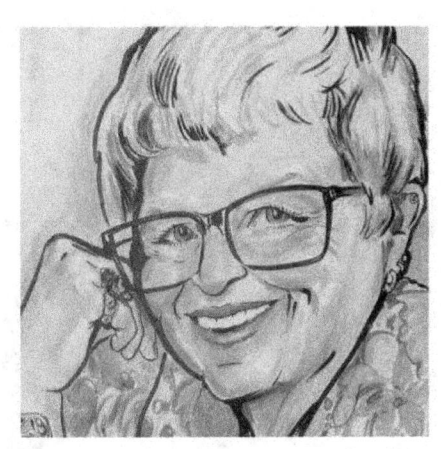

Early education is fundamental for the children in our life. The ABCs and 1-2-3s we teach them are the building blocks of their future. We first give them love and care. Then we teach them to walk and talk and right from wrong. Next is their formal education and how to socialize in their environment. It is here that my books can assist. As a mother, grandmother, and great-grandmother, I know that all kids relate to animals, and the first ones they meet are their household pets. Then as they venture out, they meet Farm animals and learn new words like duck, pig, horses, and cows, and they soon discover the habits, sounds, and colors of their new friends. Then a visit to the Zoo introduces them to the world of Nature, and it is essential to teach them to respect without touching our natural environment.

I grew up on a farm and have lived on one most of my life, so it's a subject that comes easy. My coloring books are designed to teach kids to respect the world they live in.

They are published in collectible series with different coloring pages for different ages and interests.

If you like this book, please follow my other series, and if you would give me a good review as an author, I would greatly appreciate it.

UNIVERSAL

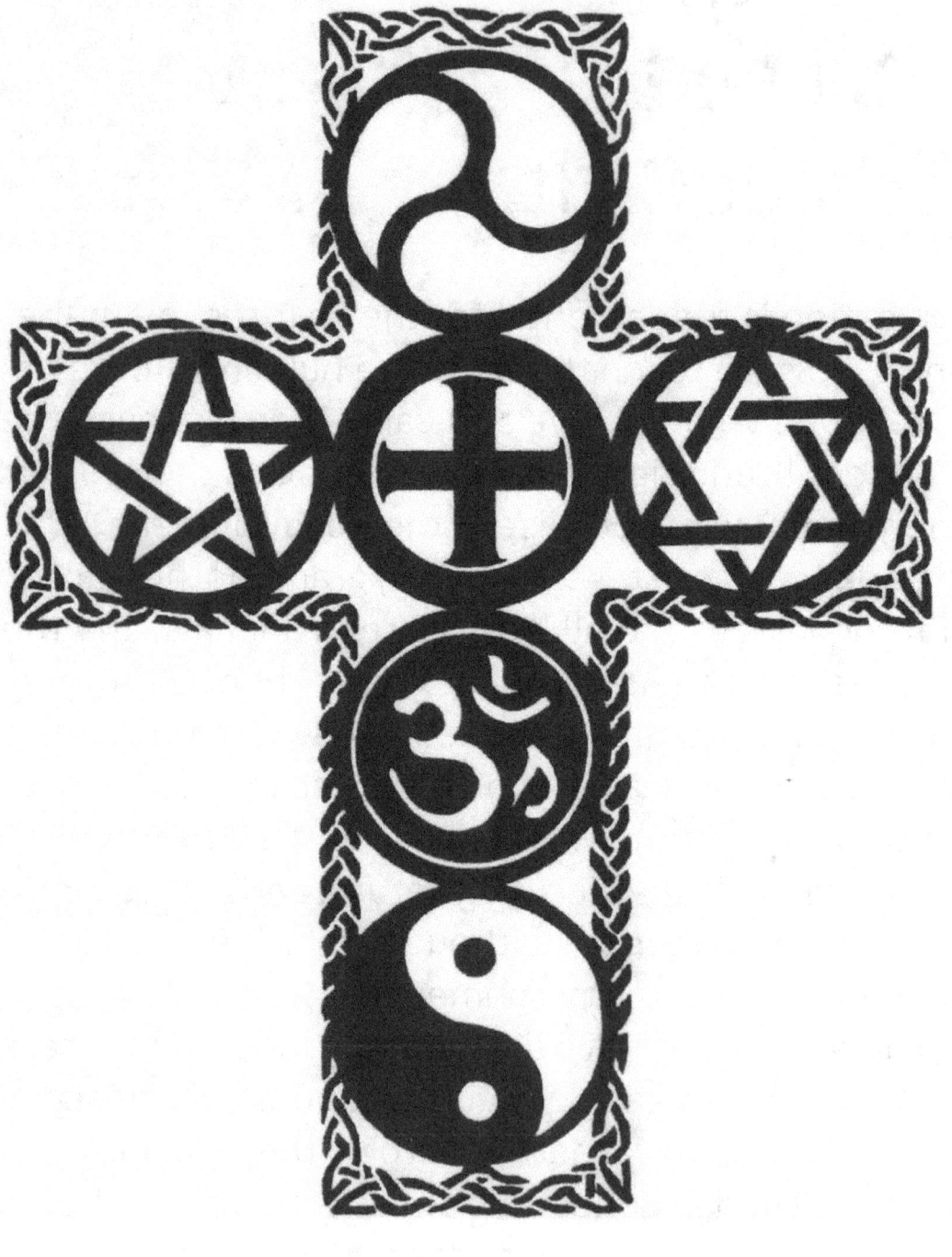

PEACE